The Princeton

Cracking

THE
GOLDEN STATE
EXAMINATION

Economics

by DAVID Anderson, PhD; and John Gilleaudeau, PhD

Random House, Inc.
New York
www.randomhouse.com/princetonreview

Princeton Review, L.L.C.
2315 Broadway
New York, NY 10024

E-mail: comments@review.com

Copyright © 2000 by Princeton Review Publishing, L.L.C.

All rights reserved under International and Pan-American Copyright Conventions.

Published in the United States by Random House, Inc., New York.

ISBN 0-375-75355-9

Editor: Gretchen Feder
Production Editor: Kristen Azzara
Designer: Stephanie Martin

Manufactured in the United States of America.

9 8 7 6 5 4 3 2 1

First Edition

The Independent Education Consultants Association recognizes The Princeton Review as a valuable resource for high school and college students applying to college and graduate school.

Dedication

For Kristen

Acknowledgments

Barbara Carmack and Patsi McAfee are appreciated for their irreplaceable secretarial assistance at Centre College and Davidson College.

Contents

PART I: CRACKING THE SYSTEM 1

  1 The Mystery Exam: About the Golden State Examinations 3

  2 What's on the Economics GSE: Structure and Strategies 11

  3 Cracking the Multiple-Choice Section 21

  4 Cracking the Essay Section 27

PART II: ECONOMICS REVIEW 35

  5 Economics 37

  6 Markets 43

  7 An Alternative View of Markets 57

  8 Measuring the Economy 63

  9 Economic Problems and the Business Cycle 71

  10 Fiscal Policy 79

  11 Money 87

  12 Monetary Policy 97

  13 Economic Growth 103

  14 Distribution of Income 111

  15 International Trade 115

  16 International Finance 123

  17 Ideology 131

  18 Market Structure 141

  19 Labor Markets 149

PART III: THE PRINCETON REVIEW GSE ECONOMICS PRACTICE TESTS 155

  20 The Princeton Review GSE Economics Practice Test I 157

  Practice Test I: Answers and Explanations 169

21 The Princeton Review
GSE Economics Practice Test II 179

Practice Test II: Answers and Explanations 191

22 The Princeton Review
GSE Economics Practice Test III 201

Practice Test III: Answers and Explanations 213

23 The Princeton Review
GSE Economics Practice Test IV 223

Practice Test IV: Answers and Explanations 235

About the Authors 245

Part I

CRACKING THE SYSTEM

Chapter 1

THE MYSTERY EXAM: ABOUT THE GOLDEN STATE EXAMINATIONS

WHAT ARE THE GOLDEN STATE EXAMS?

The GSEs were established by the State of California Board of Education in 1983 (so your parents never took them—that's why they have probably never heard of them and may not understand how important they are). The tests are designed to offer a rigorous examination in key academic subjects to students in grades 7 to 12. Students who pass have a variety of advantages over those who don't—including the fact that their school transcripts will be more attractive to college and admissions boards. The tests provide an opportunity for students to demonstrate outstanding levels of achievement in a particular subject area.

The GSE program has grown in the last few years, both in the number of different exams offered and the number of students who take at least one test. During the 1999–2000 academic year, thirteen different GSE exams will be administered, and California students will complete more than one million. In 1998 more than 2,100 graduates earned the Golden State Seal Merit Diploma, which recognizes students who have "mastered their high school curriculum" (see the following pages for more information on the Merit Diploma).

Many students are given the GSE without advanced knowledge or without specific preparation for the test, which brings us back to the benefits of this book. You probably purchased this book because a teacher recommended it or because you were told to get ready to take a GSE. Congratulations! This is the most thorough guide you can own to prepare for the Golden State Examinations. Our goal is simple—to get you ready for the Golden State Examination in Economics.

WE'RE HERE TO HELP

The GSEs are somewhat of a mystery to students, particularly because there aren't any official practice tests that you can study. We're here to change all that. Our research and development teams have spent countless hours to ensure that this is the most complete guide available for the Golden State Examinations. All of the information that is released about the GSEs is in this book. We've also spoken to students and teachers about their experiences with these tests and designed our content review around their feedback. In short, we have the inside scoop on the Golden State Examinations, and we're going to share it with you.

What's So Special About This Book?

Golden State Examinations test your knowledge of a subject, and your ability to apply that knowledge. The goal of this book is twofold. First, we want to help you remember and relearn some of the key components of the subject material that's covered in the exam. Second, we want you to become familiar with the format and structure of the GSE, so that you'll know exactly what to do on test day.

We at The Princeton Review aren't big fans of standardized tests, and we understand the stress and challenge that a GSE presents. But with our guide and some work on your part, you should be able to do well on these tests. Our proven strategies and techniques will help you in your preparation. There's just one more thing you might be wondering—why *should* I take the Golden State Examinations?

WHY SHOULD YOU TAKE THE GOLDEN STATE EXAMINATIONS?

There are many reasons why you should spend time and energy getting ready for the GSEs. They include:

- **Qualification for a Golden State Merit Diploma**

  The Golden State Merit Diploma is one of the—if not *the*—highest academic awards given by the State of California. In the pages that follow, we will discuss in detail how you can qualify for a Merit Diploma.

- **Recognition on Your Transcript**

  If you perform well on a Golden State Examination, you will receive recognition on your high school transcript. We'll tell you later how the scoring system and award processes work on the pages that follow.

- **College Admissions Committees Will Love You!**

  A strong performance on the Golden State Examinations will make you look great to colleges and universities. These are academic awards that will demonstrate to schools that you can excel in an academic environment.

- **They're Risk Free!**

  First, there is absolutely no fee to take a Golden State Examination, so you won't need to worry about spending money on these tests. Second, there is absolutely no penalty if you do not perform well on a Golden State Examination. If you don't earn an award, nothing will appear on your transcript. In fact, only you will know if you did *not* pass a Golden State Examination. Translation—you've got nothing to lose, and a lot to gain!

- **All the Things Your Teacher Would Say**

  There are academic benefits to passing the tests as well. If you asked your teacher, "Why should I take these exams?" your teacher would probably tell you that, in addition to all the benefits listed above, "These tests provide a great opportunity for you to demonstrate what you have learned throughout high school, with the possibility of receiving numerous awards and titles for strong academic performance. The Golden State Examinations are an academic challenge that can enrich your high school experience."

Although we'll be a little less formal in the way we say it, we agree with the teacher's advice. The GSEs are your chance to show off what you know. You should receive recognition for all your hard work, and we're going to give you every tool we can to ensure that you do well.

HOW ARE STUDENTS RECOGNIZED FOR THEIR PERFORMANCE?

If—or should we say when—you score within the highest levels on any one Golden State Examination, you will receive one of three awards: high honors, honors, or recognition. Say you take three GSEs, one in economics, one in biology, and one in written composition, and (because you used The Princeton Review test-prep books), you are among the talented minority who passes, you have earned the awards listed below:

Test	Award
Written Composition	High Honors
Economics	Honors
Biology	Recognition

See how it works? These awards are formally called Academic Excellence Awards. Students who receive one of these three awards will receive an Academic Excellence Award from the State of California. This will be recorded on your high school transcript, and you'll receive a gold insignia on your diploma if you attain a score of high honors or honors.

HOW MANY PEOPLE EARN AWARDS AND WHAT DO THE HONORS REALLY MEAN?

According to the administration of the Golden State Examinations, only about one-third of the students who take an exam receives credit (one of the three honors) for any one GSE. Here's a description of these honors:

- **High Honors:** This is the most prestigious award given to students on the GSE Economics. It will be given to approximately the top 8 percent of students. If you receive "high honors," you will receive a special gold seal on your high school diploma, and your award will be placed on your permanent transcript. Even if you've already applied to college by the time you get your score back, you can still let the schools know about this achievement. Further, you can use this result as part of the requirements necessary for pursuing the ultimate award, the Golden State Merit Diploma.

- **Honors:** This is the second most prestigious award given to students on the GSE Economics. It will be given to approximately 12 percent of the students who take the exam (students who score in the 78th to 90th percentile). If you receive "honors," you will receive the same rewards as students who achieved a score of "high honors" (so, read above to see what you get).

- **Recognition:** This is the final type of Academic Excellence award given to students on the GSE Economics. It will be given to approximately 15 percent of the students that take the exam (students who score in the 66th to 78th percentile). If you receive an award of "recognition," you will receive notification of this achievement on your high school transcript. Further, you can use this result as part of the requirements necessary for pursuing the ultimate award, the Golden State Merit Diploma.

Any one of these awards can signal high achievement to colleges, universities, and employers. Golden State Scholars are also eligible for a Golden State Seal Merit Diploma.

What is the Golden State Seal Merit Diploma?

In July of 1996, the State of California developed a Golden State Seal Merit Diploma program to recognize high school graduates who demonstrated high performance in several different academic areas. The Golden State Merit Diploma is the most prestigious award you can receive. In 1997, the first year the Golden State Seal Merit Diploma was issued, more than 1,300 high school seniors received the award. This number jumped to more than 2,100 in 1998 and will continue to increase as more students take the Golden State Examinations.

In order to receive the Merit Diploma, students must receive high honors, honors, or recognition designations on *six* Golden State Examinations. The specific tests and requirements are described below.

How Can You Get a Golden State Seal Merit Diploma?

You must complete four required examinations, plus two elective exams, and receive at least recognition for them. You do not need to apply to receive a Golden State Seal Merit Diploma. School districts track the performance of each student and submit the information to the California Department of Education.

The four exams that students must pass are:

1. One English exam (Written Composition or Reading and Literature)
2. U.S. History
3. One Mathematics exam (Algebra, Geometry, or High School Mathematics)
4. One Science exam (Biology, Chemistry, Physics, or Coordinated Science)

In addition to the four required exams, you will take two other GSEs, selected from the following: Economics, Spanish Language, or Government and

Civics. You may also elect to complete an additional science, mathematics, or English exam as one of your electives. For example, let's say you complete both the Algebra and Geometry examinations. In this case, one of them will be counted as the mathematics *required* exam and the other as an elective.

WHAT MATERIAL IS COVERED ON THE GSE?

The Golden State Examinations are developed by a committee of teachers, university professors, and other education specialists. Each examination is designed and tested so that the content reflects the state standards and curriculum framework for each subject. In general, you should expect that the information tested on a GSE will be similar to what you've been tested on during the academic year. The style and format of the GSE may be different, but the material should be just like the stuff you studied in class. Unlike many other high school examinations, the GSEs are not designed to trick or trap you. Most examinations consist of one day of multiple-choice questions, followed by one day of written work. Of course, certain exams will have a different structure when appropriate, but all Golden State Examinations consist of two 45-minute parts. In Chapter 2, we'll discuss the specific format, structure, and scoring of the Golden State Examination in Economics.

> Remember that only about one-third of all test takers are honored for their performance on the Golden State Examination. Translation: Two-thirds don't pass and receive no recognition! These tests aren't a shoo-in; you need to know the material and be familiar with the structure to pass. This book is your key to being among the well prepared.

SO, HERE'S THE LOW-DOWN ON THE TEST

Below are all those so-called "frequently asked questions" about the administration of the GSEs. If there's anything we don't cover or if you're still confused, ask your guidance counselor or teacher.

How are GSE Exams Scored?

Every Golden State Examination has specific scoring criteria based on its format, structure, and level of difficulty. See Chapter 2 for more specific information about how the GSE Economics is scored.

As we mentioned, there is no penalty whatsoever for poor performance on a Golden State Examination. If you fail to receive one of the honors designations, there will be no mention of it on your academic transcript. Further, students who do not receive an honors designation on one GSE should still take additional GSEs. Each test is scored independently—performance on one GSE will have no impact on the scoring of any other GSE.

When Will I Receive My GSE Results?
Results from the Golden State Exam are first sent to your school district. If you take a winter test, you should expect to hear about your results in May. If you take a spring test, you should expect to hear about your results once you return to school in the fall.

If you have any questions regarding your performance on a GSE, contact your high school counselor for a copy of your results.

Can I Take the Tests More Than Once?
No. Students are eligible to take each GSE only one time. For this reason, be sure that you have learned the appropriate material before you take the test. If you're holding this book, you're well on your way!

How Can I Keep Track of All the Tests and Requirements?
Determining which GSEs to take, and when to take them, can be a confusing process. The California Department of Education has designed some worksheets for students to use that will help you keep track of this information. Ask your high school counselor for a copy of these worksheets.

How Do I Inform Colleges About My GSE Awards?
If you are applying to a college, university, or military academy, you will want to make sure that any awards you received on the Golden State Examinations are included in your application. If you received high honors, honors, or recognition on a GSE, this will be noted on your high school transcript. In addition, you can get a form called the *GSE Status Report for College Applications*. This form is available from your high school counselor, and along with your high school transcript, it will ensure that admissions boards notice your performance on these tests.

> For additional information about the GSE program, contact the Standards, Curriculum, and Assessment Division of the California Department of Education:
>
> phone: (916) 657-3011
> fax: (916) 657-4964
> email: star@cde.ca.gov
> Internet: www.cde.ca.gov/cilbranch/sca/gse/gse.html

HOW THIS BOOK IS ORGANIZED
The next chapter of this book is devoted to giving you the specifics about the test you are about to take. We will discuss test structure and scoring, and we'll also talk about some techniques and strategies that can be helpful to you as a test taker. Our goal is to provide you with a "bag of tricks" you can use throughout this exam. These tricks are actually helpful tools and tips that make it easier to take a standardized test.

We will then provide a specific content review of the subject material that's covered on the GSE. Rather than giving you lists of things to know, our goal is to give you information so that you can apply it to the specific way it's asked on the GSE. How do we know what is tested on the Golden State Examinations? We have carefully studied California State Curriculum Standards and Golden State Examination questions, surveyed high school teachers, and reviewed textbooks to determine exactly what is covered on each test.

Finally, we have prepared and constructed four full-length (practice) tests based on the GSE in Economics. We will provide you with detailed explanations to each problem, and sample written work, when appropriate. Use these tests to because familiar with the exam and to recognize the areas in which you need improvement.

Using all the elements in this book will prepare you to tackle anything the Golden State Examination throws your way.

WHAT IS THE PRINCETON REVIEW?

The Princeton Review is the nation's leader in test preparation. We have offices in more than fifty cities across the country, as well as many outside the United States. The Princeton Review supports more than two million students every year with our courses, books, online services, and software programs. In addition to helping high school students prepare for the GSEs, we help them with the AP, SAT-I, SAT-II, PSAT, and ACT, along with many other statewide standardized tests. The Princeton Review's strategies and techniques are unique and, most of all, successful.

Remember, this book will work best in combination with the material you have learned throughout your high school course. Our goals are to help you remember what you have been taught over the past year and show you how to apply this knowledge to the specific format and structure of the Golden State Examination.

AND FINALLY...

We applaud your efforts to spend the time and energy to take the Golden State Examination in Economics. You are giving yourself the opportunity to be rewarded for your academic achievement. Remember that the GSEs are not designed to trick you or test you on information you have never seen before. A strong year in your academic subject, combined with a review of the material and the test-taking strategies in this book, will leave you more than prepared to handle the GSE. Don't become frustrated if you don't remember everything at once; it may take some time for the information to come back.

We're rooting for you. We've designed our GSE series specifically for students who feel they are missing something in their preparation for these tests. Stay focused, practice, and try to have fun working through this book. And finally, good luck!

Chapter 2

WHAT'S ON THE ECONOMICS GSE: STRUCTURE AND STRATEGIES

It may seem pretty intimidating that only one-third of all students who take the GSEs receive any sort of honors. You might be wondering whether or not you can be one of them—of course you can! Just remember that most students don't prepare at all before taking the GSEs, so you're already ahead of the game. Our strong content review, in conjunction with our practice tests and proven techniques for scoring higher on standardized tests, will enable you to *crack* the Golden State Exam in Economics. Not only *can* you be in the top one-third of test-takers, we *expect* you to be!

In this chapter, we'll tell you which economics concepts are tested, and how. We'll also give you an idea of the scoring process, the structure and format of the test, and teach you The Princeton Review's proven strategies and techniques that will help you earn a higher score.

WHAT IS TESTED ON THE ECONOMICS GSE?

The content of the Economics GSE is in alignment with the State Board *California History–Social Science Framework for California Public Schools*. This means that what is tested on the Economics GSE will be similar to what you learned during the school year. The review in this book will cover in detail even the most challenging concepts you may have just touched on in class. This is so that once you master our review and the sample questions in the practice tests, the actual GSE should seem relatively easy to you. Specifically, the following content areas are covered in this book:

- **Fundamental Economics**

    This section tests the basic rules of economics. You probably learned this information at the start of your economics class. Below are some topics and definitions that are tested:
    - economics as the study of the scarcity of resources
    - the necessity of choice due to scarcity
    - economic specialization and efficiency
    - productive resources vs. final goods and services
    - introduction to the supply and demand market system
    - opportunity cost, marginal benefit, and marginal cost

- **Microeconomics**

    Many students learn microeconomics in combination with many formal statistical and mathematical models. While there are some calculations required in microeconomics questions, you will not be asked to perform any derivatives or fancy statistical operations. The following are some microeconomics topics that will be covered:
    - in-depth examination of the demand and supply market system
    - forms of business organizations (single proprietorships, partnerships, corporations, etc.)
    - market structures (perfect competition, monopolistic competition, oligopoly, and monopoly)
    - employment and wages, and their determinants
    - distributions of income, plus redistribution through taxes and transfer payments

- **Macroeconomics**

    All macroeconomic questions will be about the current United States economic system. Some international economics questions will appear, and those are described in the international section below:
    - economic measures such as gross national product and consumer price index

- aggregate demand and aggregate supply
- fiscal policy and the federal budget
- monetary policy and the Federal Reserve
- measures to study inflation, economic growth, and unemployment

- **International Economics**

    You will be asked a few questions about various international policies. All international trade questions will involve the United States as a participating country:
    - foreign exchange, exchange rates
    - comparative advantage, absolute advantage
    - balance of payments and trade
    - tariffs, quotas, and trade restrictions
    - international trade policies

- **Comparative Economic Systems**

    Questions in this area will focus on alternative economic systems, such as free market, traditional, and command economies. Additional questions will focus on the decision-making process of economic policies (decentralized decision making or command economy decision making).

HOW IS THE ECONOMICS EXAM STRUCTURED?

The Golden State Examination in Economics is two parts, administered in two 45-minute sections, each on a different day. For example, Part I may be on a Tuesday, and Part II on a Wednesday.

Part I consists of approximately 30 multiple-choice questions. These questions are designed to test your knowledge of a wide range of economics concepts. You will probably find several of these questions easy. However, you might have looked at the outline of topics above and seen a few topics that you weren't familiar with. Don't worry, we'll review all the material you need to know. Be sure to use this book in conjunction with your economics textbook to get the most thorough review possible.

Basically, the multiple-choice questions emphasize the concepts and principles of economics. Each of these questions consists of four answer choices. Later, we'll talk about how to use the answer choices to your advantage.

Part II consists of two essay questions that you must complete in 45 minutes each. You'll be asked to write essays that emphasize analysis and draw logical conclusions that are supported by sufficient and accurate detail. The score is on a 1–5 scale and will be determined not only by the conclusions you make, but by how well you support them.

HOW IS THE TEST SCORED?

A machine will score all of the multiple-choice questions in Part I. The written-response portion of the GSE Economics will be scored by economics teachers and other professionals. Your overall score will be a combination of your Part I and Part II scores.

CAN I USE ANY NOTES OR BOOKS FOR THIS EXAM?

No. This is a closed-book test. You will not be allowed to bring any reference material into the testing session.

CAN I BRING ANYTHING ELSE?

Of course you should have a few #2 pencils with erasers. You will need these to complete Part I and the written-response questions in Part II. In addition to pencils, the directions recommend that you bring a ruler or a straightedge. This can be helpful during the written-response question. For example, drawing supply-and-demand graphs may add support and credibility to the conclusions you present in your written response.

WHERE CAN I FIND A REAL GSE EXAM?

Sample copies of the real GSEs are not available, but you should get enough practice from the four practice Economics GSEs in the back of this book, which are followed by explanations and sample student written responses. These tests simulate the format and kinds of questions you can expect to see on the GSE.

YOUR BAG OF TRICKS

Have you ever seen the cartoon Felix the Cat? Felix fought crime, solved problems, and got his way out of difficult situations by reaching into his bag of tricks. In this special bag, he'd find the exact tool he needed to resolve any situation. With his bag of tricks, Felix was invincible.

We're going to help you fill up your own bag of tricks. What will be in there? We'll provide you with strategies and tools for handling the different types of questions on the GSE Economics, as well as general strategies for how to take the test. It is important to know that being a smart test-taker is just as important as knowing the material tested. Managing your time, knowing when to guess, and taking the time to figure out what the questions are *really* asking are skills that we'll teach you. These tools will help you earn more points in applying the material that you already know. You'll see there's a difference between knowing the material and *applying* it to the test. Let's take an example of two students, Gretchen and Laurie, each with the same amount of economics knowledge. Now, Gretchen took the same econ class as Laurie, but Gretchen has additional training. She has learned to think like the people who write the GSE: she understands the common mistakes, the ways to eliminate answer choices, and the best techniques to use for certain types of questions. In short, she has learned how to become a solid test-taker. Gretchen, with her bag of tricks, is now going to do much better on the GSE than Laurie. Why? Not because she knows more, but because she knows how to take this specific test in a smarter way than Laurie does. She understands the rules of the game. Once you know the rules of the game, you know how best to apply your skills to the test.

General Strategies

Now that you know what is tested on the GSE Economics, and in what format it is tested, we need to talk about the best way to take this test. Certainly, your overall score will be determined primarily by your knowledge of economics. However, learning how to take what you know and applying it to the test is a skill that can help you accumulate more points on this exam. In this chapter, we'll discuss some general tools for you to use as you proceed through the test. In the chapters ahead, we will discuss specific strategies for particular types of questions. For now, we're going to arm you with some tools to put in your bag of tricks to use throughout the test. Using these can help you become a better GSE test-taker.

An Empty Scantron Sheet Is a Bad Scantron Sheet

In the past you've probably taken a standardized test that had a guessing penalty. This penalty means that points would be subtracted from your raw score if you answered a question incorrectly. Guessing penalties are meant to discourage test-takers from answering every question.

But, guess what? There is NO guessing penalty on the GSE! Your score is only determined by the number of questions that you get correct; it doesn't matter how many questions you get incorrect. So, when you take the GSE, there is one thing that you must do before you turn in your test: You Must Answer Every Single Multiple-Choice Question! There are approximately 30 questions on Part I of the GSE Economics. Before you turn in your test, make sure that you have selected an answer for all 30. Earning an Academic Excellence Award may boil down to just one additional point, and leaving a question blank guarantees a wrong answer.

So, now you know that you must select an answer on every question. Great. Now, let's talk about how to be an intelligent guesser.

Process of Elimination (POE)

Try the following question:

> What is the capital of Malawi?

Unsure? Do you know even where Malawi is located? If not, don't panic. Geography and world capitals are not topics tested on the GSE. If you had to answer this question without any answer choices, you'd probably be in trouble. You'd just randomly pick a city, and most likely guess wrong.

Of course, on the GSE, you will have four answer choices to choose from. Rather than closing your eyes and selecting a choice at random, take a look at the choices—you might find some information that can help you:

> What is the capital of Malawi?
>
> A. Paris
>
> B. Lilongwe
>
> C. New York
>
> D. London

Now do you know? Can you identify any answer choices that you know are wrong? Sure! You can probably eliminate A, C, and D. Although you probably didn't know that Lilongwe is the capital of Malawi, you could tell that it was the correct answer by eliminating incorrect answer choices. This procedure is called Process of Elimination, or POE for short.

Process of Elimination will help you become a better guesser. This is because it is easier to spot incorrect answer choices than to know the correct answer. Remember to cross off any answer choice that you know is incorrect, then if you still need to make a guess, select an answer from your remaining choices.

It is unlikely that POE will actually help you eliminate three answer choices like we did in the sample problem above. However, every time you get rid of one answer choice, the odds of getting that question correct go up significantly. Instead of a 25 percent chance of guessing correctly, you will often find yourself guessing with a 50 percent (1 in 2) or 33 percent (1 in 3) chance of getting a question right.

Process of Elimination is such an important concept that we'll be referring to it throughout this book, including in the explanations provided to the practice tests. There are also some specific POE strategies for certain economics questions that will be presented in the chapters ahead. It is important that you practice using POE, because getting rid of incorrect answers is a powerful tool on the GSE.

You Don't Have to Start at Number 1

Some tests contain an order of difficulty within each section. On these kinds of tests, the first question is generally very easy, and the questions become progressively more difficult, with the last few questions being the hardest. On the GSE Economics, however, there is no order of difficulty on the multiple-choice section of the exam. Questions will vary in difficulty throughout the test in no particular order. So doing the test straight through, from 1 to 30, may not always be your best strategy. Your goal on the test is to work as rapidly as you can without sacrificing accuracy. This means that if you find that a question is difficult for you, leave it for later, and move on to another question.

The Two-Pass System

Have you ever been given a question that stumped you, but you were sure you could answer it? Have you ever said, "Just one more minute.... I know I can figure this out!" Well, we all have, and we know that one more minute sometimes means five more minutes, and often, we don't end up with the right answer at all.

Don't let one question ruin your whole day. No one question is that important. You've got a certain number of questions to tackle, and allowing one to throw off your timing might set you back. Here is a general rule for the multiple-choice section:

If you haven't figured out the correct answer in 90 seconds, skip the question and come back to it later. We're not telling you to give up on it. If you can't answer the question, make a small mark on your answer sheet so you can come back to it later. After you complete the section, go back to the questions you weren't able to answer. Remember to use POE on these questions, and make sure you have selected an answer choice for every question before time is up.

We call this strategy the two-pass system. The first time you go through a section, try every question. If a question seems too difficult or stumps you, move on. Once you've completed the section, go back to those questions. If you still aren't sure how to answer them, use POE and make a guess.

Often times, when you go back to a problem a second time you'll have a revelation about how to solve it. (We've all left a test and said, "Oh yeah! Now I know what the answer to number 5 was.") Skipping the questions and then going back to them might give you a chance to have this revelation *during* the test, when it's still useful.

Follow the Template

A lot of students think the written-response section of the GSE Economics is the most difficult section of the examination. Students usually find two major problems with the written-response question. First, they are uncomfortable with the format. (What if you are not familiar with the economic issue that is presented in the question?) Second, they tend to give up on the question as soon as they run into some problems.

Below is a reprint of the directions that appear with the written-response question found on Part II of the Economics GSE:

The essay portion of the examination will give you an opportunity to analyze and synthesize economic evidence, to demonstrate a chain of reasoning, and to justify your conclusions. You will want your essay to be clear and well-organized.

1. Read the following essay topic.

2. Plan your answer carefully before you begin to write. It is recommended that you outline your essay.

3. Allow at least 20 minutes to write your essay.

4. Use specific economic concepts, line graphs, terms, and policies to support ideas.

5. Avoid digressions. Stay focused on the topic and support your ideas with sufficient facts and reasons.

Later in the book, we will spend time practicing exactly how to approach these written-response questions, so that you will be comfortable with them by the time the actual test day comes. For now, you need only to remember the most important thing about answering a written-response question: **Provide explanations to the claims that you make!!**

To receive a high score on the written-response section, you will need to provide explanations for the material, arguments, and conclusions you present. When you make a claim, be sure to cite economic policies, graphs, or charts to document your claim. Supply-and-demand graphs, utility curves, and production charts are just a few examples of tools you can use to support a written-response question. Even if your claim is not that strong, you can receive some partial credit on this section for providing sound explanations, even if you do not end up with the best answer. Students who leave parts blank because they aren't sure of the answer cost themselves lots of points on this section. The reverse is also true: students who are able to give a correct answer often lose points for not providing a complete explanation. This is one area where showing your work is not only helpful, it is vital to scoring well on the exam.

Further, one of the greatest challenges on Part II of the GSE Economics is to organize your thoughts into a well-constructed explanation within a quick, 45-minute time frame.

We will discuss other strategies for the written-response questions in more detail as we move throughout the review of economics concepts.

YOU ARE IN CONTROL

We know that taking the Economics GSE can be a stressful process. With all this built-up pressure, it might feel like this test is totally out of your control. But, the opposite is true—you are in control. Although you can't decide what number pencil to bring to the exam (you must bring a #2) or where to sit during the test, you can decide how you take the GSE. Let's review what we've discussed in this chapter:

- First, you must take advantage of the multiple-choice format of Part I. There's no guessing penalty, and you can use Process of Elimination to add points to your score, even without knowing the correct answer.

- Second, you can answer the multiple-choice questions in any order you want. Spend time with questions that you're comfortable with. If question 12 is really stumping you, move on to question 13, but save 12 for later.

- Third, you can gain points on the written-response section by providing clear explanations and supporting your claim with graphs or charts.

As you build on your economics knowledge by reviewing the chapters ahead, you'll gain more confidence in your ability to handle the questions presented on the GSE.

Bag Of Tricks Summary

Here's a list of tricks you'll find in that bag of yours. Be sure to make good use of them on the test:

- Leave no questions blank.
- Use Process of Elimination (POE).
- You Don't Have to Start at Number 1.
- The Two-Pass System.
- On the written-response questions, provide thorough, well-reasoned answers even if you can't answer all parts.
- You control how you take the test.

Chapter 3

CRACKING THE MULTIPLE-CHOICE SECTION

In Chapter 2 we introduced you to your bag of tricks. In this chapter we are going to show you how to apply those tools specifically to GSE Economics. But no matter what test you are taking, there are certain principles and procedures that will increase your chances of success. These include such things as eating a healthy diet, consistently exercising at least at a moderate level, and making sure you get adequate sleep. All of these help your body—and especially your brain—to work more efficiently. You should absolutely make sure that you get adequate sleep the night before the exam itself. At some point, whatever studying you have managed to accomplish will be done, and any additional study time will only yield diminishing returns, relative to those of a restful night's slumber. A well-rested mind is a significantly more efficient one. You will make far fewer careless errors, and you will be able to recall what you learned while studying much more rapidly. This is a fact, so get to bed early the night before the exam. The return will be a quantum boost in your performance.

While we are on the subject of efficiency, let's not neglect your study habits. Though self-discipline may be required, it is probably no secret to you that consistent, concentrated study is the golden road to learning and success. Instead of trying to pack it all in during one cram session, study small amounts of material, without distractions, on a regular basis throughout the year and particularly in the weeks preceding the exam. If you study smaller amounts of material at one time, you will be less likely to become bored. Even if you study intensely, it takes less time to review a year's worth of economics in shorter stints. Instead of gobbling the course whole and thus becoming intimidated and overwhelmed, you will slowly but surely build a core of knowledge in your subject.

Another benefit of the consistent study method is that the longer you live with the material, the more likely it will become permanent knowledge. You'll get to the point where you make associations based on your newly acquired knowledge. You'll consciously and subconsciously be living with and mulling over the new ideas until they become deeply ingrained in your mind and you completely understand them. At that point, you can more easily apply your knowledge of economics, which has become second nature to you. It will give you a wider view of the world and the issues that drive its political economy.

MULTIPLE-CHOICE QUESTIONS

The multiple-choice section on the GSE Economics consists of 30 questions that you have 45 minutes to answer. That gives you 90 seconds per question. However, you probably don't want to spend much more than one minute on any individual question. You should try to save time to go through the multiple-choice section twice. Go through the first pass carefully but quickly, only answering the questions that are relatively easy for you. Spending too much time on any one question will just increase the likelihood that you will not get to read all the questions, and thus miss the opportunity to answer a few easier questions that may appear near the end of the multiple-choice section.

Use Process of Elimination

The second pass is the time to try to answer the difficult questions that you skipped on the first pass. As you reread the difficult questions, be careful to determine exactly what is being asked. Then, use process of elimination to help you choose the right answer from among the choices that are given. It's often easier to eliminate some choices than it is to see the correct answer outright. For every answer that you can eliminate, you significantly increase your odds of guessing the correct answer. Here's an example:

If a price floor is set above the equilibrium price in a market, then

A. a surplus of goods will exist

B. a shortage of goods will exist

C. there will be upward pressure on price in the market

D. it will encourage increased consumption of goods

E. both B and D

Note, a price floor does not allow the price to fall below a certain level. If this price is above the equilibrium price, then price is already being set higher than it would have been in a free market. Thus, there would be no further upward pressure on price and choice (C) can be eliminated from consideration. It is also obvious that a high price would never encourage more consumption, as consumers prefer low prices. Thus, choice (D) can also be eliminated, as can choice (E), which includes (D) as part of the answer. Now, you have only two possible choices remaining: (A) or (B). If you had no idea before, you now have a 50/50 chance of choosing correctly. Setting a price higher than its equilibrium level must cause either a surplus or a shortage. And if you think just a little more on the subject, it might even become clear that (A) is the correct choice, because a price that is set too high will naturally encourage production as it discourages consumption. There will be more brought to the market at this artificially high price than consumers are willing and able to buy.

Read Carefully

Make sure that you read the questions and all of the answers carefully before committing to one answer. Here's an example:

If a nation's current account is in balance, then

A. its exports are greater than its imports

B. capital inflows outweigh capital outflows

C. there are no barriers to trade

D. the nation is following its comparative advantage

E. none of the above

Reading carefully, we note that the question asks about the current account when it is balanced. Even if you do not realize that this means the nation's imports and exports are essentially in balance, and that it would imply the same for the capital inflows and outflows, (A) and (B) can be eliminated as unlikely candidates because they clearly speak of imbalances. (C) says there are no barriers to trade, like tariffs or quotas, but it should be clear that whether a nation has barriers or not does not necessarily imply imbalance or balance in its accounts. For (D), following one's comparative advantage may be efficient, but nations motivated by inefficient criteria are just as likely or unlikely to experience balances in their international financial flows as are nations motivated by efficiency. If one does not panic and assume that one of the vague answers must be the right one, then it becomes clear, through knowledge and using Process of Elimination, that there really isn't a good answer given. That is, with the exception of (E), which states none of the above.

Be Aware of Qualifiers

Make sure that you are exceptionally careful to look for qualifiers in questions. Words such as *biggest, best, optimal, compare, contrast, not* can change the entire meaning of the question. Here's an example:

> Which of the following is NOT a reason for preferring perfect competition to monopoly?
>
> A. it is self-regulatory
>
> B. greater levels of total production
>
> C. maximum profits experienced in the long run
>
> D. more employment of labor
>
> E. greater allocative efficiency

If you don't notice the word *not*, or realize that the question draws a comparison between perfect competition and monopoly, you might get lost in the choices above.

All of those choices have such a positive ring to them. However, if you read carefully and note all qualifiers and comparisons, it is clear that only 1 of the 5 answers is a reason NOT to prefer perfect competition.

Perfectly competitive industries are composed of many firms, which produce a homogeneous product, and whose obstacles to entry are nonexistent. Because of the many firms, the markets need little regulation or policing. Thus, (A) can be eliminated.

Because of the degree of competition, all other things being equal, the total production in the industry is driven upwards. Thus, (B) can be eliminated. To produce a larger amount of product, such an industry will tend to make fuller use of available labor. Thus, (D) can be eliminated. The pressures of competition also drive firms to utilize their productive capacity to its utmost extent, and to set prices consistent with the costs of production. In a few words, perfect competitors are allocatively efficient. Thus, (E) can be eliminated. The only remaining answer is (C).

The ease of entry and exit tends to cause firms that are competitive to break even in the long run. Monopolists, with their singular control of the supply side of a market, tend to ration production, keep price higher than cost, and to maximize profits in both the short and long run. (C) is the correct answer.

Answer Every Question

Because there is no penalty for guessing, don't let time run out on the multiple-choice section without filling in an answer for each and every question. Do not leave any questions blank!

To summarize:

- Pace yourself for two passes.
- Use the process of elimination to increase your odds.
- Read questions and answers carefully and completely.
- Leave no blanks.

Check out the next chapter for some tips on cracking the essay portion of the GSE!

Chapter 4

CRACKING THE ESSAY SECTION

The essay section of the GSE consists of two essays that you only have 45 minutes to answer. That means that you'll have 22.5 minutes to allot to each question. This is not enough time to create a masterpiece, and the question will probably reflect this by being rather focused. The exam readers will expect you to be both concise and precise in your explanation. With 22.5 minutes per essay, you need to prepare your prewriting steps quickly and then systematically answer the question. Below we'll teach you a strategy that will make this process easy.

HOW ARE THE EXAMS SCORED?

You will receive between 1 and 5 points for each of the two essays that you write. To earn 5 points, you need to do the following:

- Show that you can analyze the topic by using fully developed, clear interpretation and argument.
- Support your analysis with specific and applicable details.
- If required, include graphs that are correct and fit into the essay appropriately.

- Show an excellent understanding of the topic and use economic terminology properly. (Don't throw in smart-sounding econ terms if you aren't positive that you are using them correctly!)

If you fulfill the above requirements but make a few factual errors, you most likely will receive a 4. Also, if you answer all parts of the question, but focus too much on one aspect and not as much on the others, you will receive a 4. If you do not present a clear argument, do not complete all parts of the question, or do not show a solid grasp of the concepts, you will receive a 3. You'll get a 1 or 2 for an essay that displays little understanding of the topic or one that rambles and doesn't clearly answer the question.

Make sure that you answer both essay questions! If you don't answer one, you are guaranteed a 0. Most likely, if you attempt to answer the question (even if your answer is confusing and mostly just restates the question) you'll get at least one point.

WHO ARE THE GRADERS AND WHAT ARE THEY LOOKING FOR?

The essay part of the GSE will be graded by a group of economics teachers and professional economists. These graders will read hundreds of essays. For each essay, they have to decide whether the essay is excellent (5 points), good (4 points), mediocre (3 points), not very good (2 points), or bad (1 point). Eventually, after reading a hundred sloppy, confusing essays they'll be thrilled to read a clear, well-argued essay. A great essay makes the grader's job easy; he or she can read it quickly without getting confused, give it a 5, and move on to the next essay.

Many essays are on the border between two scores, and the grader could feel just as confident giving those "border dwellers" the lower score. Some graders get in a rut and can mark several exams in a row the lower score. A clear essay with a good structure will break them out of that rut. You need to use the exam grading process to your advantage by making the grader's job easy. All you need to do is follow our steps to success and keep reminding yourself to be straightforward—oh, and knowing a few economic concepts can't hurt either.

> We'll say it again: the graders like reading clear well-structured essays because it makes their job easier, so they'll be happy to give it a 5.

THE FOUR STEPS TO WRITING A FIVE-POINT ESSAY

The following are the steps you need to follow to rack up the points in the essay portion of the GSE. Even if you don't completely know the answer to the question, by following these steps you'll certainly be able to earn a few points for each essay.

STEPS TO SUCCESS

Step One: Read Carefully

The first step to writing a successful essay is to carefully read the question. Try to understand exactly what the question is asking and always keep that in mind. It will help you from straying wildly off the topic or from adding unnecessary information to your answer. While you are reading it, underline the components of the essay, so that you can see them clearly.

Step Two: Brainstorm

The second step to success is to devote just a couple of minutes to brainstorming.

Once you are certain what the question is addressing, write down a quick list of ideas you associate with that topic. This might include key terminology, graphs, and/or historical examples. It depends on the particular question which of these may apply.

Step Three: Edit and Organize

The third step involves editing and organizing this quick list you wrote so that you show a logical and coherent line in your reasoning and argument. Here's an example:

> For most of the 1990s Japan has been mired in recession.
>
> a) Explain what it means for a nation to be in recession.
>
> b) Offer some possible policy solutions to Japan's woes.

Note, the question involves a nation in recession. Part A essentially wants you to define and describe what a recession is, and part B wants you to propose typical solutions to such a problem.

You should spend the first two minutes jotting down a quick list like the following:

Define recession
> Falling real GDP
> High unemployment rates
> Wasted resources
> Lower standard of living
> Graph of dip in business cycle
> GDP gap increases

Solutions:
> Expansionary fiscal and monetary policies
> Lower taxes…increase government spending
> Increase money supply leading to lower interest rates
> Keynesian Cross diagram
> Aggregate supply/aggregate demand diagram
> Show recessionary gap, and boost in AD

You don't necessarily have to use all the information you thought of, but a well-conceived essay that incorporates several of the items above and that is supported with clearly drawn diagrams will score big points.

Step Four: Write the Essay

When writing the essay, use a simple and short opening introduction that clearly states your objective. The body of your essay should consist of from 2 to 4 paragraphs that clearly make and develop your arguments. Again, stick to using simple, direct, clear language and sentence structure. Make sure you use proper grammar and neat handwriting. Verbose and florid prose can be misunderstood and misinterpreted. The reviewers want a clear impression of your knowledge. They are not mind readers, and will not work overly hard to try to interpret your confusing words. They will view confused prose as a reflection of a confused student, who has yet to master the subject.

Your conclusion should be a strong but short summary statement. Don't waste time or energy here. Just reassert your basic premises and be done.

Here's another example with an answer that would be well-received by the GSE graders:

> Graph and explain the impact on the personal computer market of using less expensive semiconductor chips in the construction of personal computers.

Semi-conductor chips are a vital input in the production of personal computers. As such, when chip cost declines, it has significant effects on the personal computer market.

Whenever an input's price is reduced, it has a positive effect on the production, or supply, of the good it is helping to produce. In this case, semiconductor chips have become less expensive, and so the cost of producing a personal computer has fallen. Such a cost reduction will lead to an increased supply of the good, as producers with lower costs are willing and able to produce more of the good at any particular price.

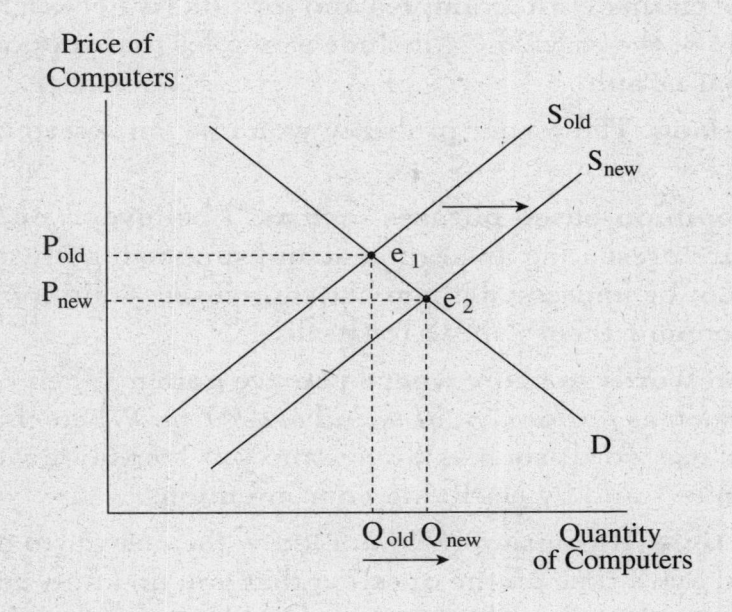

Note, on the graph above, when chips decline in price, and the cost of producing a personal computer declines, the supply of computers increases, represented by a shift of the supply curve out to the right. The new supply curve crosses the demand curve at a new, different point of agreement, or equilibrium. The new equilibrium price of computers has fallen, and the new equilibrium quantity has risen.

In short, because of lower costs in production and a consequent rise in supply, prices of computers will drop and will induce greater sales of computers in the marketplace.

ESSAY-WRITING ADVICE

Keep sentences and paragraphs simple. Avoid run-on sentences or confusing paragraph structure. You must make your essay easy for the grader to read. Do not use words if you are unclear on their meaning or usage.

Use good penmanship. The graders don't want to strain their eyes while they try to figure out chicken scratch penmanship. If your handwriting makes reading the essay difficult, it may have an adverse effect on your grade.

Follow the introduction, body, and conclusion structure. The grader will be impressed if the body of your essay sticks to the ideas presented in your introduction and follows through to the conclusion.

Support your claims with examples and graphs (if necessary). Each paragraph in the body of the essay must include examples that support the first sentence of the paragraph.

Avoid using slang. The reader probably won't be impressed by the use of slang.

Avoid using opinion-based phrases such as "I believe..." or "I think..." In your essay, you are presenting an argument and supporting it with evidence. The grader will not be impressed if you blatantly insert your opinions into your essay. Let the economic theory speak for itself!

Use transition words to show where you are going. When continuing an idea, use words such as *furthermore*, *also*, and *in addition*. When changing the flow of your thoughts, use words such as *however* and *yet*. Transition words make your essay easier to understand by clarifying your intentions.

Budget your time. If you simply do not know the answer to one question, you should spend extra time on the question that you do know so that you can earn 5 points. Remember, though, that you should answer the question that you don't know anyway. You'll most likely pick up a few points if you make an attempt.

Let's review some important points for a successful essay:

- Read the question carefully and focus on what it's asking.

- Brainstorm to make a quick list of ideas related to the topic.

- Organize ideas and supporting material, such as graphs.

- Reserve almost 20 of your 22.5 minutes to write the essay.

- Start simply and directly; the body should be objective and clear; the conclusion a strong summary of what you have demonstrated in the body.

- Keep sentences short and sweet; use good grammar; write with good penmanship.
- At all times, remain logical, focused, and clear.

If you follow these tips, you should be able to write a logical and clear essay. Good luck!

Part II

ECONOMICS REVIEW

Chapter 5

ECONOMICS

Economics is the study of how we allocate our limited resources to satisfy our unlimited wants. This seems like a simple enough sentence, but let's dissect it a bit.

In some shape or form, we all desire to get what we want, when we want it. These are the unlimited wants that we referred to above; however, we live in a world of scarce resources. So, we have a problem, the economizing problem or problem of scarcity, because we cannot have everything we wish for in the real world.

In the real world, there are only so many people, with just so much skill, energy, and ambition. In the real world there is only so much raw material that nature provides. And in the real world, there is only so much machinery that is only at a certain level of technological advancement. These resources are often referred to as labor, land, and capital, and they are limited or scarce.

With scarce resources, or inputs, there can only be so much output—the goods and services that satisfy our needs—produced. So, again this leads to our problem, the economizing problem.

If you cannot have everything you desire, should you give up? Of course you shouldn't! And economies, which are a collection of human interests, do not give up either. They attempt to do the best that they can achieve, given the limits they face.

When an economy does the best it can, it achieves full production. Full production means that all resources are being used completely and efficiently, and, as a result, the greatest possible level of production for a particular nation in a particular year has been achieved. The nation has reached its economic potential.

PRODUCTION POSSIBILITIES

A nation can use its resources fully and efficiently in many different ways, producing many different combinations of goods while reaching its economic potential.

Economists often depict the various combinations that a nation can produce at full production with a production possibilities curve (PPC), which is sometimes called a transformation curve.

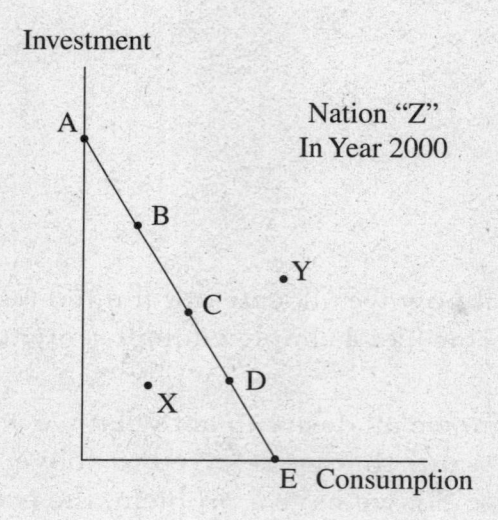

Every point on the PPC shown above represents a point of maximum, or full, production for nation Z in the year 2000. Points on the graph such as A, B, C, D, and E have something in common. Any one of them represents a full and efficient use of the resources of nation Z in the year 2000. But they have important differences too. Each represents a unique mix of consumption and investment goods that can be produced:

- Point A uses all the nation's resources for investment-oriented goods. These are goods like infrastructure—such as roads and bridges—education, training, and other goods whose benefits will largely enhance a nation's growth and wealth in future time periods.

- Point E uses all the nation's resources for consumption-oriented goods. These are goods like food, clothing, entertainment, and anything else that tend to enhance the current standard of living in a nation. The benefits are felt largely in the short run.

- Points B, C, or D each represent production of a mix of consumption and investment goods, but the proportion of one to another varies from case to case.

Notice what the curve implies: if any of these points completely exhausts the resources of a nation, and any single point differs as to how those resources are used, then a choice must be made. A nation cannot be at A and B, or any other two points at the same time, any more than an individual can be at home taking a nap and simultaneously attending economics class. The nation and the student must make a choice.

Nations, like individuals, will choose a point at which to aim based on their subjective preferences and perceived needs. If they wish to grow more quickly, they may choose something farther up and to the left (such as point B), where greater expenditure on investment will help them get to this point. Whereas, if they want a quick and current boost in their material well-being, they may shoot for more consumption to meet this need (point D). Either way, since a nation can only use its resources fully one way, it must make a choice.

And, as you may have suspected, no matter what a nation hopes to achieve, it may fall short of its goal. Points lying beneath the PPC represent such disappointments.

Point X is just one of the infinite number of points that represents falling short of full production. And how is it that such a thing occurs? Look at unemployment. When people are willing and able to make a productive contribution to a nation's output, and yet they are excluded from participating in the economy, they are unemployed. They are in a bad position, but so is society at large, for having squandered a valuable resource. A nation with high unemployment will not reach full production.

By the same token, if someone has excellent skills that are being underutilized or if another person would like to make a larger effort but is kept from doing so, then we could say these people are **underemployed**. Nations with large amounts of underemployment will not achieve full production. Thus, we have our answer: Nations fall short of full production any time they have unemployment or underemployment. In other words, when a nation wastes its resources, it does not *do the best it can*.

That explains points like X, but what about points like Y, which lie above and beyond our PPC? Quite simply, these are points of production that are currently impossible for nation Z to reach. Naturally, with investment, a nation may grow, and a point like Y, which is unattainable today, may be easily reached in the future. But for now, it's simply out of reach.

Why the Negative Slope?

A negative slope runs down as you move from left to right. It indicates a negative, or inverse, relationship. This means that as one of the two variables goes down, the other goes up. This might make it obvious to you why a PPC has a negative slope. If all points on a PPC represent full and efficient use of resources, then as nation Z moves from one point to another, gaining one good, it must necessarily divert resources from the other good and thus its production will fall.

In the PPC diagram, as nation Z moves down the curve, it is gaining consumption at the expense of investment. If it had gone up the curve, it would have gained investment, but at the expense of consumption. This must be so, since the only way to have a fully employed economy is to take some resources—labor, land, and capital—from some other sector where they were already making a contribution. This also illustrates an important basic principle of economics, which says "there is no such thing as a free lunch." By choosing to produce one good, you have given up the opportunity to produce the other good. This is known as the **opportunity cost** associated with the production of that good. You never get something for nothing. In a world of scarcity, you must always choose, and in so doing, you must forego other possibilities. You are reading this book now. What have you given up at this moment to read this book? You are not reading another book. You are not taking a nap. You are not socializing with your friends. Do you see how pervasive opportunity costs truly are?

Back to Choice

Earlier we mentioned the economizing problem, which exists because we live in a world of scarcity. Thus, we are confronted with choices, one of which concerns the economic systems we pursue.

Traditional economic systems, although more common long ago, do still exist. These systems do not allow for much freedom or flexibility, but in a world of famine, disease, low technology, and short life spans, they guarantee that a certain predictability could be maintained. If all children follow their parents in a line of work, then the system would be unlikely to ever have a complete shortage of that sort of worker. If rules of inheritance remain rigid and consistent, then property, as a basis for early society's wealth, will not be threatened. Traditional economic systems, for all their shortcomings, do suit certain circumstances better than we sometimes appreciate.

In more recent times, the two great "-isms" that have struggled for ascendance are socialism and capitalism. **Socialism** is considered a stepping stone to the more idealistic extreme of pure communism. Under socialism, most property and the means of production are held by the state. There are strict limitations on variation in wages among and between jobs. Price controls and planning are universally used, and the individual is considered to be in service to the greater good of society as a whole. A central planning committee decides what is to be produced, how it is to be produced, and for whom.

The downfall of socialism in recent years became manifest because too many systems that were socialistically constructed failed to use their sometimes abundant resources efficiently. This, however, should not be a surprise. Limiting compensation and private ownership limits incentives for the individual to contribute. Trying to plan every detail in a complex and ever-changing modern economy is old-fashioned at best, ludicrous at worst. Setting prices leads to surpluses and shortages whenever those prices do not reflect market conditions.

On the other hand, **capitalism** is based on private property and initiative. It allows individuals the freedom to participate in markets, buying and selling their property, to the extent that it serves their own interest. This is known as **free enterprise**. Because all individuals have the right to private property, and can freely buy and sell it, the inevitable result is competition and the rationing of property to those who are best able to manage it. Does this lead to a society of "haves" and "have-nots"? Not according to capitalist theory.

With free markets and self-interest in operation, the great eighteenth-century economist, Adam Smith, said there is a kind of "Invisible Hand" at work. Smith essentially said, I don't work so well or so hard for any other reason than for my love of myself and those of my immediate concern, such as my family. However, the only way for me to be rewarded more for my efforts would be to channel my time, talent, and energies into activities valued by society as a whole. By following self-interest, I am inclined to enhance the wealth of society at large. I will provide services for which society will reward the "Love of my life," which is me! And as long as government stays out of the way, not regulating or taxing the operation of these markets, then efficiency and production, individual incentive, and initiative will be maximized.

Shortcomings of Capitalism

Nice theory, capitalism, but does it work? To a large extent, yes, but there are significant qualifications to be made. For instance, aren't there lottery winners among us? Not many, but they do exist. What did these lucky winners do productively to deserve such rewards? The answer is—nothing! Of course, this seems like a silly case to cite because it is rare and insignificant. But what about the other "lottery winners" among us, like children who stand to inherit fortunes just because their talented, hard-working parents are rich.

Let's not forget to mention all forms of discrimination and bias founded on any other basis but productivity. Through much struggle and work, bias and discrimination have abated tremendously in our nation in the last few generations, but they still exist and infringe on the possibility to establish any capitalistic ideal.

Mixed Enterprise

Modern nations have a choice to make because we live in a world of scarcity. One of these is which economic system to choose. There never has been a purely communist or capitalist country on earth, and perhaps there never will be.

The economic systems from which nations actually choose are differing degrees of mixed enterprise, and in recent years most nations have favored a brand of mixed enterprise strongly inclined toward the capitalist end of the spectrum, not unlike the U.S.

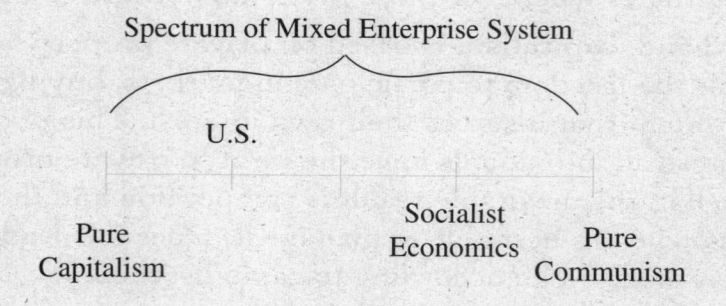

Spectrum of Mixed Enterprise System

U.S.

Pure Capitalism — Socialist Economics — Pure Communism

In the U.S. we have an economy of largely free and unfettered markets, where overwhelming proportions of all kinds of property are held by private citizens or privately owned institutions. We do, however, have significant taxation, regulation, and government programs to modify our predominantly capitalistic culture. We support a system based largely on individual incentive, but recognize the need for some social/welfare modifications.

The U.S. federal government has a budget of close to 2 trillion dollars with programs ranging from social security to welfare, which, taken together with national defense and debt service, dominate the outlay of this enormous fund. One could easily argue for a more efficient social welfare system. However, one would be hard pressed to make an argument for its complete abolition.

Chapter 6

MARKETS

Markets are places where buyers and sellers meet, negotiate, and exchange goods, services, or resources. Every market has two sides: a buying side (the demand-side of the market) and a selling side (the supply-side).

Quite naturally, buyers and sellers—demand and supply—have different interests and inclinations for participating in markets. Neither will receive their most extreme hope and desire. Through negotiation, however, they may achieve a mutually satisfying balance—called the **equilibrium**—of their competing interests. Let's look at each side of the market in isolation, so that we better understand the differences and how they ultimately reach their agreement.

DEMAND

By using various statistical techniques, the reactions of a consumer, or a group of consumers, can be represented by a **demand schedule**. The demand schedule shows, in tabular form, the varying amounts of a good that a consumer is willing and able to buy at different prices.

Law of Demand

As $P \uparrow Q_d \downarrow$ and as $P \downarrow Q_d \uparrow$

P = price of good/service
Q_d = quantity demanded of a good/service

It is typical for the consumer to be willing and able to buy more of a good as its price falls. Conversely, as price rises, it is a discouragement to the buyer. When translated graphically, this inverse relation, known as the **Law of Demand**, will be illustrated with a curve of negative slope—that is, a slope that falls as you move from left to right. This is known as a **demand curve**.

The Law of Demand states that there is an inverse relation between the price of a good and the quantity demanded of that good. Simply put: all other things being equal, as price rises, consumers are less willing and able to buy a good. As price falls, they are more willing and able to buy a good.

Demand Schedule:

Price of Oranges $	Quantity of Oranges Demanded	PT.
5	10	A
4	20	B
3	30	E
2	40	C
1	50	D

Demand Curve:

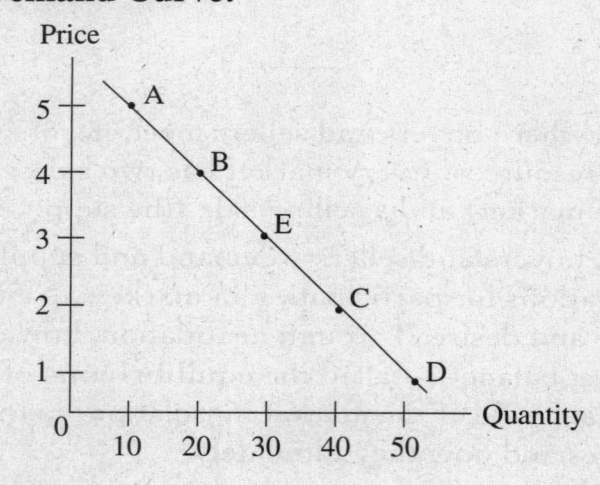

SUPPLY

The reactions of producers can also be estimated and presented in tabular form. This is known as the **supply schedule**. This supply schedule indicates the various amounts of a good that a producer is willing and able to provide to the market at different prices. Producers are inclined to love high prices, as there is prospectively greater profitability. At high prices, the producer is willing and able to provide more to the market. And low prices, acting as a discouragement, will reduce the tendency of producers to provide goods to the market. This direct relationship between price and the quantity supplied is known as the **Law of Supply.**

> **Law of Supply**
> As $P\uparrow Q_s \uparrow$ and as $P\downarrow Q_s \downarrow$
> Q_s = quantity supplied of a good

The graphical representation of the supply schedule is a positively sloped **supply curve**, one that slopes upward as you move left to right.

The Law of Supply states that there is a positive, or direct, relation between the price of a good and its quantity supplied. Simply put: other things being equal, as price rises, so does the willingness and ability of producers to bring goods to the market. When price falls, so does the inclination of producers to provide goods.

Supply Schedule:

Price of Oranges $	Quantity of Oranges Demanded	PT.
5	50	F
4	40	G
3	30	E
2	20	H
1	10	I

Supply Curve:

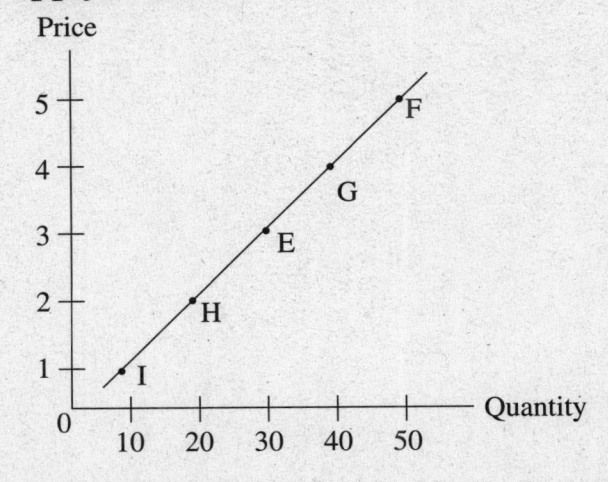

MARKET EQUILIBRIUM

Now that we understand a little more about the tendencies of supply and demand, we can bring them together in the market. Recall that demand and supply curves taken alone, in isolation from each other, do *not* reflect the market as a whole. They only outline the inclinations of the two competing interests that participate in the market. The buyers will not receive immense quantities of goods at zero cost, and sellers will not be able to sell enormous amounts of goods at extremely high prices. It is obvious that these are two distinct groups, with different objectives. They must engage in a struggle to find some middle ground, which is mutually satisfying to each, or the transaction of goods will not take place. This struggle, or negotiation, between the competing interests of demand and supply is known as the **price mechanism**. It sets the actual price and quantities of goods that will represent equilibrium in free markets.

In its simplest form, when quantity is fixed and only price is negotiable, the price mechanism is a game that we have all witnessed many times. It is a game of "you come down a bit, and I'll come up a bit." For instance, suppose I have an old car I'd like to sell. I'm the supplier and love high prices. I'd like to start the bidding high, and if possible, keep it there. On the other hand, suppose you are interested in buying a used car. You are the demander and as such, hate high prices. You'd like to start the bidding low, and if possible, keep it there. As the negotiation commences, I may come down a bit. You may come up a bit. If we hit a mutually satisfactory point, and exchange the car at an agreed on price, then we have found an equilibrium, a balance of our competing interests. The struggle that led automatically to this balance is called the **price mechanism.**

Even though suppliers and demanders have differing objectives in markets, they can find a mutually beneficial point, an equilibrium, at which to exchange.

Below is a combination of the demand and supply schedules and curves, so that you can see just how automatically this mechanism brings about equilibrium when both price and quantity are undetermined.

Demand & Supply Schedules:

Price of Oranges ($)	Q_d	Q_s	Surplus or Shortage	Pressure on Price
5	10	50	Surplus 40	Down
4	20	40	Surplus 20	Down
3	30	30	Equilibrium	None
2	40	20	Shortage 20	Up
1	50	10	Shortage 40	Up

Market Diagram:

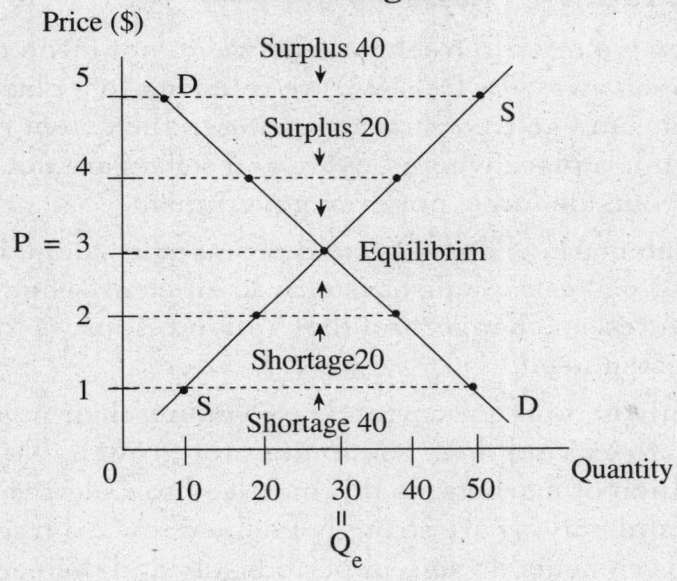

The equilibrium occurs at a price of $3.00 and at a quantity of 30 oranges. If this market operates freely, then this is the price and quantity at which exchange will be made. Any deviation from this point signals a divergence of interests between buyer and seller, and either too much or too little would be available in the market.

More specifically, suppose the price was set at $5.00. This relatively high price encourages supply, but simultaneously discourages demand. Thus, a surplus ($Q_s > Q_d$) of 40 oranges would exist, if the seller insisted on keeping the price so high. Of course, who likes rotting, smelly fruit and financial losses? The price will inevitably drop toward the equilibrium.

MARKETS ◆ 47

The price could have been set at $1.00. And such a low price would surely encourage demand, but discourage supply. In this case, many people who want oranges will not have them, and many providers who could have sold them profitably will not.

Can you see how this shortage ($Q_s < Q_d$) of 40 oranges will lead to rising prices, which would ration available oranges and lead to greater orange production and distribution?

Surpluses drive prices down, while shortages drive prices up. Neither surplus nor shortage will persist in a free market for long, as neither serves the self-interest of the buyer or seller.

WHEN MARKETS AREN'T FREE

As you know, when we refer to free markets, we do not mean to imply that goods are being given away for free. We are referring to a place where buyers and sellers can come and go freely, participating to the extent that it serves their own self-interest. It is a place where buyers and sellers are not compelled to act in any way by any outside force, not even government.

Not only do such markets thrive on and promote freedom, but they are also at the heart of what makes capitalist systems so efficient. They allow for rapid adaptability to unforeseen change, and they ration resources to those areas where they are most in need.

This is why many nations are currently expanding their involvement with free markets, so as to expand their possibilities for growth. No one advocates complete deregulation of markets, as this may lead to excesses of other kinds. Thus, most successful nations are strongly inclined toward free market economies; however, governments do step in periodically and deliberately interfere with the free exchange that takes place in some markets.

Below are two classic examples from our own economy.

Price Ceilings

A **price ceiling** occurs when the government sets a maximum price at which goods may be exchanged. This does not affect the operation of a free market unless the maximum price is lower than the equilibrium price, in which case it encourages buying, discourages selling, and results in a shortage. Rent control or stabilization programs are examples of a price ceiling that local governments establish. In most instances, such programs set a price of housing—a rent—that is deliberately lower than the price in a free market.

Rent Control

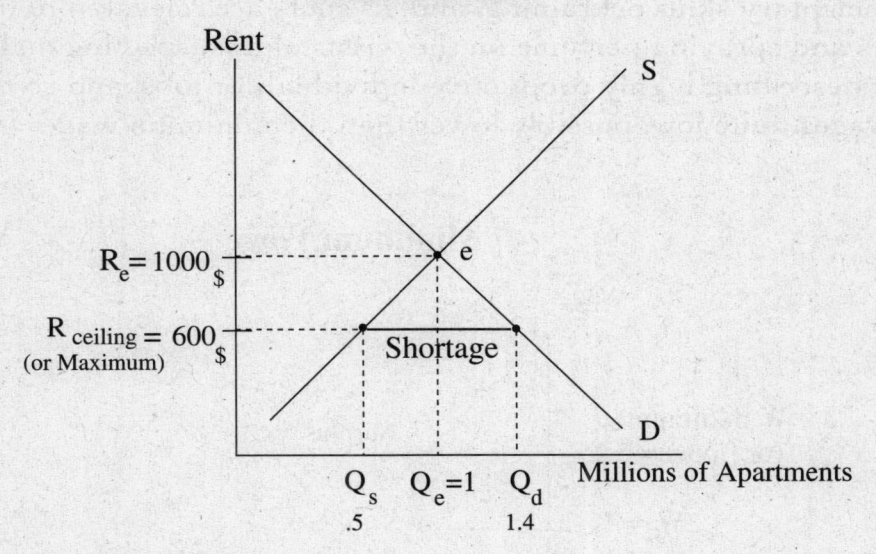

```
Rent
                              S
R_e = 1000 $ ----------- e
R_ceiling = 600 .------·------·
(or Maximum) $      Shortage
                              D
              Q_s  Q_e=1  Q_d   Millions of Apartments
              .5          1.4
```

As you can see in our hypothetical market above, the equilibrium rent is $1,000. At that price, there is an agreement between buyers and sellers as to how many units of housing to exchange. If the government were to step in and set a rent ceiling at $600, then it is clear that renters would be willing and able to buy more units, but that the landlords would be less willing and able to provide units. The result would be a shortage of housing.

By taking the profit out of owning and operating rental property, the government has reduced the incentive to provide housing units. The problem lies in the fact that many who qualify for the benefit often do not need the subsidy; it is also clear that when resources are shifted away from rental housing, it is the poor who suffer disproportionately. It is this realization that has caused the elimination, or scaling back, of many of these programs.

It is important to note that there are benefits when using a price ceiling; however, the cost of interfering with a free market usually outweighs the benefit. This is clear in the case of rent control because of the shortage of decent apartments.

Price Floors

A **price floor** occurs when the government sets a minimum price at which goods can be exchanged. This has no impact on a free market unless this minimum price is set higher than the equilibrium price, in which case a surplus will result.

When the federal government sets a minimum wage for an hour's work, it is setting a price floor on labor. Note that the minimum wage does not affect labor markets for doctors, lawyers, baseball players, accountants, teachers, or any other professionals for which the equilibrium wage is set much higher than $5.15 per hour. But let's not forget teenagers. Teens *usually* have a poor work ethic and few complementary skills or training, and, as such, are relegated to flipping hamburgers and spraying perfume on the wrists of unsuspecting mall-strollers. We are not describing highly productive individuals or jobs, and so the market sets their wages quite low, possibly lower than the minimum wage.

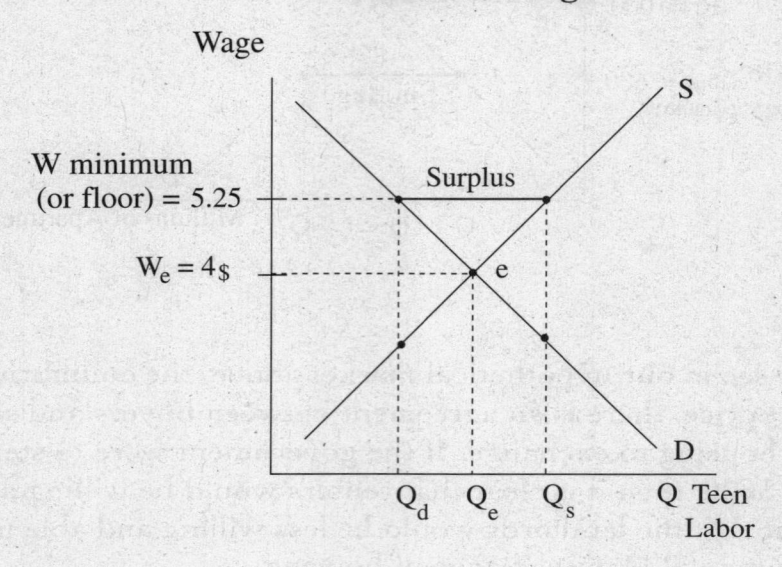

Minimum Wage

W minimum (or floor) = 5.25

$W_e = 4\$$

Surplus

Q_d Q_e Q_s Q Teen Labor

As you can see above, if the legal minimum is set above the market equilibrium wage, it encourages greater participation by teens in the labor market but it has a chilling effect on employers. The employer is not interested in paying a premium for less productive workers, and so the necessary result is a surplus of teen workers. This means very high rates of teen unemployment. Indeed, at the peak of the last recession, unemployment in general reached approximately 8 percent in the U.S., but it was only about 1 percent for college graduates, while in some major urban centers, teen unemployment reached nearly 50 percent.

It is important to note that there are benefits to imposing a price floor. In this case, some teen will find a job and make another $20–$30 a week because of this market intervention. Some other teen, however, who would have found a job at $3 or $4 an hour, will find no job at all. This is not as simple as right and wrong. The intelligent debate involves weighing the benefits versus the costs and deciding what makes sense for each individual community taken in its entirety.

CHANGING EQUILIBRIUM

Until now, we have spoken about the equilibrium point as something that you can't escape. As long as the market remains free, self-interest drives you back to the equilibrium. Yet prices change—going up and going down—sometimes with great rapidity. How can this be explained? Well, suppose those demand and supply curves started moving around. They wouldn't keep intersecting, or agreeing, at the same point. If we can understand what may cause such shifts in supply and demand, we will understand how prices in free markets may vary. Let's look at one side of the market at a time and then we'll bring them together.

Shifting Demand

Demand depends on many things. One of them is the price of the good. But with respect to the two dimensions of our graph, we can gauge the response of a consumer to a change in price merely by moving up or down a single demand curve. This **change in the quantity demanded**, which occurs inversely in relation to price, is the Law of Demand as described above. This is the reason why almost all demand curves are negatively sloped. You might have wondered: Why is the demand curve so steep or so flat? Why is it more or less curved? Why is it so far in or so far out? In other words, the placement of any particular demand curve may have made you wonder. The placement, position, and nature of any two-dimensional demand curve is affected by other factors; among them are the following.

Income: As income rises, any price is less of a discouragement than it was before, and in most cases, demand will shift to the right.

Tastes and preferences: As perceived quality rises, if I like something more, this too could cause an expansion of demand, a shift to the right.

Consumers: With greater populations, all other things held constant, there will be greater demand.

Expected prices: If I believe the item I am interested in buying will be more expensive tomorrow, then I'll be inclined to buy more of it today at any price.

Taxes: Any tax that falls on consumers discourages them. Conversely, by removing or reducing a tax, one can encourage consumption.

Prices of substitutes: A substitute is a good you can use instead of the original good. If the substitute became expensive, it would drive up demand for the original good.

Prices of complements: A complement is a good that is used with the original good. If a complement becomes less expensive, it will encourage the use of the original good.

Price ↑ Minimum Wage
(shift right)

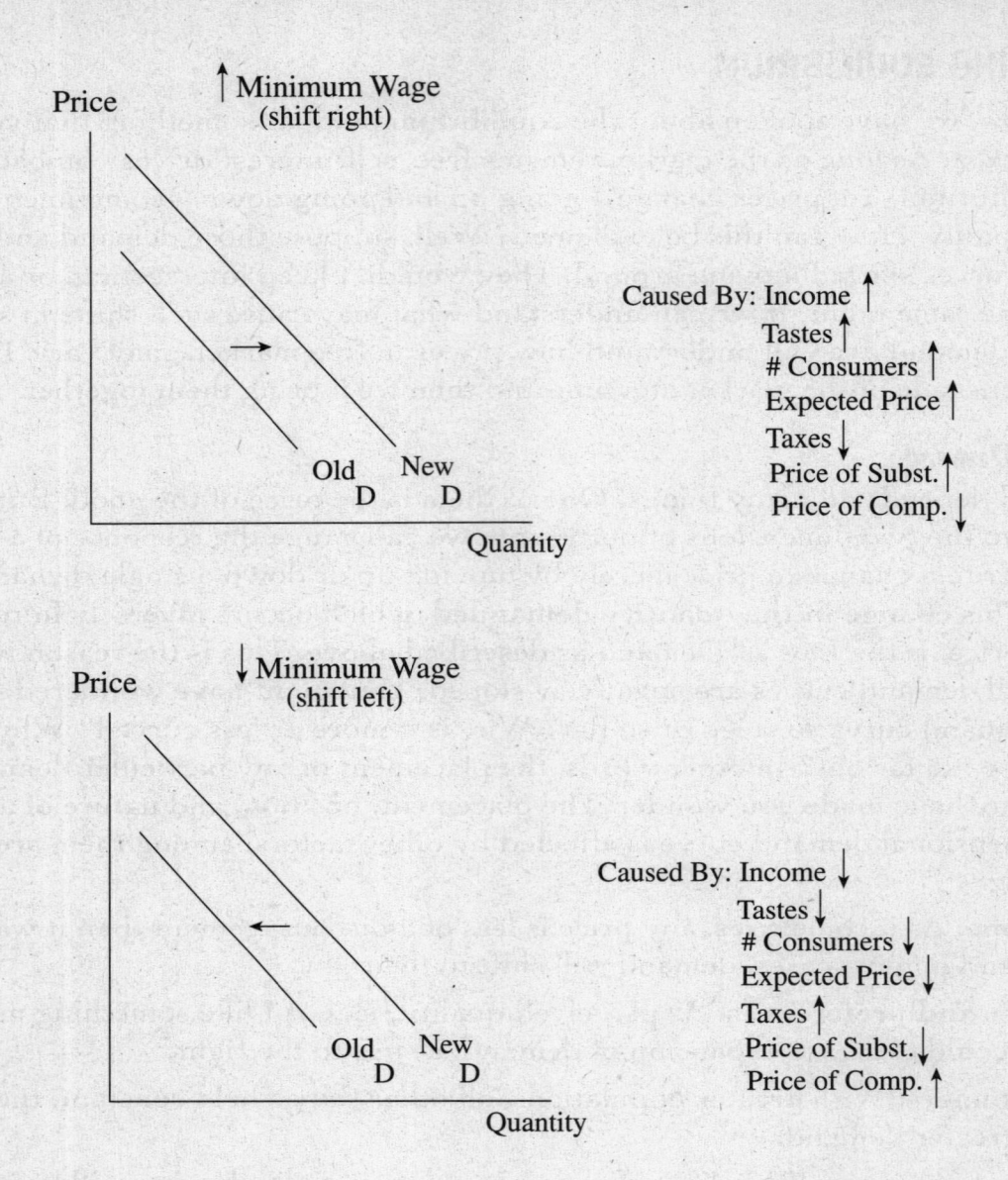

Caused By: Income ↑
Tastes ↑
Consumers ↑
Expected Price ↑
Taxes ↓
Price of Subst. ↑
Price of Comp. ↓

Old D   New D
Quantity

Price ↓ Minimum Wage
(shift left)

Caused By: Income ↓
Tastes ↓
Consumers ↓
Expected Price ↓
Taxes ↑
Price of Subst. ↓
Price of Comp. ↑

Old D   New D
Quantity

Shifting Supply

As with demand, any change in the quantity supplied can be shown on the two-dimensional axis as a sliding up or down of a single curve in response to a change in price. There are, however, other factors that influence supply; among them are the following.

Costs of production: Reduced costs of production, in the form of lower wages, rents, or interest payments, enhances the ability to produce profitably at any given price. The supply will expand to the right.

Technology: Better technology allows a producer to do more with less, to be more productive and cost effective. The supply will move to the right.

Producers: More producers in a more competitive market will generally, though not necessarily, lead to an expansion of supply.

Expected prices: As a producer, if I think I can sell my products for less tomorrow than today, I'll be inclined to sell them today. Current supply will increase.

Taxes: Any tax that is felt by a producer is similar to an increased cost of production and will discourage supply. By eliminating taxes on producers, one may encourage supply.

Prices of alternatives: Most producers can shift their resources seamlessly between several activities. These are the productive alternatives. If one of these alternatives became less expensive to the consumer, the producer would shift resources away from this good and into the original good and other more highly priced activities (for example, toward beef and pork, away from chicken).

Prices of by-products: Secondary products that occur during the production of a primary good are called by-products. If a by-product (for example, beef and leather) becomes more expensive, then it will enhance incentives to produce the original good (cattle).

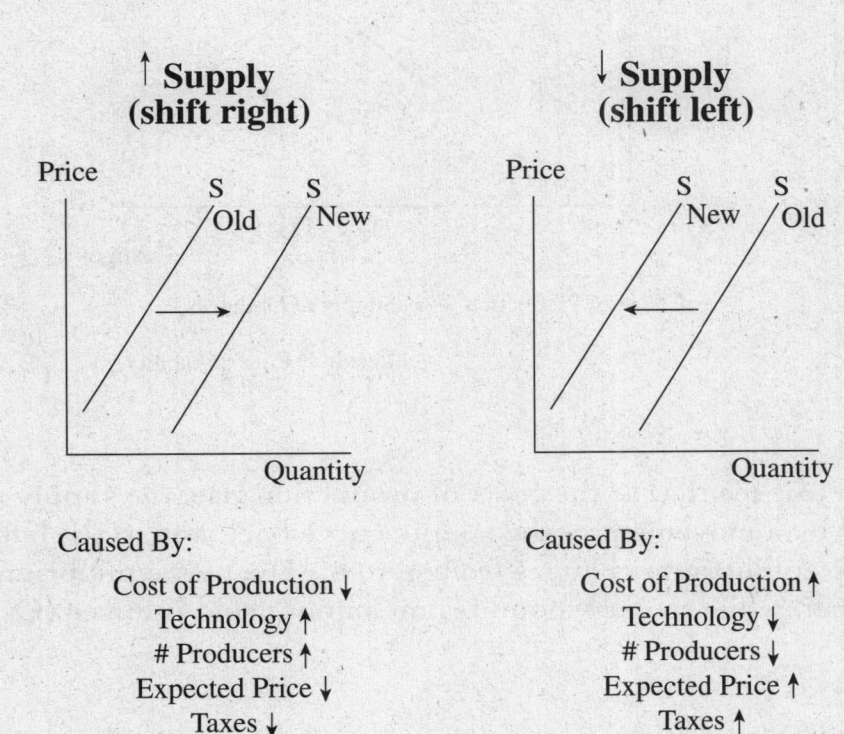

↑ **Supply (shift right)**

Caused By:
Cost of Production ↓
Technology ↑
Producers ↑
Expected Price ↓
Taxes ↓
Price of Alternatives ↓
Price of By-Products ↑

↓ **Supply (shift left)**

Caused By:
Cost of Production ↑
Technology ↓
Producers ↓
Expected Price ↑
Taxes ↑
Price of Alternatives ↑
Price of By-Products ↓

APPLICATIONS

Let's apply some of the concepts we just reviewed to a few examples of changing markets.

Case One—Florida Oranges

Suppose next winter a sudden and bitter frost sweeps Florida. Will this affect how much people like orange juice and other orange products? Of course not, but it will certainly increase the costs of production, as orange farmers hustle around the clock to salvage as much of their crop as possible.

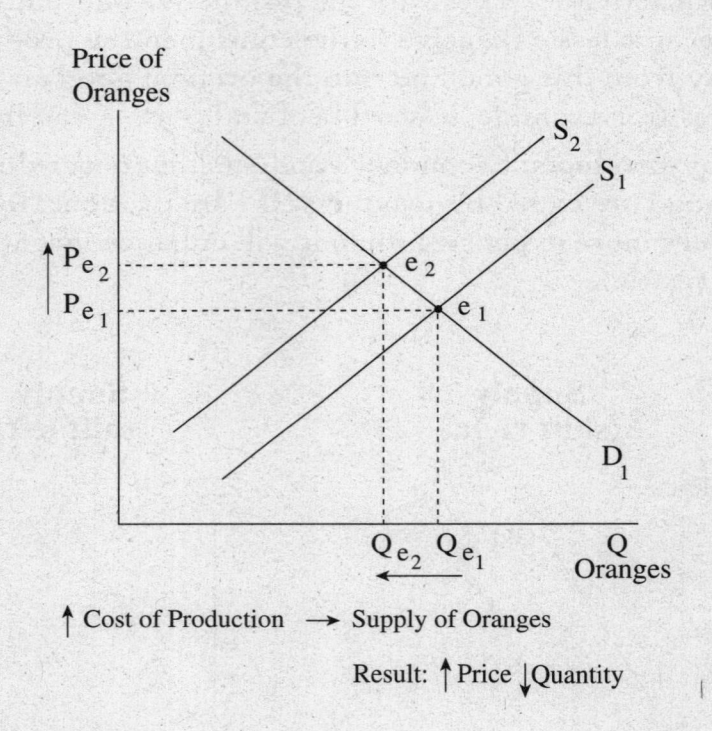

↑ Cost of Production → Supply of Oranges

Result: ↑Price ↓Quantity

Above, you can see that as the costs of production rise, the supply is reduced as represented by a movement of the supply curve back and to the left. When this occurs, the equilibrium changes from e_1 to e_2. The new equilibrium price of oranges is higher, while the new equilibrium amount sold is lower (Q_{e_1} to Q_{e_2}).

Case Two—Coffee and Sugar

Suppose we look at the *coffee* market and find that in the next few months *sugar* prices will rise precipitously. You may ask, "Why even mention sugar?" Sugar is a complement to coffee. Many people use at least some sugar in their coffee to enhance the pleasure they extract from its consumption.

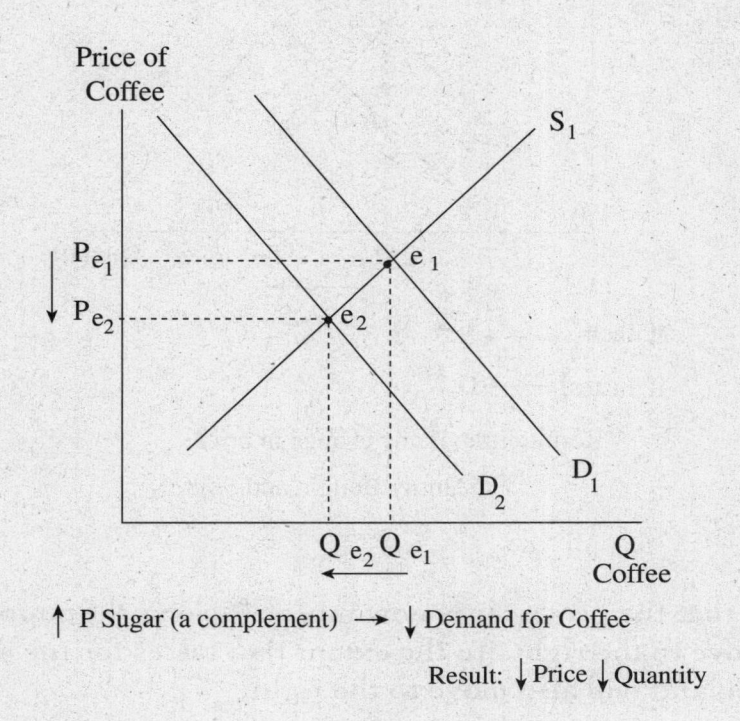

↑ P Sugar (a complement) → ↓ Demand for Coffee

Result: ↓ Price ↓ Quantity

Above, when a complement's price rises, it reduces the demand for the original good. When sugar gets expensive, the demand for coffee falls, or moves to the left. The result is that the new equilibrium price of coffee is lower, while the new equilibrium amount sold will be less.

Case Three—Technology

Suppose the technology in producing some good was much improved, and resulted in an improved product that appealed to a much larger consuming public.

Price

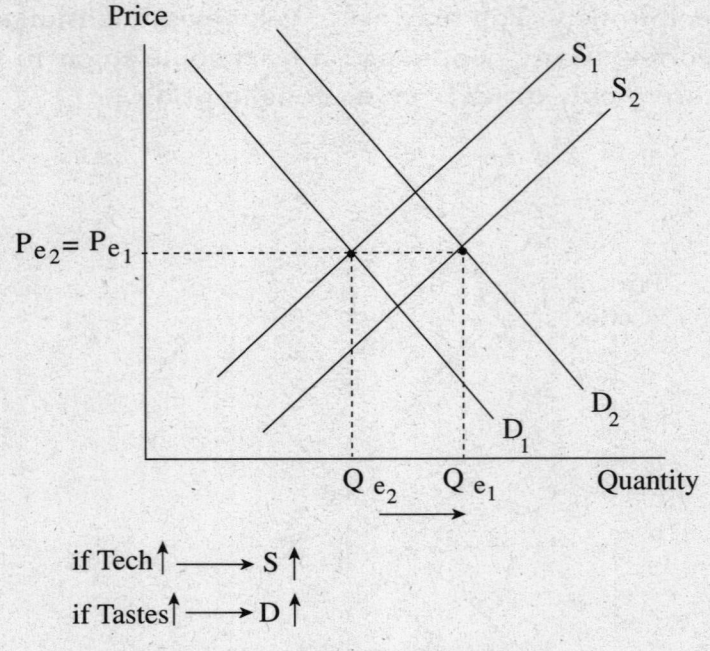

[Diagram: Supply and demand curves showing S₁, S₂, D₁, D₂ with $P_{e_2} = P_{e_1}$ and Q_{e_2}, Q_{e_1} on the Quantity axis]

if Tech ↑ ⟶ S ↑
if Tastes ↑ ⟶ D ↑

Result: little, if any change in price
↑ Quantity Bought and Sold

To the extent that the producer is now more efficient, the supply will be enhanced and move to the right. To the extent that tastes for the good have been enhanced, the demand will also move to the right.

You will note that these have offsetting impacts on the price of the good. Without more detailed information, we can only say that price will probably not change greatly. On the other hand, these movements affect quantity sold. Even without more detailed information, we can be confident that once these changes occur, consumers will be buying and producers will be selling many more units of this good.

To be prepared for the GSE, practice drawing these market diagrams, recalling crucial information as you go. Demand has a negative slope. Supply has a positive slope. Where they intersect, they agree to exchange. At prices that are too high, a surplus will occur. At prices that are too low, a shortage occurs. Make sure you know the other factors that affect the placement of the demand and supply curves, and practice shifting them about and observing the resulting change in equilibrium.

Chapter 7

AN ALTERNATIVE VIEW OF MARKETS

We live in a world of limits:

- We can never have *everything* we want, when we want it.

- We must make choices as to **what to produce, how much to produce,** and **for whom to produce.**

- Markets are the best way we know for balancing the competing interests that exist in this limited world. Markets provide a way of rationing our time, energy, and efforts such that we experience our maximum net total benefit.

Our net total benefit depends on the difference between the total benefits associated with consuming goods and the total cost of providing those goods. If total benefits exceed the total costs by the greatest margin, then net total benefits have been maximized.

$$\text{Net Total Benefit} = \text{Total Benefits} - \text{Total Costs}$$

Interestingly, to maximize this difference, one must not necessarily focus on totals at all, but rather on marginals.

In economics, the word **marginal** is often used to describe the extra, or additional, of something. In the case of markets, the **marginal cost** is an additional cost of providing the last unit of a good. A supplier must be compensated for this additional cost of provision, or she will cease to provide. In other words, the supply curve shows the price that must be charged for producers to bring each additional good to the market. The supply curve is proportional to the rising additional cost of providing increasing amounts of goods to the market. By the same token, it is clear that with each additional unit of a good consumed, its additional benefit decreases. This additional benefit is the **marginal benefit**, and it declines as additional satisfaction would, with each additional good consumed. The demand curve traces the path by which consumers are willing and able to pay for this ever less rare, less additionally satisfying good.

The typical supply and demand curves in terms of markets reflect the rising marginal cost and the declining marginal benefit of additional goods being provided and consumed in the marketplace.

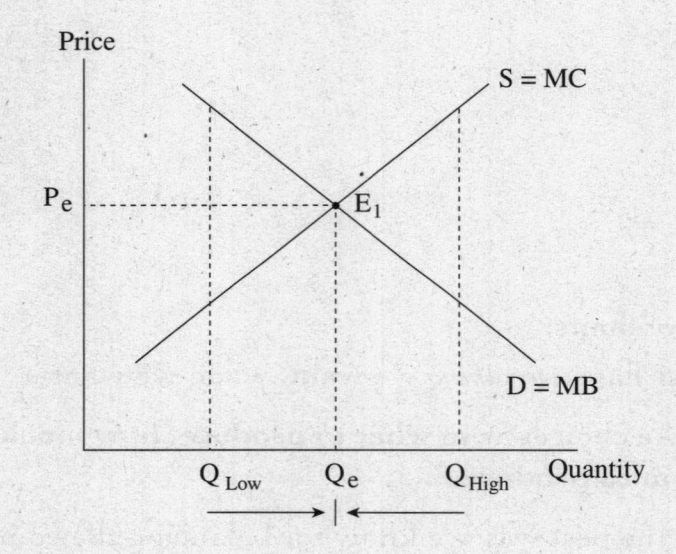

At low levels of production, the additional benefit of the good exceeds its additional cost (point B is above point A). Whenever the marginal benefits exceed the marginal cost (MB > MC), there is a positive addition to net total benefits, and this is a signal that more should be produced. Similarly, at high levels of production, the additional benefit of the good is less than its additional cost (point C is below point D). Whenever marginal cost exceeds marginal benefits, it indicates that there has been a reduction in net total benefits (MB < MC), and that production should be reduced. With this new perspective, the emphasis is placed on appropriate levels of production, and the best, or optimal, level is found when marginal benefit and cost are equal (MB = MC). This occurs at the equilibrium level where net total benefits are maximized. We can now use this approach to better understand how markets may fail.

MARKET FAILURE

Markets fail whenever they do not consider all of the costs and benefits associated with the production and consumption of a good or service.

A market always has two sides—supply and demand. As we have already said, these two parties have competing interests that motivate the negotiation between them when finding an equilibrium. But what if there were third-party costs or benefits that were not considered? If an equilibrium failed to reflect these, then it would represent a sub-optimal level of production. **Third-party costs** are those costs that affect others whose interests are not directly linked to the negotiation in a market. For instance, car producers have explicit costs of providing cars, and car buyers have tangible benefits associated with owning a car. The costs and benefits of the two parties involved will determine the result of the negotiation that takes place in markets. But what about the pollution that reduces the standard of living and raises health costs for those who live near the factory that produces the cars? These third parties do not necessarily work at the factory or own stock in the company. They do not necessarily buy cars made at the factory, but they are getting sick more often and dying younger than if there was no factory and no pollution. These third-party costs are real, but are not considered by the supply and demand parties in their negotiation. Such costs are called **external costs**. And if there are external costs, then there are additional external costs, or **marginal external costs (MEC)**, that must be considered to find the true marginal social cost of providing an additional good and to determine what is truly optimal for society as a whole.

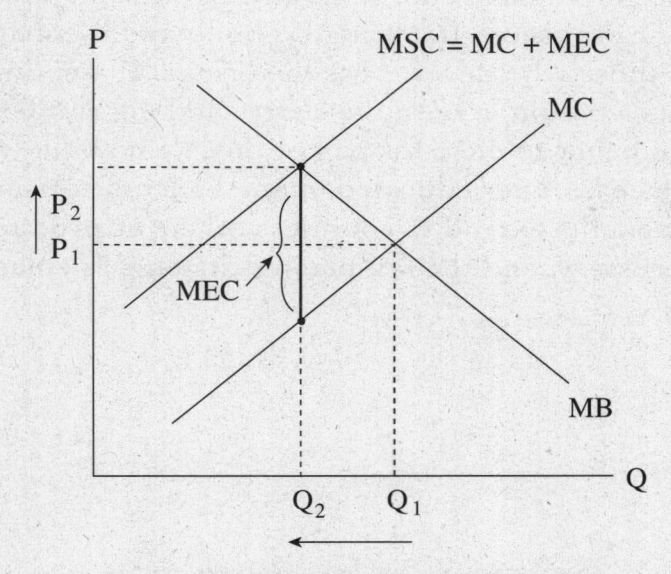

A market with external costs will lead to overproduction of the good unless the external costs are internalized.

AN ALTERNATIVE VIEW OF MARKETS ◆ 59

Note above, that if external costs are present, but unrecognized, then the market will produce too much to be socially optimal (Q_1). In order to "internalize" these externalities, a government may choose to tax, regulate, or penalize producers in proportion to the estimated additional cost. In the case of pollution, devices may be required to reduce it to a tolerable level, or having failed compliance, a producer may face fines to aid in the financing of a cleanup. Either way, the external costs are now explicit to the producer, who will then share some of the burden of this additional cost with the consumer of the good. This will be done in the form of higher prices for an activity that truly costs society more than previously accounted for in a simple two-party negotiation. The additional costs are reflected in the shift of the supply curve to the left. The new equilibrium output quantity is Q_2.

Similarly, there may be significant third-party benefits in markets. These external benefits accrue to parties outside those of demand and supply. When such benefits are unrecognized, society may enjoy less of a good than would have been optimal or appropriate (Q_1 rather than Q_2.) Many **public goods**—goods that have nonexcludable benefits—fall into this category. For example, air, once having been cleaned (or kept from being dirtied), cannot be kept from consumers who did not pay for its cleaning any more than from those who may have. The benefit of clean air is nonexcludable. This also means, however, that it will be impossible to charge customers for this service—and that it will be impossible to make a profit in the private sector—by contributing to clean air. Thus, if markets were kept exclusively private, there would be an underprovision of this very valuable commodity.

Public goods also often have enormous and significant external benefits associated with their provision. If a bridge is built, and it enhances commerce, it will do so even for those who never cross the bridge. If a national defense is provided, it benefits a nation in both the short and long run far beyond those who are engaged in being soldiers for pay or those who build weapons for delivery. And if a populace is better educated, many benefits accrue to the one who is educated, but the benefits extend to countless others as productivity rises, fewer prisons become necessary, and the tax-paying citizenry is enlarged.

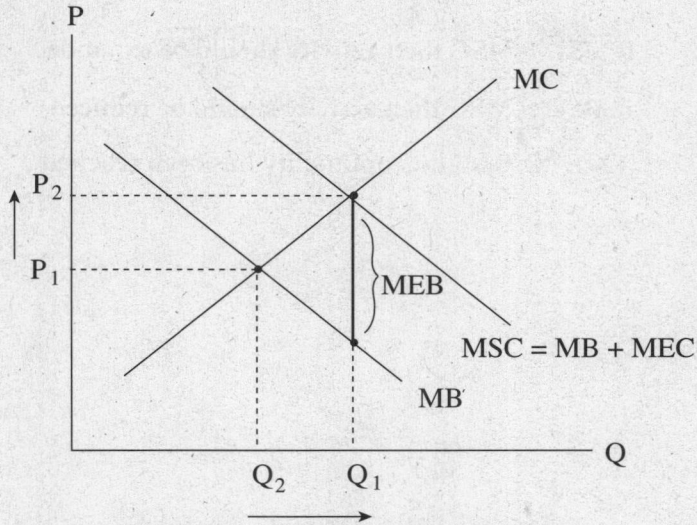

A market with external benefits will lead to underproduction unless the external benefits are internalized.

Note above, that if there are external benefits associated with an activity, then there are marginal external benefits associated with it. This means that the marginal social benefit would exceed the simple marginal benefit of providing that good. If these benefits are unrecognized, society will not choose to produce enough of these goods (Q_1). Such would be the case with public goods and semi-public goods, like education. If external benefits are not incorporated into the debate over how much to produce, then there will be an underallocation of resources to this activity.

> Let's sum up some of the topics we've discussed in this chapter:
> - Markets fail whenever they do not consider all costs and benefits of an activity.
> - If external costs are excluded from consideration, society will devote too many resources and produce too much of the good.
> - If external benefits are excluded from consideration, society will devote too few resources and produce too little of the good.

To "internalize" external benefits, governments may choose to provide or subsidize an activity in proportion with those additional benefits. In the case of education, building a public school system is the outright supplemental provision of the service. Alternative plans are underway to subsidize and encourage more provision in the private sector. Either way, government is trying to encourage society to allocate more resources to activities that are undervalued because some of their benefits are not fully recognized. The new equilibrium quantity with all benefits internalized will be Q_2.

AN ALTERNATIVE VIEW OF MARKETS ◆ 61

SUMMARY:

if MSB > MSC then activity should be expanded

if MSC > MSC then activity should be reduced

When MSB = MSC optimality has been reached

Chapter 8

MEASURING THE ECONOMY

Although the exact systems of accounting vary distinctly from the private to the public sectors of the economy, like a business, government tries to keep track of how the nation is doing through a system called **national income accounting**. The single-most quoted statistic in all of national income accounting is the **gross domestic product** (GDP). The GDP, and its close relative, the **gross national product** (GNP), are measures of the value of all finished goods and services produced in a nation in one year. This is not a measurement of an amount, but a measurement of the total value of an amount of goods and services produced.

Suppose two countries each produce a single unit of a single good. Are these nations equally productive? The answer is—not necessarily. One nation may have produced a single baseball, while the other produced a single Cadillac. Obviously, there is a lot more value, output, and income generated in the second case. In economics, one does not always equal one.

Although the above definition is generally accurate for both GDP and GNP, there is a distinct difference between the two measures. GDP (also sometimes called nominal GDP or current dollar GDP) measures the value of output produced within a nation's borders, whether or not the productive entity is domestically owned or not. Thus, the proceeds from a Japanese-owned Toyota plant in

Kentucky will be counted but the proceeds from an American-owned IBM plant in Tokyo would be excluded from the U.S. GDP. On the other hand, GNP focuses on any output or income from businesses owned by citizens of a particular nation, regardless of where the output generator is be situated. Thus, the proceeds from businesses owned by Americans will count in our GNP, even if they operate offshore, while those proceeds from foreign-owned properties will not count, even if they operate within our borders.

You may ask, which measure, GDP or GNP, most accurately assesses the economic state of one nation. The answer is GDP because what happens within your borders largely affects you and your destiny, much as what happens within your home affects you. Does it matter that the neighbor's child sets a fire in your living room? It is still your living room that caught fire and is damaged. In turn, does it matter that the majority stockholders of a plant in Kentucky live in New Zealand, considering that the output, income, wages, employment, and complementary spending is being done overwhelmingly in and around Kentucky?

Historically, GDP and GNP figures for the U.S. have not diverged greatly. What was excluded or included in the U.S. measures tended to offset each other to a large degree. Other nations, however, especially those with large guest-worker populations and high proportions of foreign investment, experience a significant divergence between the two statistics. In this case, the GDP is a better—not perfect—but better reflection of the performance of those nations.

EXCLUDED ITEMS

When calculating the GDP or GNP there are certain other items that are not counted.

Let's refer back to the definition of these terms. GDP is the value of all finished or final goods and services, but what is a **finished or final good**? It is one that is ready to be used or consumed in the final marketplace. When tallying the GDP, one would exclude any **intermediate goods** that may have contributed to the final good's value. For instance, I wouldn't want to count the value of all wheat production, and then count all the bread and all the cereal. This would be double-counting since bread and cereal have a final market value that is partially dependent on the contribution of wheat. Double-counting exaggerates the capacity of the nation to produce.

This distinction between final and intermediate goods is not always as simple as it would appear. For example, do you count spark plugs as a final or intermediate good? The spark plugs that contribute to the final value of a new car are intermediate goods and should be *excluded*, but the spark plugs that are produced to be used for tune-ups are final goods and should be *counted*. Careful accounting is necessary here, but the point is that a good is not inherently intermediate or final, but is considered as such depending on its use.

Another excludable item is resold goods. The GDP's only interest is in finding the *productive* capacity of a nation in a specific year. Although used car and used home sales measure in the hundreds of billions of dollars annually, GDP excludes them because it is not a statistic that keeps track of the transfer of depreciated or appreciated assets. It is a statistic that attempts to indicate a nation's current ability to produce.

Intermediate goods and resold goods are excluded by design. Excellent records for these items exist, but we choose not to include them in GDP because we don't want to exaggerate our nation's capabilities. In addition to these items, there are others that are excluded because, by their very nature, they are "off the books" and therefore difficult to gauge with any accuracy. One such category is the underground economy, which includes any activity illicit or otherwise for which there are no official records kept or recorded. Innocuous activities, like an 11-year-old who works part-time in a shop and is paid "under the table," fall into this category. Less innocent activities, however, like the enormous market for illegal drugs, dominate this category. Estimates for the size and impact of illegal activity in the U.S. vary from 3 percent to 8 percent of the officially reported GDP. Even 1 percent translates into nearly 100 billion dollars in illegal activity. Which estimate is best—the low-end, the high-end, or something in-between? There is no sure way to know, so failing accuracy, illegal activity is considered too speculative and inexact to merit inclusion in the GDP.

Another item that is difficult to gauge by its very nature is the household contribution, which includes all activities that are done by individuals outside of markets and for themselves. When you fix your own computer, change your own light bulb, or raise your own children, you are engaging in this type of activity. The value of raising our own children, although an enormously important positive contribution, is somewhat intangible, especially with regard to its current value. Thus, it fails the test of statistical rigor, and is excluded. We can only hope that the negative aspect of the underground activity and the positive aspect of household contributions, both of which are excluded from GDP, may tend to offset each other, leaving us with a good—if not perfect—GDP statistic.

Items Excluded From GDP:

Items	Reason
Intermediate goods	Avoid double counting
Resold goods	Avoid double counting
Underground economy	No accurate estimates
Household contributions	No accurate estimates

It is important to note that any statistic is only one indicator of a nation's condition. And as important as GDP is, it is only one statistic. We will review a way to improve GDP and other matters such as distribution later. Before we get to these topics, bounce this question around in your mind: Two nations may have the same GDP, but are they equally well off if one concentrates all the wealth in relatively few hands, while the other has a more equitable dispersion of returns?

TWO APPROACHES

There are two approaches for calculating GDP. One is the **incomes approach**, and the other is the **expenditure approach**. The terms themselves are fairly self-defining. For example, the incomes approach starts with the premise that when you add all payments to all resources for their productive contributions, then you have the total value of output produced. Adding wages (the payment for labor) to rents (the payment for fixed resources) to interest (the payment for use of capital) to profit (the return to entrepreneurs), the sum is the **national income** (NI). Making further allowances for indirect business taxes (sales and excise taxes, and tariffs), and also for depreciation, you determine the GDP.

$$\text{Wage} + \text{Rent} + \text{Interest} + \text{profit} + \text{Indirect business taxes} + \text{GDP}$$

To determine GDP using the expenditure approach, start by adding together all the major subcategories of spending to attain the total value exchanged in the final market, the GDP. These major subcategories include:

- **Consumption**, which makes up about two-thirds of all spending in developed economies;
- **Investment**, which is present spending for future growth;
- **Government**, which includes spending for public goods; and
- **Net Exports**, which is the difference between a nation's yearly exports and imports.

$$\text{Consumption} + \text{Investment} + \text{Government} + (\text{Exports} - \text{Imports}) = \text{GDP}$$

Starting from different perspectives, you can check and countercheck the GDP of a nation, using one method and then comparing to the other.

OTHER IMPORTANT INCOME MEASURES

Of all the output produced and of all the income generated, a large share—but not 100 percent—is received by the private sector. After factoring out many items such as depreciation, indirect business taxes, and retained corporate profits, and after factoring in various redistributions via transfers from one sector of the economy to another, personal income is left. Subtracting personal income taxes from personal income leaves the so-called **disposable income** of a nation. This income is what remains for the private sector to use as it chooses after all adjustments have been made. There are but two basic activities that can be pursued: consumption and savings.

Consumption is spending directed to immediately enhance our current standard of living. It includes what we wear, eat, entertain ourselves with, etc. **Savings** is idle money. It is that part of the income at our disposal that we have chosen to set aside. Somewhere down the line, this idle money may be reinjected into the economy as investment but before anything else happens to it, it must be set aside and therefore constitutes savings.

Consumption + Investment + Government + (Exports − Imports) = GDP

The importance of disposable income and its components rests on the fact that most of the income that is generated will eventually be distributed as disposable income. Depending on whether the economy is thriving or failing, the disposable income and what citizens do with it is probably a significant—and possibly the dominant—factor in explaining this economic fate. What the private sector chooses to do with disposable income becomes even more important when we discuss policy. If the government wishes to adjust or fine tune an economy that is not operating at peak efficiency, its efforts would be inaccurate and ineffective if it had no idea of where or how 75 percent of all income was being distributed and used.

Imagine trying to get your car fixed by a mechanic who refused to even look at 75 percent of the engine. What chance would the mechanic have of properly diagnosing and fixing your auto? Obviously, those odds would be dramatically lower than they would if he had inspected 100 percent of the car. The same could be said of an economy in need of repair. The government needs to know where and how most income is generated and used in order to make effective adjustments.

REAL GDP

Another important consideration is to have the best information available. Part of this problem involves having statistics that represent, or come close to representing, what they claim to represent. GDP, as we have defined it, has a major flaw in this area. It purports to represent the productive capacity of a nation in a year. Presumably (if in most cases more is better than less) as GDP rises, it should indicate an increase in economic welfare; however, this may not always be the case.

Let's use a simple illustration to clarify this: suppose you go to the school bookstore to buy a new notebook. As you approach the books, you notice they are listed at $4 each. But just as you are about to reach out for one, a stealthily quick stock-person reaches the pile first and changes the price to $5 each. Now you have to shell out an extra dollar for the same notebook. Is it a better notebook? Did it magically spawn new pages as the stock-person stamped the new price on it? Or is it just a bit more expensive? Now, suppose the government reports that the economy has a much higher GDP now than it did ten years ago. Part of the reason could be that we have more stuff now than before, but part of the reason could be that the stuff has been marked up a few times in ten years. GDP can be increased by greater amounts produced, but also by inflation. Inflationary prices, however, are not a good indicator of being better off. Were you better off when the price on the notebook changed from $4 to $5?

We would like to correct this flaw by extracting inflation, leaving us with a statistic for the value produced that is only sensitive to changes in quantity. This new statistic is called **constant dollar GDP** or **real GDP**. The technique for calculating real GDP requires you to choose a **base year**—a reference year from which all prices in compared years are measured—and reapply that year's prices to other years.

Nation Z — Produces only 3 final goods

GDS	1999 Prices	Quantity	Total Value	2000 Prices	Quantity	Total Value
Bread	1$	1000	1000$	2$	1000	2000$
Water	.5$	2000	1000$	1$	2000	2000$
Cars	1000$	1	1000$	2000$	1	2000$

$GDP_{1999} = 3000\$$ $GDP_{2000} = 6000\$$

Real $GDP_{2000} = 3000\$$

In the example above, the GDP doubled but it was completely the consequence of prices having doubled in nation Z. Having designated the year 1999 as the base year, and reapplying its prices to the year 2000, you can see that the Real GDP has not risen. Real GDP is not a perfect indicator of economic well-being, but it is a large qualitative improvement over the GDP we introduced at the outset of this chapter.

OTHER IMPORTANT STATISTICS

There are three important price indices with which you should be familiar. The first is the **implicit price deflator**, or simply **price deflator** (PD). Like any price index, it is a measure of the average level of prices in the economy. Particularly, the PD includes the influence of the prices of all final goods and services based on the ratio of nominal to real GDP (NGDP/RGDP). Such an all inclusive index is a good reference point, but may be less relevant than a more focused index when gauging the cost of living for an average urban working family. The index designed to address this question is the **Consumers' Price Index** (CPI).

The CPI represents a weighted average of the prices of a basket of goods that are typically consumed by an average urban working family. This average was determined by proportions that were estimated from an early 1980s survey. Therein lies some controversy. Although the CPI more appropriately focuses on ham sandwiches, gasoline, and fresh produce, as opposed to helicopters, supercomputers, and cargo vessels, one could argue that the survey estimating the proportions of consumption is outdated. Additionally, the index assumes a family will stick to the proportions they reported to the survey, but when prices rise for something I like, I buy less of it. Don't you? This means that any fixed proportion scheme that does not allow for dynamic movement among goods as their prices change will have a serious upward bias. It will tend to exaggerate inflation by as much as 1 percent according to some estimates. Simply, when the CPI says we've had almost 1 percent inflation, we've probably had no inflation at all.

One other price index should be considered. It is the **producers' price index** (PPI). Mathematically it is similar to the CPI, in that it focuses on a smaller subset of goods and their prices, as opposed to all prices. The subset PPI focuses on the prices of goods that are the cost and concern of manufacturers and business owners at the wholesale level and input level. As such, PPI can be used to some degree as a barometer for future retail inflation. If costs of production and distribution rise today, you can be sure that business owners will try to pass this burden along to the consumer in the form of higher retail prices somewhere down the road. And naturally, even a little information about the future movement of the economy can be exceedingly valuable to businesspeople and policy makers.

Let's look at one last statistic, the **Index of Leading Economic Indicators**. A leading economic indicator is one that tends to move prior to the movement of the general economy. By observing the ups and downs of a leading indicator like stock prices, unemployment compensation claims, the money supply, consumer confidence surveys, and others, we might be able to anticipate the next movement of the economy. No single indicator is as reliable as an index, or weighted average, of all such indicators. This explains the great popularity of, and high regard for, the Index of Leading Economic Indicators. If this index rises for several months in a row, it usually means good times will continue for some time into the future. If it falls for several months in a row, watch out for the next recession. The economy hasn't always moved according to this pattern, but more often than not, with such strong indications, it has. Single up or down monthly movements, however, mean next to nothing as a predictor of future economic activity, and even the strongest and most consistent patterns have sometimes proved misguided.

Once again, even our best statistical tools are flawed to some degree, and no single number, not even a pile of numbers, will sufficiently tell the whole story of an economy and where it may be headed. But that is what is so tantalizing about economics, and so, we keep trying our best.

Chapter 9

ECONOMIC PROBLEMS AND THE BUSINESS CYCLE

Two economic difficulties that concern us are **recession** and **depression**. A recession is usually defined as occurring any time the real output of a nation falls for a half year or more and is usually accompanied by rising unemployment. In other words, if the real GDP drops for two quarters consecutively, or any time longer than that, the nation is said to be in a recession. Although no standard definition exists for what constitutes a depression, let's just say that a depression is a severe recession, and that most will know it when they experience it.

Whether an economic problem is classified as a recession or as the more severe depression, they both mean that the economy has fallen below its production possibilities curve, many resources have been wasted, and unnecessarily high rates of unemployment exist.

Unemployment is what captures most of our attention, as it is the most direct indication of the human suffering caused by an underperforming economy. There are more than 270 million people living in the U.S. More than 150 million people participate in our labor force. Thus, if unemployment were to rise even an additional 1 percent, it would mean an additional 1.5 million people would be without work. Then we can multiply this number times the number of people who are affected by each person being out of work. Usually it's not just one individual who depends on the income generated from a single job to maintain his or her standard of living, it is an entire family.

Economists make distinctions among several types of unemployment; some are considered more harmful than others. For instance, **wait-unemployment** is when an individual is gainfully employed in a seasonal enterprise like construction or farming. This person may have to wait for the busy season to come around to return to work. Being an efficient farming nation (or being able to efficiently build roads and bridges) is a strength of our economy; however, cold weather in the winter months tends to slow down this activity on schedule every year. We should not obsess over such temporary and predictable reversals.

Search unemployment is when someone who possesses skills finds him/herself temporarily out of work. Again, positive attributes of our economy, such as having a large mass of the population graduate from secondary schools and colleges, contribute to this type of unemployment. It can take some time for all the newly skilled labor to find its way into a productive niche in the economy, but you wouldn't say that *not* educating a larger proportion of the population is a better path. Some nations have other solutions to the influx of an educated populace; they aggressively channel individuals from school to particular jobs, thus abridging some of their freedom. Note again, that search unemployment—also called functional unemployment—is generally temporary, and of little concern to most policy makers.

Structural unemployment occurs as a result of a change in the patterns of demand for labor, which in turn often has something to do with changing technology in a progressive economy. For example, when the car was invented and later cheaply mass-produced, do you think that blacksmiths were thrilled? Of course not. Their particular livelihoods depended on skills that were of use to a horse-driven culture. On the other hand, do you think we would have been better off without the advent of all technical advances, the car among the rest? Probably not, because even though these technologies have posed their own attendant difficulties at times, they are also the basis for the greater number of jobs that exist, the higher standard of living enjoyed, and the abundance of leisure time that we have. An invention like the car may make it necessary for blacksmiths to get reeducated, relocated, or to fall back on their next best alternative occupation, but it would be the bane of civilization to restrict all such advances, as their benefits far outweigh their costs.

Economists often group types of unemployment, such as those mentioned, and refer to the result as the **natural rate of unemployment**, which can be viewed as the lowest sustainable, noninflationary rate of unemployment a nation can enjoy. In other words, when we say a nation is fully employed, there will always be some unemployment due to the reasons cited above. It will not consist of the same individuals in the long run. There will be turnover in the masses who are unemployed for the reasons mentioned. A fully employed economy means that everyone has jobs except that percentage explained by the natural rate of unemployment. This is why the natural rate is also sometimes referred to as the

full employment rate of unemployment. It may vary from nation to nation according to their differing cultures and institutions. It may vary within a nation over time as demographics or other variables shift. But every nation has a natural rate of unemployment, and though it is hard to estimate, it is a crucial consideration of policy makers, as we will see.

Speaking of policy makers, there is one form of unemployment that concerns them greatly—it is the kind particularly associated with a recession, or downturn in the economy. It is called **cyclical unemployment**, something that is caused by insufficient aggregate demand, or more simply—too little total spending. Note, if people don't spend on goods, then more goods need not be produced, but then you also need not hire as many workers to produce the lesser amount of goods. Cyclical unemployment is unemployment caused by too little spending. It is a prime target of policy makers because the higher the cyclical unemployment goes, the more wasted resources, the lower the levels of output and income, and in turn, the lower the standard of living of a nation's inhabitants.

INFLATION

The other major problem concerning our economic authorities is **inflation**, which is a rise in the general, or average, level of prices. Alternately, it can be viewed as a decline in the purchasing power of a unit of currency: If prices are, on average, higher, any single unit of currency will buy less. Why should we care about this phenomenon? Do not prices and wages rise similarly, on average, in the long run? The answer is yes; however, no individual is average and we all live in the short run, which significantly complicates the situation.

One group that is hurt by inflation consists of people on fixed incomes. Anyone whose income does not change will lose the ability to purchase goods as inflation advances. In the U.S., millions of people earn incomes that are at least partially fixed and who made sound economic choices assuming there would be little or no inflation. If inflation comes roaring back, they will pay the price in the form of diminished living standards.

Other groups who may be hurt by inflation are creditors and lenders. For example, if you lend money to someone for one year at a flat interest rate of 5 percent, but then 5 percent inflation occurs, you may be repaid promptly with a larger absolute number of currency units, but it doesn't buy any additional goods. You have been given a 0 percent return for your risk and forbearance. Of course, lenders are prepared for inflation. Once inflation occurs, they tack the **inflation premium**, to which they believe they are entitled, on to the interest rate. For example, a lender may believe she should earn a real return of 5 percent, but she also expects 5 percent inflation in the coming year. Therefore, she will charge 10 percent for money she lends out: 5 percent will be her return, and 5 percent will protect the return against the onslaught of inflation. This is the inflation premium.

No one has a crystal ball, and borrowers will want a low premium tacked on, just as lenders will want a high one. The uncertainty of inflation has complicated the negotiation between savers and investors. Because of uncertainty, some deals simply won't happen. To try to avoid these lost opportunities other techniques have been developed, such as adjustable rate mortgages and derivative securities. However, these techniques are never fully effective, and divert some funds from more directly productive activity. In brief, the real cost of high- and variable-rate inflation is a reduction in the quantity and quality of investment that would help a nation grow in the long run. Remember what we said earlier: for each percentage point that slow growth causes unemployment to increase, about 1.5 million jobs are lost per year.

Models of Inflation

Remember that there are two sides to the market, and this is no less true in aggregate than on a smaller scale. Thus, there are two models of inflation, one of which emphasizes pressures from the demand-side of the market, and the other which emphasizes pressures from the supply-side of the market.

The demand-side model is known as **demand-pull inflation**. It starts with the premise that a nation may be at or near full employment and full production, when suddenly total, or aggregate, spending increases. If a nation is at full production, it no longer has the capacity to produce more goods. Thus, even if spending increases, it would not stimulate the economy to much, if any, more production; however, it would cause the prices of the existing goods to rise.

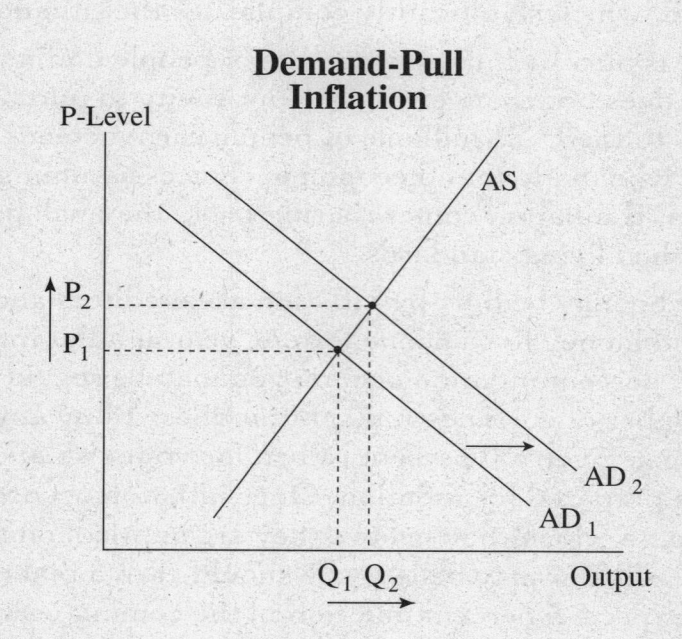

Demand-Pull Inflation

In the diagram above, you see a very steep aggregate supply curve. This is indicative of a nation that has little room to expand output in the short run. At the same time, the aggregate demand moves out to the right. This indicates the rise in general spending. Note, that under the condition of steep aggregate supply, this burst of spending does not boost output so much as it raises the price level.

This scenario of "too many dollars chasing too few goods" is the basis for the fears of current policy makers in the U.S. As we have noted, we are currently close to full production. Our rate of unemployment is hovering around most estimates of our natural rate. If too much spending is encouraged via increased availability of money and credit, it will be unlikely to stimulate our economy, but it would be quite likely to create an inflationary environment that could lead to diminished growth in the longer run.

Now, let's turn to the other side of the market. The model of inflation based on disturbances in supply is known as **cost-push inflation**. It hinges on the concept of supply shocks, which are specific labor skill or resource shortages. For example, let us consider oil. Suppose the economy has ready access to most resources it needs to thrive and grow, but there is some difficulty in getting oil. To the extent that this is true, the price of oil will rise. To the extent that oil and oil-based products are crucial inputs in many forms of production, the costs of production in many industries will rise. And eventually, that increased cost will be shared, if not completely transferred, to the consumer in the form of higher prices. The existence of supply shocks may be the basis for generally higher costs of production and a higher price level.

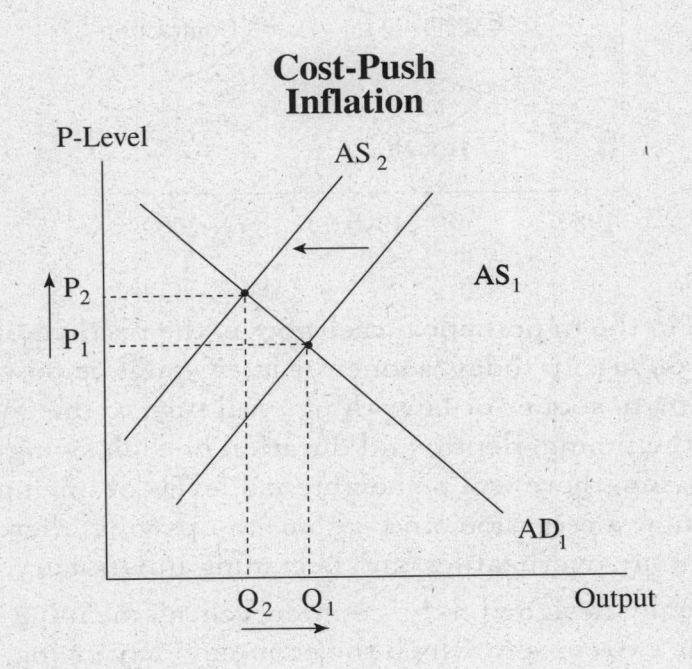

Cost-Push Inflation

In the diagram above, notice that aggregate supply is reduced as a result of higher production costs. This, in turn, leads to some diminishing production capability, but more importantly, to a rise in the general price level, which we call inflation.

To some degree, either of these models (demand-pull or cost-push) emphasizes the proximate, as opposed to the ultimate, cause of inflation, which is excessive money and credit expansion. We'll discuss money and credit more completely in later chapters.

BUSINESS CYCLE

The business cycle refers to the nonperiodic fluctuation of the economy over time. In simpler terms, the economy has its ups and downs, and they are pretty unpredictable. The ups and downs, the flux, of the economy are most often expressed in terms of some inflation-adjusted measure of output, like the real GDP versus time. Sometimes the range of time is only several quarters, but more often, it is a span of quite a few years.

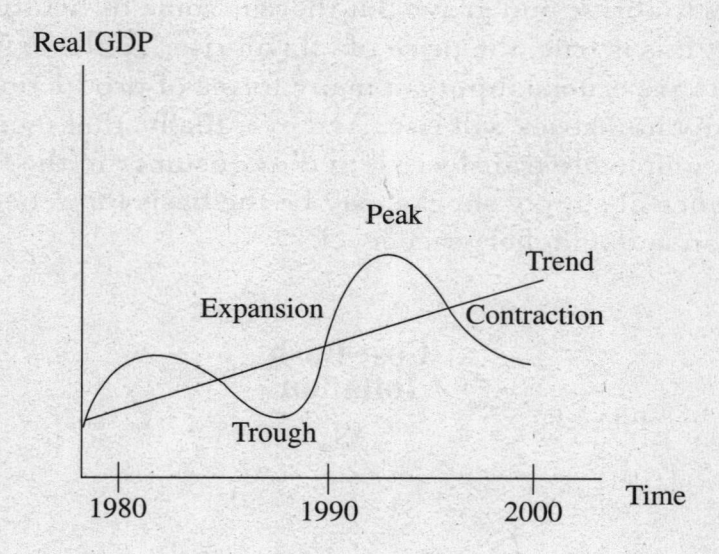

As you can see in the hypothetical case above, the predictable aspect of the process is that if you are up today, sooner or later you'll be down again, and of course, if you're down, sooner or later things will turn to the good. The unpredictable aspect is the timing, depth, and duration of each swing of the cycle. With each downswing, there will be heightened levels of unemployment and suffering as you enter a recession, and with each upswing, there will be the danger of the economy overheating, and becoming inflationary.

Policies are usually designed to be countercyclical, meaning they should work to modify the extremes to which the economy may swing, and by doing so, to reduce the tendency to experience significant levels of unemployment or inflation. However, this is not the only consideration in creating economic policy.

Another important consideration in forming policy is the trend. Note the straight line that cuts through the middle of those peaks and troughs of the business cycle pictured above. This is the trend. It doesn't say anything about the economic performance of a nation in a particular year, but it does indicate what has happened to a nation's average capacity to produce over the time period in question. In this case, since the peaks and troughs of our cycle are successively higher, the average, or **trend**, has a positive slope, indicating that the nation's ability to produce has grown on average over the time period shown. Naturally, this did not have to be the case. We could've easily imagined a different nation, with a different business cycle, and a trend that was either more or less steeply sloped. In fact, we could have introduced a trend that was flat, indicating stagnation. And worse yet, a nation may have a negatively sloped trend, indicating degeneration.

Here's the clincher: sometimes a short-run, countercyclical policy may interfere with a healthy long-term trend. For example, in our nation, if we enter a recession, more people automatically qualify for unemployment insurance and worker's compensation. Such a policy is countercyclical, because it will soften the blow of an economic downturn; however, it may also discourage individuals from making a productive contribution.

Countries like the United States, with beneficent social-welfare safety nets, actually discourage participation in the economy, raise the natural rate of unemployment, and reduce access to a subset of resources that might enable us to grow stronger more quickly over the long run. In other words, sometimes our short-run policies counter our long-term prospects as an economy. It's a razor's edge, balancing the short run versus the long run, but it is only one of many that economists must walk. A few others will be introduced throughout the course of the book.

For a quick summary of problems and basic policy prescriptions, thoroughly review the chart below. More detailed descriptions of policy will follow in later chapters.

Problem	Condition	Business Cycle Condition	Countercyclical Policy Solution
Recession	↓ Output ↓ Income ↑ Unemployment	Contraction & Trough	Stimulate Economy
Inflation	↑ P-Levels − Threatened Growth	Expansion & Peak	Slow Down Economy

Chapter 10

FISCAL POLICY

Though we live in a largely free-market economy, we are aware that the government plays a significant role in many aspects of our daily lives. The federal government alone has a budget approaching 2 trillion dollars, and when it spends, taxes, or transfers money, it is said to be following its **fiscal policy**. Further, by changing its levels of spending, taxes, or transfers, the government can play a part in adjusting the economic problems of our nation. Note: All levels of the government from local, to state, to the federal, can engage in fiscal policy making. Monetary policy, as we will see in the next chapter, can only be made by the Federal Reserve.

Government spending takes many forms, but most are obvious. When a government employee is hired and paid, when office supplies for a government agency are bought, when military hardware is purchased, or a federal road is built, each of these constitutes government spending.

Taxes are also something with which everyone is familiar. There are income taxes, corporate income taxes, social security taxes, and other less significant subcategories. If any of these grows, it deprives the private sector of some funds it could have spent. If any of these declines, it puts money back into private pockets and enhances private sector spending.

Transfers represent just that—funds that are dispensed without any exchange of goods or services. For example, most of the U.S.'s entitlement programs are transfers. If you are old enough, you are entitled to Social Security payments. If you are poor enough, you are entitled to receive some disbursement from our welfare system. Recipients of these transfers do not provide the government with a good or service for these funds. None is required to work for their transfer of funds. Transfers are like a negative tax. If taxes rise, it has the same effect as lowering transfers. Each empties the wallets of consumers and slows down their spending. Conversely, if taxes fall, it is equivalent to rising transfer payments, as each would lead to fatter wallets in the private sector and more spending. So, taxes and transfers operate in opposite directions, but via the same mechanism, the wallets of consumers in the private sector.

ECONOMIC PROBLEMS AND FISCAL SOLUTIONS

Recall the problem of recession that we discussed in the previous chapter. In a recession the economy is down and out, resources are wasted, and high rates of unemployment exist. The economy could do much better. How might government spending, taxes, or transfers help alleviate a recession? The answer is simple. The government has to pump up spending. If more goods are sold, there will be a demand for those resources that help produce them, including labor. This will lead to a reduction in the unemployment rate and a boost to the economy. Since the federal government is a big spender, it could spend more on roads, bridges, education, or any other part of its budget and stimulate the economy.

When the government spends more dollars, a chain reaction of spending occurs that has a multiple effect on the economy as a whole. If one more person gets a government contract or job, then that is one more person who can buy a house, a car, or other products. Those who sell cars, houses, or other products will then have more funds to spend in their own way, and so on down the line. A government could increase its spending by a few billion dollars and have a much greater impact on the economy than only a few billion dollars of output and income creation. This is known as the **multiplier effect**. So, the key to relieving the recession is to raise **aggregate demand**, or total spending.

The government could have achieved a similar result indirectly by fattening the wallets of the private sector by lowering taxes and/or raising transfer payments. Either of these could set that same multiple-stimulation process into motion, and in so doing, reduce the negative impact of a recession.

Now, let us consider inflation. We know that this is a rise in the general price level, and we also know that it is often the result of an overstimulated economy. So, the prescription for solving this problem will be the opposite of that for recession.

With inflation it is important to bring spending pressure down. Again, the government can contribute to this mightily by trimming its own budget, cutting certain expenditures on this or that item, having a magnified total impact on the economy.

Government could also slow spending indirectly by thinning wallets in the private sector, thus discouraging individuals from spending as much or as freely. It could achieve this by raising taxes and/or lowering transfer payments. But either way, the key to solving the inflationary quandary is to reduce aggregate demand, or total spending.

For an overview, see the chart below.

Problem	Solution	Specific Fiscal Policy
Recession	↑ Aggregate Demand	↑ Government spending ↓ Taxes ↑ Transfers
Inflation	↓ Aggregate Demand	↓ Government spending ↑ Taxes ↓ Transfers

What About Balance?

At this point, surely some of you are thinking, "Wait a minute, to spend, the government has to tax!"

You're right. In the real world there is a complex balancing act of taxes, transfers, and spending going on all the time, and much of it is motivated by concerns other than those that make sense economically. Up to now, we just wanted you to appreciate the individual impact of spending, taxes, and transfers, but now it's time to consider a more realistic assessment of the balancing act.

A **balanced budget** means that a government's outlays equal its receipts in a single fiscal year: In essence, that tax revenues after transfers barely—but completely—manage to pay for government spending in a year. This sounds like a responsible thing to do, but it does have drawbacks. One drawback of balancing the budget too strictly on a year-by-year basis is that it tends to be **procyclical**, reinforcing and magnifying the swing of the business cycle, along with the problems of recession and inflation. To appreciate this, inspect the diagram below.

Procyclical Nature of A Balanced Budget

Bad Year __ Income Falls __ Tax Revenue Falls __ Government Spending ↓

Good Year __ Income Grows __ Tax Revenue Grows __ Government Spending ↑

Notice that in bad years, when the economy needs a boost, the funds are not available. To balance the budget, the government must trim spending and cut projects and programs, just when they are needed most. This will deepen the recession.

Likewise, in good years, when the economy is expanding rapidly and may face the danger of an inflationary outbreak, a balanced budget prescribes that spending should increase, thus increasing the likelihood of a severe inflation and its negative consequences. To say that balancing the budget strictly is procyclical is to say that it makes economic fluctuations and problems worse.

The other drawback of balancing too strictly is that it weakens fiscal policy, or the government's ability to adjust economic problems. This is true because to maintain balance the government must tax and spend in the same direction, but since taxing and spending have opposite effects on the economy, this will lead to an offset. For example, suppose the government wishes to get out of a recession by increasing spending to stimulate the ailing economy. If it has to strictly remain balanced, it must also raise taxes similarly, which empties the pockets of consumers, so they spend less. Note the offsetting impact of taxes and spending that move in the same direction.

Thus, balancing the budget strictly has two serious drawbacks:

1) makes economic problems worse

2) takes away some of the government's ability to deal with those problems

You may ask, what then is to be done? Theoretically, there is a lovely solution known as **functional finance**. Functional finance stresses that although balance is an important consideration, being slightly in deficit or surplus in the short run is really no big deal. It suggests that a nation could be roughly balanced at any point in time by running surpluses in good years, deficits in bad years, and at the same time it would be following countercyclical short-run policy. This solution seems like the best of both worlds, but unfortunately, it is unattainable, as it is clear that no one gets elected by withholding funds from the public in good years. At best, if the government deems balance important, it may be intermittently achieved by unusually long and unexpected growth in the economy, or by adhering to some less than optimal rule, much like the one described earlier.

In a representative republic such as our own, it would seem that political pressures bias us toward consistently running deficits and accumulating a debt over time. What problems does this pose? Well, let's see.

Budget Deficits and the National Public Debt

In a single fiscal year, a government may take in more than it spends. This is known as a **budget surplus**. It is also possible that in a single year it may take in just enough to match its spending, in which case, it has **achieved balance**. But more often than not, over the past few decades, our government has run a **budget deficit**, which means government receipts for that year were not sufficient to finance all spending and transfers. The rest it had to borrow.

Since a budget deficit has occurred in 36 of the last 40 years, and sometimes the shortfall was hundreds of billions of dollars per year, there has been an accumulation of debt. This accumulated debt over time is the **national public debt**, and it now stands at approximately 5.7 trillion dollars! A **deficit** occurs within a year when spending exceeds revenues. A **debt** is the accumulation of yearly deficits. Of course, no one lends money without expecting to be paid back with interest, and the yearly interest on this gross debt exceeds 300 billion dollars. In fact, along with Social Security, our collective welfare establishment, and National Defense, this debt service is among the four largest yearly items in our federal budget. Considering the diversion of current funds this may create, it's clear that the consistent running of deficits and the accumulation of a debt could be a significant drag on our nation's future economic prospects.

We must, however, temper our judgement in this matter with a few important considerations.

Is the Debt So Bad?
There are several reasons why the debt and its attendant difficulties may be overstated.

1. **Consider not the size of the debt, but its size relative to the economy that accumulated it.**

In other words, although 5.7 trillion dollars is an enormous number, 8.6 trillion dollars is an even bigger one. Why mention 8.6 trillion dollars? Because that is an estimate of the U.S. GDP for this year. To put things in perspective, imagine that you had a job that generated a yearly income of $100,000 a year, but you also had debts amounting to about $67,000. Would you worry terribly? Of course not, as that proportion of debt to income, which is perfectly comparable to our nation's, is easily manageable. Naturally, you'd like to have the job without the debt, but if you could only take them or leave them together, you would be a fool not to jump at the chance to take both the job and the debt. Part of the reason the United States is as big and productive as we are has something to do with this debt of ours, which is of manageable proportions.

2. **More than 85 percent of the debt is held by Americans or American institutions.**

You may not see yourself as involved with this, but reconsider. Do you have a savings bond? Do you own insurance? Do you make contributions to a pension plan or have a bank account? Don't you know others who do? A small but significant fraction of these funds are invested in the service of government debt. In some sense then, we are paying ourselves, when we make yearly payments on the debt. And incidentally, it wouldn't much matter if we had a larger proportion of externally held debt, because to the extent that foreigners invest in our nation, they are tied to our interests and are rooting for us to succeed. The ready availability of funds only keeps things like our taxes lower, our interest rates lower, our property values higher, and our growth higher than they might otherwise have been.

3. As much as a quarter of the debt can be completely discounted as purely redistributive.

When one branch of government has a shortfall, and another has a surplus of funds, they will redistribute these already collected funds by issuing government securities. It looks like debt, but it's really just a legal accounting technique for redistributing funds to where they are needed. It represents no net burden on the American people either in the short run or in the long run.

When reports of a national debt claim numbers approaching 6 trillion dollars, they are referring to gross debt, but only the net debt represents a true burden to future generations. The net public debt is only a bit more than 4 trillion dollars, and when taken in proportion to our nation's GDP, represents a fraction closer to 50 percent than 67 percent. In other words, the debt with which we should concern ourselves is even a smaller proportion of our capacity to pay it off than the debt that is usually reported.

4. Does anyone care if we're in debt, if we put the money to good use?

Does a business hesitate to borrow millions of dollars for a new computer system that will enhance its efficiency by leaps and bounds? NO, because this investment will pay for itself with increased productivity and profit. Likewise, some of the money the government has borrowed over the years has been spent on bridges, roads, education, research, and other investments, which are partly responsible for why we have the largest and most productive economy in the history of the world. Even if the national debt were many times greater, as long as all the money were invested wisely it wouldn't present a problem. Like the computer system we mentioned earlier, it would pay for itself easily in the form of increased productivity, growth, and a higher standard of living.

To the extent that borrowed money is invested wisely, we shouldn't worry at all; however, if there is a problem with our federal budget, it may be that too little is spent on investment, and the lion's share only promotes current consumption. Borrowing money to eat a better meal today does not leave you with the ability to painlessly pay back your creditors tomorrow.

Whether a government is in debt or not, it only has three ways to pay its bills. Let's round off our discussion by looking into this matter in a little more detail.

THREE WAYS THE GOVERNMENT CAN FINANCE ITS SPENDING

Print More Money

One way in which government can get its hands on more dollars to spend is by printing more money. After all, it is the government. But even from our brief earlier discussion, you should be able to appreciate the danger of printing enormous amounts of money haphazardly just to finance any given thing. That danger is inflation.

We described the terrible costs associated with even routine levels of inflation, but printing money on a large scale can bring with it a whole new order of difficulties. When yearly inflation rates exceed triple digits—and many nations have experienced far worse than that—the circumstance is often referred to as hyperinflation. If such enormous inflation occurs, local and international communities will show a complete lack of confidence in the nation's currency. Locals will often resort to buying more respected currencies in place of their own. In turn, the local banking and financial authorities will be too weak to control what is functioning as the money supply within their own borders. Large proportions of barter will take place, but bartering—trading a good for a good—depends on a coincidence of wants, and so this further slows the number of transactions that can take place within society. Thus, the standard of living collapses.

Finally, the severe measures often attempted to reestablish confidence in a currency are themselves painful, and could only be considered the lesser of two evils. In short, if a government can avoid printing money like mad, then it should do so.

Borrow

A second way for the government to get more money to spend is to borrow it. The government can borrow by issuing debt securities of differing maturities, and in our country the most important of these are U.S. Treasury securities. Borrowing only becomes an issue if tax revenues are insufficient to finance outlays. So to say a government has borrowed money in a particular fiscal year is equivalent to saying it has run a deficit.

Running large deficits, however, means that the government is now bidding for funds in the open marketplace. U.S. Treasury securities are extremely safe, as the U.S. government has never defaulted on a payment. It always pays back what it owes. When the government is willing to pay higher interest in a certain time frame, all other riskier ventures must also promise still higher interest, or attract absolutely no funds. Some private businesses can no longer compete for funds and some capital formation doesn't take place. Other private businesses—those that still manage to borrow the funds they need to grow—do so less profitably. When an environment such as the one described above exists, it is called crowding out, because some directly productive private ventures have been "crowded out" by the government's decision to borrow funds in the private sector.

"Crowding Out"

Deficits — ↑Interest Rates — ↓Directly Productive Private Investment

If government does not use all the borrowed funds for other worthwhile investments, and we know it does not, then it has reduced the growth prospects of the nation. And this is one more criticism leveled against running excessive debt.

Taxes

One last way for government to finance its spending is through taxation.

$$\begin{pmatrix} \text{Tax} \\ \text{Revenues} \end{pmatrix} = \frac{\text{Tax}}{\text{Base}} \times \begin{pmatrix} \text{Tax} \\ \text{Rate} \end{pmatrix}$$

Note that **tax revenues**, the money collected by government, depend essentially on two things. One is the **tax base**, which is the foundation for taxation and includes any and all items that are taxed. In modern economies, most of the tax base consists of income. The other item affecting tax revenues is the **tax rate**, or fraction of the tax base that will be extracted.

If revenues are in shortfall, the natural impulse is to raise rates, as they are more responsive to proportional increase in the short run. However, the government must be careful not to squelch private economic incentives through excessive taxation, as the rise in rates may then be largely offset by a slowing economy and dwindling tax base. In some sense, taxation is the most legitimate form for raising funds by government, as it is extracting a chunk of *today's* pie, largely for *today's* purposes.

Be sure to look over the review below:

3 Ways Government Finances Spending

Method	Print	Money Borrowing	Taxation
Danger	Hyperinflation Collapsed Standard of Living	Crowding Out Could Slow Economy	Raising Tax Rates Could Discourage Private Economic Activity

Chapter 11

MONEY

Most people think that money consists of green paper and silver coins that were deliberately printed and minted for the purpose of transactions. This is partly a misconception. The paper currency and coins are only a fraction of the total money supply. Anything that acts as a medium of exchange and as a standard and store of value is, by definition, **money**. Although the printed paper and minted coins act in these ways, they are not the only things that perform these functions. The money supply is considerably broader than simply printed paper and minted coins. Money should facilitate transactions. It should be a medium of exchange. It should represent the value that is being transferred between two parties. Money should also be a standard of value—a benchmark by which we represent the relative value of all goods, thus establishing a pricing system. Finally, money should act as an efficient store of value, something that will retain value over time. If money did not perform this function, there would be no incentive to save, no ability to invest, and economies could not grow.

Another common misconception concerns the system for instilling confidence in money. Many people believe that we operate under a **commodity standard**—more specifically a **gold standard**—whereby our money supply is backed by gold and is convertible into gold. This is simply not the case and has not been the case in our nation or other developed nations for most of the twentieth century. You can buy gold with money, but the money is not backed by gold. Note, you can buy bananas with money, but we do not operate under a banana standard. Our money is not backed by gold, any more than it's backed by bananas! It is true that our country has a supply of gold. But that gold on the open market would only bring enough value to equal approximately 5 percent of our dollars in circulation.

Modern developed economies follow **fiduciary standards**, which means people have trust in the issuing authority and use money with faith and confidence. In other words, if you have faith in the stability and soundness of the American economic system and government, you will have no reservations about using American dollars as currency. This will be equally true for foreigners abroad, as well as Americans at home. So, having clarified a couple of major misconceptions, what constitutes our money supply?

DEFINITIONS OF MONEY

The answer to the question we posed above is multilayered, as it depends on how strictly you hold to the understanding of how money functions. Recall, that for money to be money, it must function in three ways: as a medium of exchange, as a standard of value, and as a store of value. Anything that operates in this manner is money. A specific definition of the money supply has been developed for accounting purposes. M1 is the strictest definition of the money supply—it says that money consists of currency, but it is dominated by checkable deposits of all kinds, as checks are safer for use in larger transactions.

$$M1 = \text{Currency} + \text{Checkable Deposits}$$

Money orders and travelers' checks could also be added; however, they make up a very small share of the total.

A less strict definition includes a few other items, which act as money to a large extent. Most of these additional items would be considered small time and savings deposits, which could be readily accessed and liquidated, or turned into cash.

$$M2 = M1 + \text{small time and savings deposits}$$

Again, there are a few other smaller components that could also be added, but they are relatively small proportions of M2 and hardly worth mentioning at this level.

A third definition of money has even more relaxed constraints. M3 includes large time and savings deposits, which are somewhat more difficult to access, yielding:

$$M3 = M2 + \text{large time and savings deposits}$$

And yes, there are a few less important and esoteric items to be added, but most of the additional items fall under the rubric of large time and savings deposits.

Notice that we have been following a pattern, one of broadening definitions of money on the basis of declining liquidity.

Definitions Of Money

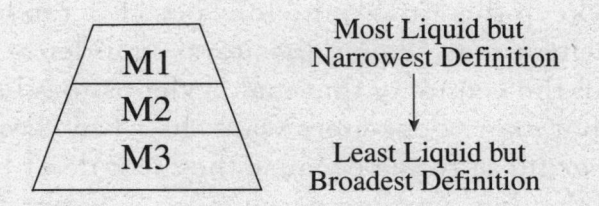

M1 — Most Liquid but Narrowest Definition

M2

M3 — Least Liquid but Broadest Definition

As we added fewer and fewer cash-like items to the mix, the definitions of what constitutes the money supply got larger. As we proceed, you will learn that which definition to use is a major complication in pursuing effective monetary policy. Controlling one definition of money does not necessarily lead to proper control of another.

Because the money supply, even in its most narrow definition, is only partially made up of cash, the key to controlling the money supply is *not* controlling the supply of cash, but rather controlling all those other items like checkable deposits that exist within our banking system. Ultimately, the proper regulation of our banking system will lead to the appropriate availability of money and credit.

MONEY CREATION

Banks, and bank-like institutions, are crucial to the economy. They act as financial intermediaries in the process of linking savers to investors and, as such, increase the growth and prosperity of our nation. For the vital service they perform, they are compensated with a "cut of the action," or profit. But they also achieve something accidentally while going about their business. They "create" most of what constitutes our money supply. Banks do not attempt to create money. Like any other business, they are trying to make a profit, which they do by lending and investing funds that have been entrusted to them, then extracting some of the return for themselves. But whether they are trying to create money or not, the fact is, they do. Every time a bank, or bank-like institution, lends or invests, they create money in the form of highly liquid credit. And these checkable deposits, and other deposits, dominate the various definitions of money.

The process starts when someone deposits cash in his or her bank account. Banks call cash, and other very liquid assets, **reserves**. Because the bank understands that not all depositors will want all their money back at once, the bank can lend or invest much of the reserves that have been entrusted to them. This is called **fractional reserve accounting**. Because banks want to make a profit, they like to lend as much of the reserves as possible. Yet they are aware of their obligation to depositors, and for safety's sake, may hold a small fraction of the reserves. This fraction is called a **reserve ratio**. Until this century, it was often left to a banker's discretion as to just how high or low this ratio would be set.

Of course, this poses a problem. Because of their interest in profit, banks would be inclined to keep this ratio quite low, possibly too low to insure the safety of deposits during times when depositors' confidence is shaken. Suppose something happens in the economy that makes depositors lose so much confidence in the banks that many depositers want their funds returned. The banks, however, fail to deliver those funds because they just don't have them. Such a scenario only causes the depositors to panic more severely, thus putting the operation and viability of responsible banks in danger. With massive bank failures, the economy would flounder, and a recession would become a depression in very short order.

This is why today, throughout the developed world, monetary authorities of respective nations set **reserve ratios**, sometimes called a **reserve requirement**. The amount of money in reserve is no longer left to the discretion of private bankers. An authority sets it, and bankers must obey. To obey this restriction or requirement, banks must hold a certain amount of liquid assets that they can neither lend nor invest. These reserves are called the **required reserves**. A bank may hold more than is necessary, and these liquid assets that a bank holds beyond its required level are known as **excess reserves**. A bank's total reserves equal its required plus excess reserves.

Under ordinary conditions, the total reserves will be almost exclusively made up of required reserves, as banks attempt to use all excess reserves for profit-generating loans and investments. When a bank approaches having no excess reserves, it's considered to be **loaned up** or **loaned out**. But conditions are not always ordinary. During a recession, banks may freely choose to hold some excess reserves. In this way, they maintain their ability to meet their obligations to depositors, even though they are operating in an environment of larger proportions of business loan defaults. During a recession, a bank may also redirect some of its funds to more secure, less risky investments, such as government securities. Because of these twin effects—holding more excess reserves and allocating more funds to the public sector—the private sector may become starved for funds to grow and expand. This is known as a **credit crunch**, and it further exacerbates the problems associated with a recession.

In fact, a bank's typical behavior, like many businesses, is quite procyclical. If left alone, banks will retreat during times of economic contraction and burst forth during times of economic expansion, causing the business cycle to swing more widely and wildly. This is all the more true because of the central role that banks play in the economy, and it's all the more reason why policy makers will encourage banks to resist their natural inclinations and act countercyclically.

We will explain some of these details further as we proceed. Let's first explore this policy-making, monetary authority, which sets reserve ratios and regulates many other behaviors of banks.

THE FEDERAL RESERVE SYSTEM

The **Federal Reserve System** started operating in 1914, and since that time its structure and powers have been significantly modified and enlarged. Every modern nation has a central bank, a financial institution that has the power to control the availability of money and credit within society. The Federal Reserve is the central bank of the U.S. Structurally, it is configured somewhat like a corporation in that it has a chairperson, who is the first among equals on a Board of Governors. This board has a majority power in establishing reserve ratios, among other things. Their influence filters down to the various regions, via the auspices of twelve regional Federal Reserve Banks, each of which enforces and implements regulation from above and fine tunes application particular to the interests of their given geographic area.

The Federal Reserve (the Fed) also holds deposits for other financial institutions. In fact, most banks keep the major portion of their required reserves on deposit at the Fed. This keeps the money safe and also makes it easier for the Fed to perform its role as a clearinghouse for checks.

When a bank does not meet its requirement, it is obliged to seek a loan from another bank with a surplus of reserves. Failing that, a bank may fall back on the Fed as a lender of last resort. The process by which the Fed loans liquid assets to banks is referred to as **discounting**.

The Fed has many other powers, some of which we will discuss later, but for now, understand that taken together, the powers of the Fed enable it to control the availability of money and credit in our society. The Federal Reserve chairperson, who has the trust and confidence of other board members, as well as the financial community, has considerably more power to influence the economic destiny of our nation than any other single individual, including the President of the United States. Our current chairperson is Alan Greenspan.

MONEY CREATION IN THE BANKING SYSTEM

Recall, we discussed the ability of any single bank to "create" money in the form of highly liquid credit whenever it extended a loan or made an investment. But realize that in the U.S. there is not only one bank. Rather, there are many thousands of banks and bank-like institutions with this same power. When a bank makes a loan to someone, that person wishes to spend the money. When they spend the money by writing a check, reserves are deducted from the bank that has backed them. But someone else has received the check, and when that second individual places most or all of the funds into his bank, a second bank now has enhanced reserves. The second bank is in the same business as the first: it makes profit the same way; it is regulated in the same way; and it will behave very much the same way. The second bank, like the first, will take whatever excess reserves it has, and it will loan or invest those funds. Then the process repeats itself. Someone writes a check. Someone else receives a check. When it is deposited in a third bank, that third bank has the same abilities and inclinations as the previous two banks. When it makes a loan or an investment, the process is once again repeated, and so on down the line.

Even a small amount of reserves injected into any bank in the banking system will lead to an enormous amount of loans and credit. The larger the injection of reserves, the larger the multiple expansion of credit throughout the system. The reserves are the raw material for loans and investments that lead to the creation of most of our money supply.

There is one hindrance to this mechanism. It is the reserve requirement, which has been set by the Federal Reserve. This requirement restricts any bank's ability to use the reserves it receives for loans and investments. If the reserve requirement is high, it's like telling every bank in the banking system that they must hold most of what they receive and not make too many loans or create too much credit. Conversely, a low requirement allows each bank in the system to use more of the liquid assets they receive for loans, investments, and the creation of credit.

It is clear that the Fed's ability to raise or lower reserve ratios grants it the power to influence how much money is created within the banking system. But this is only one way, and not even the most important. Let's review all the techniques the Fed may use to control the money supply.

CONTROLLING THE MONEY SUPPLY

There are three ways for the Fed to control the amount of money floating about the economy. The first one we have already discussed—through the reserve ratio.

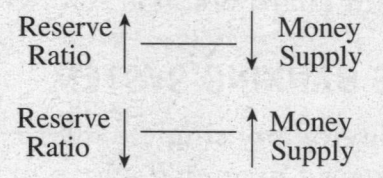

$$\text{Reserve Ratio} \uparrow \quad \longrightarrow \quad \text{Money Supply} \downarrow$$

$$\text{Reserve Ratio} \downarrow \quad \longrightarrow \quad \text{Money Supply} \uparrow$$

As you can see above, high reserve ratios mean less credit creation, and low reserve ratios lead to more credit creation. But it is important to note that the

Fed has seldom, or significantly, varied this ratio to influence the amount of money. Reserve ratios help maintain safety and confidence in the banking system. Thus, maintaining liquidity in the banking system is the primary purpose of setting reserve ratios.

The second way for the Fed to influence the money supply would be through discounting. You already know that when banks do not meet their required reserves, they must borrow from other banks that have a surplus of these funds; however, they may not be able to find such a bank, and may fall back on the Fed as a lender of last resort.

When the Fed lends to these banks, it does not do so for free. It charges them an interest rate, known as the **discount rate**. By lowering or raising the discount rate, the Fed can either encourage or discourage banks from pushing their limits, and in turn, from borrowing reserves.

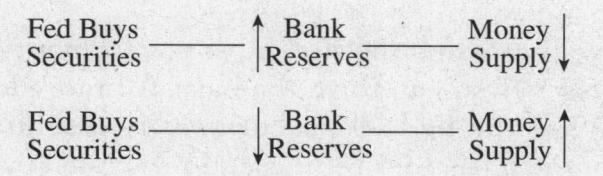

```
Fed Buys ─────── ↑ Bank ─────── Money ↓
Securities        Reserves         Supply

Fed Buys ─────── ↓ Bank ─────── Money ↑
Securities        Reserves         Supply
```

If the discount rate is high, it discourages banks from borrowing reserves. With less reserves, fewer loans will be made, and less credit will be created. Conversely, if the discount rate is low, it encourages banks to borrow reserves, and with more reserves, more loans can be made, and more credit will be created.

When the Fed was first established, the process of discounting was seen as its primary means to influence the money supply. However, through experience, it became obvious that this channel was less effective in practice than in theory, largely because the initiative remained with the banks themselves.

Let's look at a brief illustration. During a recession, the Fed may lower the discount rate to enhance banks' ability to loan, invest, and promote growth in the economy. But during a recession, banks tend to retreat, as many loans default and many prospects seem less than optimistic. Waving "cheap" funds in front of the banks during a recession is similar to waving a sandwich in front of someone who has already eaten a three-course meal. It may still encourage some banks to indulge, but not to the extent one may have hoped. They are already full. This is not to say that adjusting the discount rate is not effective. We do see variation in the discount rate used to affect money creation; however, it is usually done as a signal of the Fed's well-thought-out intentions or as a supplement to the third and most important method the Fed uses to influence the money supply—open market operations.

Open market operations involve the Fed buying or selling government securities in the open market. Sometimes the operation takes place with a bank directly but more often with a **treasury dealer**, a specialist in the marketing of government debt. Either way, when the Fed buys securities, it leads to increased reserves in the banking system and more money creation. And when the Fed sells, it has the opposite effect.

Open Market Operations

Fed Buys Securities ——— ↑ Bank Reserves ——— Money Supply ↓

Fed Sells Securities ——— ↓ Bank Reserves ——— Money Supply ↑

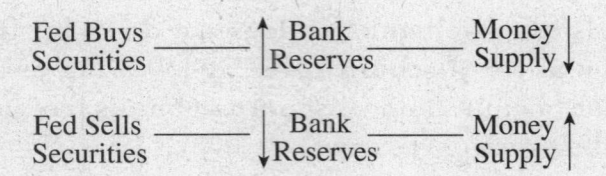

Above, you'll notice that when the Fed buys government securities, it pays for them with liquid assets that can form the basis for more loans, investments, and credit creation. When the Fed sells securities, it's essentially providing an asset that cannot form the basis for credit creation, while absorbing some of those reserves that could have served that purpose.

When the Fed operates in the open market, it is exercising monopolistic control over the availability of unborrowed reserves. Because those reserves form the basis for interbank loans in the very first instance, the Fed exerts control over the cost of these funds.

The funds that banks loan to each other are called **federal funds**, and the rate they charge each other for these overnight loans is called the **federal funds rate**. The demand and supply of these funds in the market determine this rate. It is not correct to say this rate is set. It is determined by market forces; however, since the Fed can estimate the demand for these funds, and at the same time has monopolistic control over their supply, it is correct to say the Fed controls this rate. To the extent that the federal funds rate forms the foundation for rates in general, other rates will be influenced too. But note, these other rates, like the **prime rate**—the rate banks charge their best corporate customers—are farther removed from the direct influence of the Fed. Such influences demonstrate how complex the Fed's job can be.

The Fed controls nonborrowed reserves in relation to the demand for such funds. This establishes a price for these funds, but other interest rates for other loans with differing characteristics fall farther afield of the Fed's direct influence, and so are harder to control with any accuracy.

Aside from controlling the amount of money and credit in circulation, the Fed can also exert influence over the direction and use of credit. This power is usually informally exerted through persuasive efforts grouped under the title **moral suasion**, whereby the Fed tries to encourage banks to divert funds from some activities, while reallocating funds to others.

In addition to moral suasion, other selective credit controls exist, such as the margin requirement, which establishes a limit on the proportion of a stock purchase that may be financed with bank credit. Raising or lowering this measure does not necessarily have an impact on how much credit exists. Rather, it influences how existing credit is used.

These selective controls can play an important role in the Fed's monetary policy, but they usually pale in significance when compared to quantitative methods of control like those we mentioned earlier, and that are summarized below.

Methods of Monetary Control

Method	If	Then
Reserve Ratio	↑	↓ M^S
	↓	↑ M^S
Discount Rate	↑	↓ M^S
	↓	↑ M^S
OMO	Fed buys	↑ M^S
	Fed sells	↓ M^S

M^S ↑ —— When ⟨ r ↓ / DR ↓ / OMO Fed Buys Securities

M^S ↓ —— When ⟨ r ↑ / DR ↑ / OMO Fed Sells Securities

Now that you have a handle on what money is and how it is created, we will go on to discuss monetary policy, which involves changing the money supply to affect the economy.

MONEY ◆ 95

Chapter 12

MONETARY POLICY

Monetary policy involves a change in the money supply to affect the economy. As the central bank of the U.S., the Federal Reserve is in charge of directing monetary policy, and it can pursue either of two basic policy orientations: **expansionary monetary policy** or **contractionary monetary policy**.

EXPANSIONARY MONETARY POLICY

Initially, expansionary monetary policy involves an increase in the availability of money and credit relative to its demand. If we assume that the demand for money is stable, we can simplify our presentation and say that expansionary monetary policy involves an absolute increase in the size of the money supply. To understand the impact of such an increase in the money supply, look at the diagram below.

Expansionary Monetary Policy

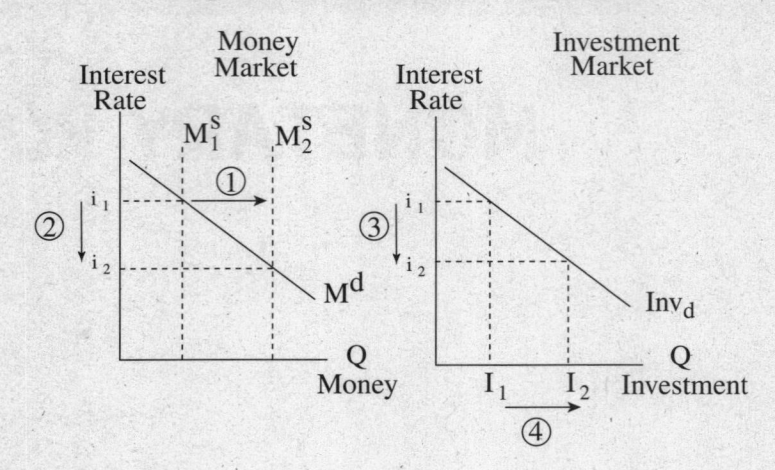

Pictured above are two markets. On the left is the money market, where the price of money (the interest rate) is set. The money supply is perfectly vertical, implying that the Fed has perfect control of the money supply and can keep it precisely at any level it chooses. Of course, this is an exaggeration, but it is not grossly inaccurate, and it aids in simplifying our analysis.

In contrast, the money demand has a negative slope because the interest rate represents the opportunity cost of holding money. In other words, as the interest rate rises, the cost of holding money in hand, without any return, rises. So, less money will be demanded at higher interest rates. Conversely, as the opportunity cost falls, as interest rates decline, it is preferable to hold more money, since it is not expensive to do so.

On the right is the investment market, where the investment demand represents the willingness and ability of business owners to borrow funds to create and expand the means to produce. As interest rates rise, it represents an increased cost of borrowing funds, and is therefore a discouragement to investors. On the other hand, low interest rates mean low cost of borrowing, and an encouragement to do so.

The money supply is like any other good. If it becomes abundant, its price will drop. And since the interest rate is the price of money, as the money supply expands, the interest rate drops. This establishes the basis for all interest rates in the economy and, importantly, those of the investment market. When the price of money drops, this means the cost of borrowing money has dropped, thus encouraging investors to borrow the cheap and available funds to expand the nation's ability to produce.

Initially, an expansionary policy refers to an expansion of the money supply, but ultimately it can lead to an expansion of the real economy, and a rise in our standard of living. Therefore, an expansionary policy would be appropriate if the goal is to stimulate the economy. This would be the goal, if the economy was in recession. To understand this more fully, inspect the chain of causation below.

Expansionary Monetary Policy

$$\text{If Recession} \longrightarrow \begin{matrix} \downarrow r \\ \downarrow DR \\ OMO \\ (\text{Fed Buys}) \end{matrix} \longrightarrow \uparrow \text{Bank Reserves} \longrightarrow \uparrow M^s \longrightarrow \downarrow i \longrightarrow \begin{matrix} \uparrow \text{Inv} \\ \uparrow \text{Cons} \\ \uparrow \text{Dur} \end{matrix} \longrightarrow \uparrow y$$

Assuming the nation is in recession, the Federal Reserve could take several actions to stimulate the growth of the money supply, and in so doing, stimulate the growth of the economy:

- The Fed could lower reserve requirements to free banks to extend more credit.

- The Fed could lower discount rates to encourage banks to borrow additional reserves for lending.

- Most importantly, the Fed could buy securities in the open market, which would provide banks with additional raw material to lend. Increased reserves for lending allow the money supply to be raised even more quickly, as banks bounce this raw material throughout the system of banks. And like other goods, abundance will lead to low price. As the money supply expands, the interest rates will fall, making it cheaper to borrow money.

This is especially important to investors who wish to expand businesses, and also to consumers who buy durables, which are goods of great durability and expense. Consumers generally have to take out loans to purchase durable goods, such as houses and cars. If interest rates are lower, these goods are effectively cheaper, and consumers will be encouraged to purchase them. With greater investment and a larger number of transactions of goods, society will experience greater levels of employment, higher wages, and a general increase in its standard of living. An expansion of money can lead to an expanded economy. Now, that sounds like a no-lose proposition. Why not blow the roof off the money supply all the time? The answer is: if it was not during a recession, or if it was a minor recession, and suddenly there was an enormous expansion of money and credit, the economy would experience terrible inflation and the "no-lose" scenario would not play out.

Expansionary Monetary Policy

If No Recession — ↑M^s — ↑Price Level — ↓i — ↓Inv, ↓Cons, ↓Dur — ↓y

Recall, if an economy is at or near full employment and suddenly general spending rises significantly, it does not stimulate the real economy. The real economy will show little or no slack that could be put to better use; however, the rise in general spending will lead to higher prices on average. With an economy almost fully employed, any large expansion of the money supply will fuel increased spending, and inevitably cause inflation. Again, remember, expansionary monetary policy is appropriate during a recession.

CONTRACTIONARY MONETARY POLICY

Contractionary monetary policy is the opposite case of expansionary. It involves a relative reduction in the availability of money and credit. If we assume money demand to be stable, which would imply that any reduction in the absolute size of the money supply would constitute a contractionary policy, this simplifies the case.

Contractionary Monetary Policy

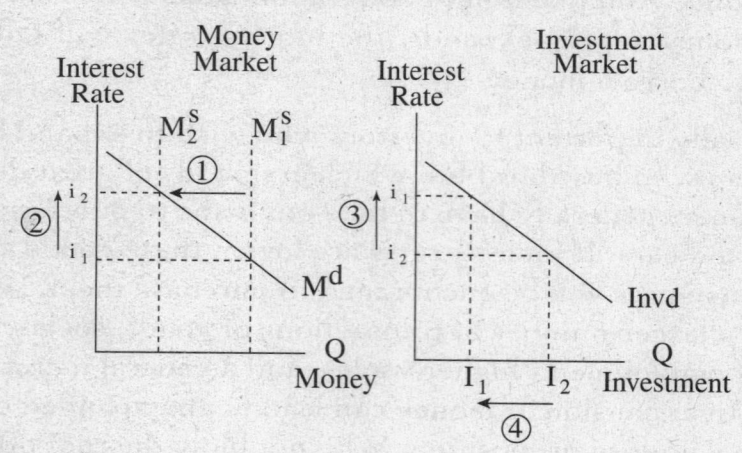

The graphs above are the same as presented before; however, this time the money supply is being reduced. And like other goods that become scarce, money's price will rise. Money's rising price is the higher interest rate, which then forms the basis for all cost of borrowing in our society. Thus, any borrower will now be discouraged from borrowing the relatively more costly funds. This is certainly true of investors, who wish to borrow funds for building businesses.

Why would the Federal Reserve want to hinder expansion of the economy? When does it make sense to slow down our economic juggernaut? The answer, if not directly obvious, is not difficult. The Fed would want to slow the economy if the economy was going too fast, which might lead to an outbreak of inflation and serious detrimental circumstances for the economy over the longer run. As before, let's inspect the details.

Contractionary Monetary Policy

$$\text{If Recession} \longrightarrow \begin{matrix}\uparrow r \\ \uparrow DR \\ OMO \\ (\text{Fed Sells})\end{matrix} \longrightarrow \downarrow \text{Bank Reserves} \longrightarrow \downarrow M^s \longrightarrow \uparrow i \longrightarrow \begin{matrix}\downarrow \text{Inv} \\ \downarrow \text{Cons} \\ \text{Dur}\end{matrix} \longrightarrow \downarrow y$$

If an economy is experiencing inflation, or is on the brink of doing so, the Fed could take several steps to slow down the money supply, which is the impetus of the problem:

- The Fed could raise reserve requirements, reducing the amount of reserves that banks could lend.

- The Fed could raise the discount rate, thus discouraging banks from borrowing as many reserves for additional lending.

- Most importantly, the Fed could sell securities in the open market, which would reduce the reserves held by banks, and therefore reduce credit creation.

With less reserves, banks can make fewer loans and investments, creating less money. With less money available, its price (the interest rate) rises. Higher interest rates make borrowing more expensive, and so investors and those who buy consumer durables will be less willing and able to do so. With less investment and transactions, the economy will slow down. This sounds very bleak, but remember the reason for slowing the economy is an attempt to combat the more serious risk of diminished long-term growth due to the presence of inflation.

Contractionary Monetary Policy

$$\text{In Longer Run} \longrightarrow \downarrow M^s \longrightarrow \downarrow \text{Price Level} \longrightarrow \downarrow i \longrightarrow \begin{matrix}\uparrow \text{Inv} \\ \uparrow \text{Cons} \\ \uparrow \text{Dur}\end{matrix} \longrightarrow \uparrow y$$

Above, it is clear that slowing down the money supply depletes the basis for any inflation. With inflation low, expectations of any inflation also drop. This means creditors will stop tacking on large inflation premiums to the interest rates they charge for borrowed funds. Lower interest rates mean lower borrowing costs. Lower borrowing costs mean more borrowing for investment and consumer durables. And this will invigorate the economy over the long run. Let's look at an analogy.

Suppose you are driving to school on the highway. In the distance, you see a flaming wreck in the middle of the road. If you try to plow through, you will become a part of the carnage; however, if you carefully slow down, change lanes, and move around the wreck, you may be slightly late to school, but you will arrive safely. Likewise, to avoid the wreck of inflation, the Fed may have to slow the engine of the economy, so as to avoid dire circumstances in the long run. By moderating the expansion of the economy—hitting the brakes so to speak—the Fed allows us to experience sustained, more vigorous growth over the long run. It may cost us many thousands of jobs in the short run, for the sake of increasing the likelihood of creating millions more jobs over the subsequent years.

As you may suspect, hitting the brakes on money growth is controversial. There is always room for debate concerning the timing and magnitude of such actions by the Fed. For it is possible to hit the brakes too hard or at the wrong time, thus creating the recessionary tendencies you were trying to avoid. Policy is like medicine. If you take too little medicine, you will not get better. On the other hand, too much medicine will poison you, possibly killing you. The trick is to take the proper dosage for the proper amount of time. With policy, too little action leaves the economy sick. Too much action can actually cause alternative difficulties.

Review the table below and keep in mind that most modern central banks, the Fed included, focus their energies on maintaining price stability in order to provide a firm foundation for investment and growth of their economies over time.

Summary:

Problem	Fed Action	Impact on Money Supply	Impact on Interest Rates	Intended Result
Recession	↓r ↓DR OMO (Fed Buys)	↑	↓	↑Loans Investment − Create Jobs − Stimulate Economy
Inflation	↑r ↑DR OMO (Fed Sells)	↓	↑	− Slow Economy ↓Price Level − Promote Long Run Growth

Chapter 13

ECONOMIC GROWTH

The output that a nation's population has to enjoy depends on the nation's inputs, also known as **resources**. All other things being equal, if there are more resources, there is a greater capacity to produce. To the extent that labor, land, and capital become more abundant, production should increase. Of course, all things are seldom equal. For example, having a small but fertile field would be far more beneficial than owning an enormous plot of land that was completely barren and destitute. It would be better to have a shovel to dig a ditch than to have an equally valued pile of spoons for the same task. And a well-educated and trained labor force would generate far more output than an even larger population of poorly educated and badly trained individuals.

The point is this: although the quantity of resources is important to production and growth, the quality of those resources is even more crucial to raising the standard of living in a nation. Without technology and without human capital—the investment in improving the labor force—there will be little growth in the truest sense of the term. More sweating backs may produce more products, but they also produce more hungry mouths to feed. The only real way to grow is through enhanced resource capability.

GRAPHING GROWTH

We have already reviewed two of the most popular ways to represent growth:

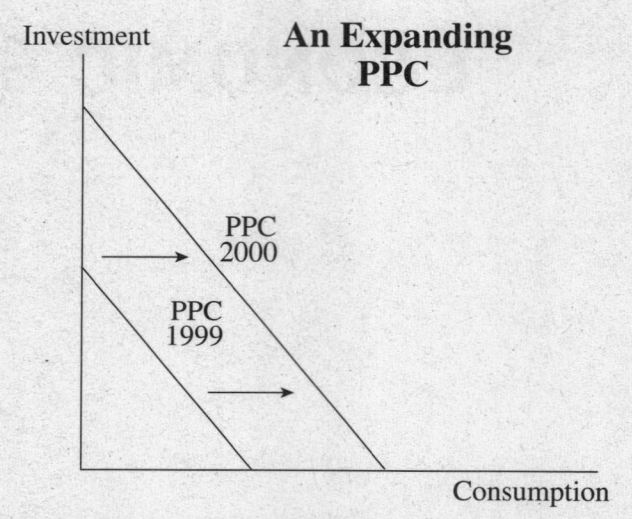

An Expanding PPC

(Investment vs. Consumption graph showing PPC 1999 shifting outward to PPC 2000)

Indicates a Nation's Potential to Produce has Risen

One way to represent growth is by an expanding PPC as the graph above shows. When technology improves, when labor is given skills, even when population expands, it increases the nation's potential to produce, which is shown as a PPC moving out and to the right. Over time, with growth, a nation may be able to reach levels of production that were formerly unattainable.

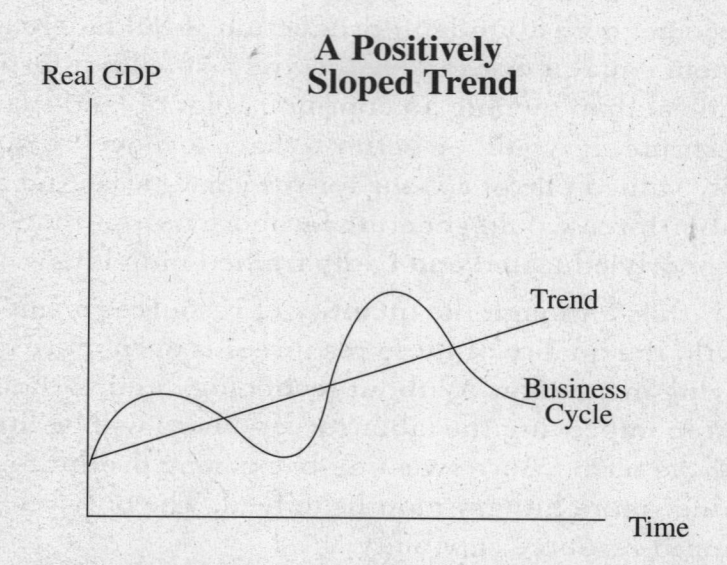

A Positively Sloped Trend

(Real GDP vs. Time graph showing a business cycle oscillating around an upward-sloping trend line)

Indicates a Nation's Average Capacity to Produce has Risen

Another popular way to depict growth is via a positively sloped trend line. Earlier we saw that when the peaks and troughs of the business cycle gravitate upward over time, this indicates that, despite the fluctuations, the nation's average capacity to produce has increased.

Note the difference in these two approaches for graphing growth. The expanding PPC gauges the potential of a nation increasing over time, while the positively sloped trend line indicates what a nation has produced on average over time. Though the approaches differ, they are both commonly used to show growth.

MEASURES OF GROWTH

Next, let's look at those statistics that are often used to define growth. The simplest measures are national output figures like the GDP. But we know that a rising GDP can be misleading, for it may be rising, at least in part, due to inflation. Even more commonly used are measures of inflation-adjusted output, like real GDP. One more rudimentary adjustment that can be made, which vastly improves this statistic as a measure of growth, concerns population.

A brief illustration will help you understand the impact of population on GDP: Suppose you are single and have a job that pays $100,000. You live quite well. On the other hand, suppose that, in addition to the high-paying job, you have a spouse and eight children to support. One hundred thousand dollars is enough for the family to get by, but you can hardly live as well as you could if you were single. After all, the same money is being spread out over ten heads, instead of only one. This same concept also applies to nations. If two nations have the same real GDP, they are not necessarily equally well off. If one nation's population is much greater, then this wealth must be spread over many more heads and support that many more lives. Thus, to better gauge such situations, one should divide the real GDP by the population, which yields the **real per-capita GDP**. The real per-capita GDP indicates how much output (or income) is available on average to a single person of the nation. Realize that an individual may receive a larger or smaller than average share. But before anyone receives anything, the output (or income) per person must exist. We will discuss distribution later in this review. Thus, of all the simple ways to define economic growth, the most common states that growth occurs when the real per-capita output of a nation rises over time.

PRODUCTIVITY

Closely tied to the discussion of growth is the concept of **productivity**, which refers to how much output can be generated per input. We can express this concept with some variety and apply it to all the different resources; however, it's most likely to refer to how much value is created with a single hour of labor.

If you were to quickly peruse popular news sources, you might get the impression that there is a crisis in American productivity. Nothing could be farther from the truth.

American productivity is higher than any other nation's on average and by a significant margin. American productivity is higher in most categories than any other nation's. And American productivity is the highest, not only currently, but in the history of the world. In brief, the typical American worker generates more output in an hour than any worker ever has, anywhere, anytime.

But if there is something to be concerned with, it's the rate of growth in our productivity. A nation's level of productivity determines its standard of living, and the rate of increase in productivity will determine the rate by which that standard of living grows. Even the slightest proportional variation will make a world of difference within a single human lifetime.

Consider the examples below.

$$\text{Real GDP} = (\text{Real Per-Capita GDP}) \cdot (\text{Population})$$
$$\parallel \quad \updownarrow \text{Proportional} \quad \updownarrow \text{Proportional}$$
$$\text{Real GDP} = (\text{Productivity}) \cdot (\text{Labor})$$

As you can see, we've presented two distinct, but equally valid, ways of breaking down a nation's real GDP. In the first case, we have the real per-capita GDP multiplied by the population, which yields the real GDP. This simply states that if you multiply how much each person has on average times the number of people who have it, the result will be everything they have. For example, maybe in a certain nation, the average person has $1,000, and there are 1,000 people in that nation. Well, 1,000 people times $1,000 yields 1 million dollars in output (or income) in total for the nation.

In the second case, we have broken down the real GDP a little differently. The second illustration shows real GDP to result from productivity times the labor force. The formula simply means you are measuring what a worker can produce on average then multiplying it by how much labor is available. Naturally, the result is all that is produced. For example, maybe the level of productivity in a nation is worth $10 of value per hour, and the labor supplied to the market in a year is 100,000 hours. Well, multiplying $10 times 100,000 hours yields a total value produced of 1 million dollars in output (or income) for that nation. Real GDP equals itself in either case, but it can be expressed as either of these two product relationships. You then might ask, "Where does all the labor come from?" You might realize the answer is: from your population! Although labor participation rates may differ over time, they do not vary dramatically in a hurry. Thus, a bigger population correlates with a larger workforce, and a smaller one correlates with a smaller workforce. The more people, the more workers. The fewer people, the fewer workers.

Now that we have determined the proportionality that exists between population and labor in the two differing product relationships, you should be able to recognize that the remaining two variables—productivity and real per-capita GDP—must also be proportional in order to yield an equivalent result. Remember we said that to grow is to have more output per person to consume (a higher real per-capita GDP), but now we are saying that in order to have more per person to consume, you must have more productive workers. The more your average worker can produce in an hour's time, the more output per person will exist. Nations with low productivity have low standards of living, and nations with high productivity have high standards of living.

To understand the importance of the rate of growth in productivity, you need to understand the "rule of 72," which is a useful mathematical rule of thumb for estimating the "doubling time" associated with any proportional process. Any process that grows at a certain rate or percentage will lead to a doubling and redoubling of the item in question given enough time. To estimate this doubling time for processes growing at reasonable percentages, you need to divide the rate into the number 72. So, if inflation was 12 percent a year, it would take about 6 years for the price level to double, because 72/12 equals 6. Or, if the return on an investment was 9 percent a year, it would take about 8 years for your money to double, because 72/9 equals 8. Or, if the population is growing at 4 percent a year, it will take about 18 years for the population to double, because 72/4 equals 18.

Let us now apply the rule to productivity. If your nation's productivity is advancing at 1 percent a year, then it will take about 72 years for your nation's level of productivity and its standard of living to double. In short, you'd be dead before you'd see the average American enjoying a standard of living that is twice as high as that enjoyed today! On the other hand, suppose America could sustain productivity growth of 4 percent during your lifetime. Then the standard of living would double every 18 years, and in those 72 years, the standard would have doubled four times. This means, the average American standard of living would not have doubled, not quadrupled, not increased eightfold, but would have risen a whopping sixteen times over! Instead of your great grandchildren living in a nation that is marginally better off than the one you now live in, they will live in a nation vastly more wealthy. And this can be achieved by raising productivity growth from a poor 1 percent a year to a quite reasonable and sustainable 4 percent a year.

Nations with high rates of productivity growth have big increases in their standard of living, and the difference between lousy productivity and great productivity is a measly few percent. Thus, the rate of productivity growth always concerns us.

ECONOMIC GROWTH ◆ 107

DIMINISHING MARGINAL RETURNS

In economics, there are very few laws, ideas that work just about everywhere and at any time, but diminishing marginal returns is one of them. The **Law of Diminishing Marginal Returns** states that there is a tendency for marginal, or extra, production to eventually and inexorably fall as more abundant resources are added to the less abundant, or fixed, resources. Basically, everyone tries to do the best they can with what they have available. Naturally, people use the resources that they can easily obtain in greater and greater abundance than those resources that are not so easy to obtain.

Only a certain plant size exists in the short run for large corporations in the modern economy. To maximize the intensity of production, corporations hire more and more labor—the resource that is more easily varied in the short run. Sooner or later, however, increasing labor stops helping as much and, in extreme cases, could even hurt total production. Imagine an increasingly crowded factory floor—this could be a factor leading to this consequence.

Of course, large companies can circumvent the problem in the long run, by dividing their efforts among divisions and building new plant with the aid of previously accumulated profits. So, do these large corporations consider diminishing returns? Yes. Is it a tragedy for them? No, as they have the means to avoid its most dire consequences over the long run.

Poor nations, which depend on primitive, labor-intensive agriculture for their livelihood, have it much worse. Labor is their variable (abundant) resource. If food is even barely sufficient, population will grow, and with it, the labor force. As the populations of these limited and fixed lands grow, diminishing returns ensues rather early in production and the consequences are harsh. Keep in mind the previous point about productivity and the standard of living. If the additional production that a worker contributes is falling, what must eventually happen to the average production of workers in general and to the standard of living of the average consumer within that nation? If your last (marginal) test score kept getting lower and lower, would it not pull your average down? Nations that experience large increases in population and commensurate reductions in marginal productivity also pull down their average productivity and, with it, their standard of living. A man named Malthus published one of the earliest and most influential analyses of this topic 200 years ago. His legacy lives on.

MALTHUS' TREATISE ON POPULATION

Thomas Malthus was a clergyman and a prominent economist, who first gained notoriety with the publication of his work *An Essay on the Principle of Population*. Originally published in 1798, largely as a response to the overoptimistic assertions of some early industrialists in England, he revised it several times prior to his death in 1834, but it remained essential and straightforward throughout.

Malthus' treatise starts with two premises: that food production grows slowly and population grows quickly, as long as it is sustained by food. Eventually, ever-growing populations become more difficult to sustain, and so nature provides certain natural correctives, namely, famine, disease, and war, all of which contribute to reducing the surplus population. Malthus stated that ultimately the world would have a sort of miserable equilibrium at high, but stable, levels of population. He thought the average person would receive a "subsistence wage," which meant receiving barely enough to sustain life.

Malthus' work influenced Wallace's and Darwin's views on natural selection. Modern theories of how the world is running down are often referred to as Malthusian, because though they may differ on details, they come to the same dismal conclusion as Malthus' work.

Malthus is often criticized for not recognizing the enormous contribution of technology to transforming the entire dynamic process. This criticism may be a bit unfair, as Malthus witnessed so little technical change in the world of his day. The onset of the Industrial Age moved at a snail's pace by the standards of today's computer age. Refer to the chart below to more fully appreciate the role of technology.

Illustrating Malthus' Theory

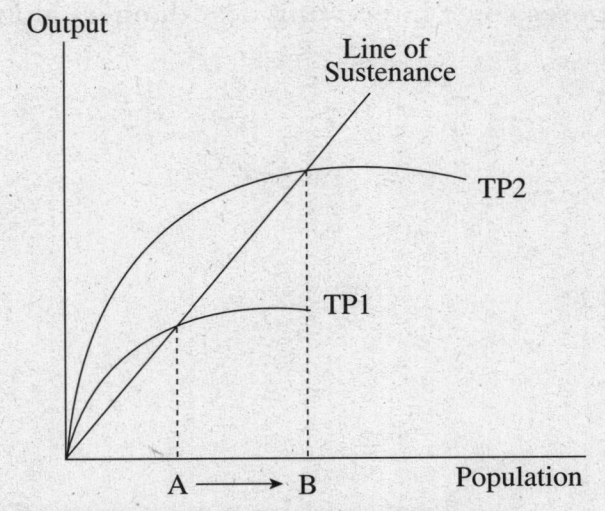

Higher Technology Leads to Higher Production
And Higher Standards of Living

As you can see, there is a certain ratio of output to population necessary for sustenance.

ECONOMIC GROWTH ◆ 109

The diagonal ray that originates at the vertex of our graph represents this. Additionally, we assume there are diminishing marginal returns. You can see this in the total product curve, which rises as population rises, but more and more slowly. Those product curves are leveling off because each additional labor unit is not contributing as much as the labor unit that preceded it. Note that when the total product curves exceed the sustenance curve, populations can grow; however, when total product curves fall below the sustenance curve, populations will begin to starve and dwindle. Thus, given a certain level of productivity, populations tend to gravitate toward the level where they are barely sustained, as Malthus predicted.

If we assume a low level of technology, perhaps we would see a product curve like TP1. But if technology were to improve, perhaps a larger, higher product curve, such as TP2, would more accurately represent the situation. Note that with lower levels of technology, a lower sustainable population exists, point A. But as technology grows, more population can be sustained, point B.

Clearly, with increased technology, greater populations can be supported, and we can imagine that if high technological growth can continue indefinitely, we may be able to "stay ahead of the curve." In other words, with high technology growth, it's possible that we could maintain levels of production that outstrip our populations' capacity to ever catch up. Thus, a higher standard of living could be forthcoming indefinitely.

But let's not dismiss Malthus too quickly, as the world does have limits. And technology itself poses some interesting new dangers along with all its promise.

Chapter 14

DISTRIBUTION OF INCOME

During our discussion of growth, we stressed how important it is to raise the real per capita GDP because this allows more output (or income), on average, per person to enjoy. Even if we raise the average, some people will receive more than this average and some will receive less. The range, or dispersion, from the low end of the scale to the high end of the scale is known as the **distribution of income.**

Consider two nations with the same real per-capita GDP, one of which distributes its income fairly evenly, and the other which concentrates the proceeds of production in just a few hands. Is it fair to say that these nations are equally well off? Hardly, since in the first case many are served by the wealth that has been generated, while in the second case only a small number of individuals have benefited. Don't be misled: some of the disparity between rich and poor is necessary to provide incentives for growth in general. For instance, if individuals were rewarded equally for working or not working, for working very productively or for working less productively, then why would anyone make the effort to get ahead, get educated, or get trained—all things that require significant time and energy regardless of a person's innate talents? The simple answer here is that people would minimize such efforts.

To promote maximum total effort and constructive contribution in a society, there must be some gradation of rewards. The more equal the rewards, the less total wealth that will be generated, and citizens will not enjoy being equal if it means being equally poor. Society only has the luxury of providing for the legitimately downtrodden and luckless among its population if a vast majority of its people is making contributions to expand the general wealth that exists. The most reliable way to encourage such contributions is to appeal to self-interest in largely free markets. Thus, some disparity of payouts must exist for the entire pie (the amount of available income) to grow large enough for all to feast.

Distribution of Income

	Quintiles	% of Disposable Income Recieved	Cumulative% of Income Recieved
Poor	1	4	4
	2	10	14
	3	16	30
	4	24	54
Rich	5	46	100.0

Above you have approximate data for the distribution of disposable income in the U.S. in the 1990s. Actual data varies slightly from year to year, and more so in the long run, but the figures presented are close to those that have existed in the U.S. in any given recent year. The scale moves from the poor to the rich end of the spectrum, and the categories are quintiles, which means that any category contains one-fifth, or 20 percent, of all American families. Breaking the data down like this correlates with those clichéd categories often cited in association with income and wealth: poor, lower middle-class, middle-class, upper middle-class, and rich. The data are also presented in two different ways; the first, as a simple distribution of income, pointing out what proportion of income was received by each quintile; the second, as a cumulative distribution of income, designating what proportion of income was received up to and including the quintile in question. Whichever way it's presented, it's the same data which clearly demonstrates that the distribution of income is quite wide. For instance, notice that the rich quintile received more than eleven times the income of the poor quintile. We already understand that some of this disparity is warranted, and it's a matter of opinion if less disparity would be better.

Over the past quarter century, the dispersion has been widening slowly but surely. Does this mean that the poor get poorer and the rich get richer, or that the rich are getting richer at the expense of the poor? The answer to both questions is, not necessarily. In the first case, you must recognize these statistics as representing the *relative* dispersion of income. In other words, these percentages are shares of a particular existing income, one that we know has grown significantly in our nation over the years. So, having a slightly smaller percentage share of a much bigger pie still means you get more pie. To provide a drastic illustration, would you like to have 100 percent of nothing, or 1 percent of something? Some poor individuals have seen their standard of living improve, even with their share of national income falling. Others have not been so lucky. The "poverty level" is set at three times the minimum food budget as established by the Department of Agriculture. Between 1976 and 1996, the number of individuals living below the poverty level increased from 24,975,000 to 36,529,000 and the percentage of the population living below the poverty level increased from 11.8 to 13.7 percent. It can be argued that some poverty and inequality results from the exploitation of labor and government policies favoring the rich, such as tax loopholes and corporate welfare. However, the ability to receive higher incomes is an impetus for hard work and innovation. In our efforts to reduce income inequality, we must be careful not to remove incentives for entrepreneurs to take risks and create jobs.

Other things that have contributed to the widening of this wealth spectrum are based on how we choose to live our lives and how the data reflect or fail to reflect those choices. For example, today's economy has a lot of double-income yuppie families. They marry late and deliberately choose not to have children (or limit the number of children they do have) to pursue careers with greater vigor. Add these two very good incomes together, and you get a family that has a fantastic income, often belonging to the richest quintile.

On the other end of the spectrum, this country has had a huge increase in unmarried teenagers becoming parents. With the limited availability of childcare and other types of support, these young parents are often unable to receive the education and training they desire in order to pursue successful careers. As a result, some become stuck in poverty.

Such recent changes to our economy can make the relative distribution of income wider.

LORENZ CURVE

Lorenz was an early-twentieth-century economist who decided to quickly and easily summarize the distribution of income using a graph. He thought that by graphing out changes in data over time, trends would be easily noticed and understood. If we take the cumulative distribution of income, as expressed in the last column of the chart above, and graph it in two dimensions, we have the Lorenz curve.

The Lorenz Curve:

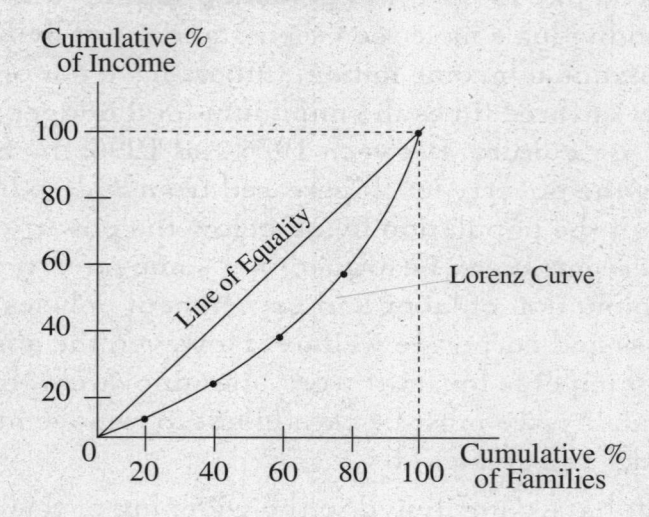

As a visual aid, we have extended lines at 100 percent of cumulative income and at 100 percent of families receiving income, which are parallel to their alternate axis. In this way, we have formed a kind of box. By cutting through the heart of that box, connecting vertex to vertex, we get the so-called line of equality. We know that incomes are not equally distributed. We know they should not be artificially equalized at the expense of incentives for effort and risk taking; however, as a reference line, it's useful to envision how a graph of the cumulative distribution would appear if such equality existed. It would be a line like the one above, because if shares of income were perfectly equal, then 20 percent of families would receive 20 percent of income. Forty percent of families would receive 40 percent of income. Sixty percent would receive 60 percent, and so on. Thus, a straight, diagonal line with a slope of one would be traced out. The line of equality is only a line of reference, but an important one.

The actual graph of the cumulative distribution of income is the Lorenz curve, and because shares of income are unequal, it has a "belly," which bulges away from the line of equality. Note that if the government transferred tax revenues from the rich to the poor, or imposed a "progressive tax," which collected a higher percentage of income from the rich than from the poor or middle class, the distribution of income would be less dispersed. Graphically, the Lorenz curve would move back toward the line of equality.

Alternately, any trend or policy that would lead to a wider dispersion of income would cause the belly of the Lorenz Curve to get bigger and move farther away from equality.

Chapter 15

INTERNATIONAL TRADE

The dominant economic reason for trade is that nations can gain from it. It's not a gamble or a dangerous game. It's possible for one nation to gain at the other's expense, but when markets are free and fair, it's a safe game and, by playing, all nations involved raise their prospects of winning something.

In the simplest cases, it's easy to see how these mutual gains are made possible. Nations merely follow their **absolute advantage** in the production of a good. In other words, if one nation is better, faster, and more efficient in producing computers than another nation, then that nation should specialize in and export computers to the second nation. Likewise, if the second nation is better, faster, and more efficient in producing cheese than the first nation, then the second nation should specialize in and export cheese to the first nation. As long the two nations trust one another, they can each focus on an area of production in which they are absolutely more productive, and therefore, less wasteful.

By allowing nations to focus their resources and energy on areas in which they are highly productive, the world's production will rise. And the prospect for mutually advantageous trade and a rising global standard of living will be forthcoming.

Sometimes, however, a developed nation with absolute advantages in all areas trades with a less developed nation with absolute disadvantages in all areas. For example, when the U.S. trades with South Pacific islands that have small economies, it's likely that any and all products could have been produced more efficiently in the U.S. However, the United States' advantages in some areas may be larger than in others, as the South Pacific island's *dis*advantages may be *less* in certain areas. Therein lies the explanation for such trade, and how it may still be beneficial to both parties. You see, there is a more general principle at work here called **comparative advantage**, which states that a nation should specialize in and export goods for which it has the least opportunity cost. Absolute advantage is merely a special, more obvious subcase of this more powerful and inclusive principle. It's clear that if one nation is better at producing computers, then it wastes less time and energy producing them and exporting them. If another nation is better at producing cheese, then it wastes less time and energy producing cheese and exporting it. The exchange of cheese and computers leaves both nations better off than before.

But now we have said that it is possible for one nation to be better at everything than another, and still have the prospect of gaining from trade with that less-productive nation. Let's look at an example to demonstrate this scenario. Suppose that the U.S. and China wish to trade, and their economies produce only wheat and automobiles. The U.S. has 100 million hours of labor available in a year's time, and China has 400 million hours. Finally, let's suppose that in the U.S., in one hour either 8 autos could be produced or 4 tons of wheat, while in China an hour of labor will yield either 1 auto or 2 tons of wheat.

	wheat	autos
U.S.	4	8
China	2	1

Immediately, something is clear. In one hour, the U.S. economy can produce more autos than China, and it can also produce more wheat than China, meaning that the U.S. has an absolute advantage in both wheat and autos, while China has an absolute disadvantage in both wheat and autos. Despite this, these nations can trade, and both nations can gain by following their area of comparative advantage, the area where they give up the least to specialize. In the U.S., the absolute advantage is greater in auto production, and so by focusing our efforts on autos, we waste less time, energy, and resources than if we produced wheat, an area where our absolute advantage is less. By the same token, the Chinese are less disadvantaged in wheat. The production of wheat would be their area of comparative advantage because by focusing their efforts on wheat, they would be losing less ground than if they had spent their resources on the production of autos.

To further aid understanding, inspect the graphs below. They represent the production possibilities curves (PPCs) of the U.S. and China, respectively.

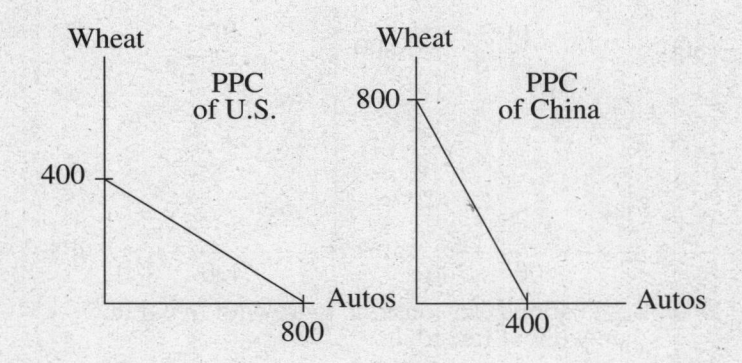

```
   Wheat                        Wheat
           PPC              800 ┤\     PPC
           of U.S.              │ \    of China
                                │  \
    400 ┤\                      │   \
        │ \                     │    \
        │  \                    │     \
        │   \                   │      \
        │    \                  │       \
        └─────\──── Autos       └────────\──── Autos
              800                        400
```

Notice that in the U.S., one extreme point of full production would occur if all its time was spent on auto production, and at 8 autos an hour times 100 million hours, one point of full production would be 800 million autos and nothing else. Another extreme of this sort would have occurred if the U.S. had exclusively produced wheat, and at 4 tons an hour times 100 million hours, one point of full production would be 400 million tons of wheat. Without trade, the U.S. would probably choose a point of full production where they produced a mix of autos and wheat. All such points are represented along the straight line connecting the extremes we have described. The entire line, end-points included, constitutes the U.S. PPC for a certain year.

Similarly, much the same could be said for China. It could use its 400 million hours to produce only autos, and at 1 auto per hour, that would be 400 million autos. Instead it could use all its labor to produce wheat, and at 2 tons an hour, that would be 800 million tons. But like the U.S., if there was no trade, China would probably choose a full production point where they produced a mix of autos and wheat. Again, these would be the points that connect the two extremes we mentioned. And taken together, all these points, extremes included, would constitute the PPC of China.

With free and fair and trusting trade, the U.S. could focus on its area of comparative advantage—autos—while the Chinese could focus on their area of comparative advantage—wheat. In fact, with perfect trust and constant costs, the U.S and China both would move in the direction of producing at the extreme ends of their possibilities. The U.S. would exclusively produce 800 million autos, and China would exclusively produce 800 million tons of wheat. Having used the world's resources more efficiently, the total pile of wheat and autos available is now so large as to make many different levels of trade beneficial.

**Consumption Possibilities Curves
With Free Trade**

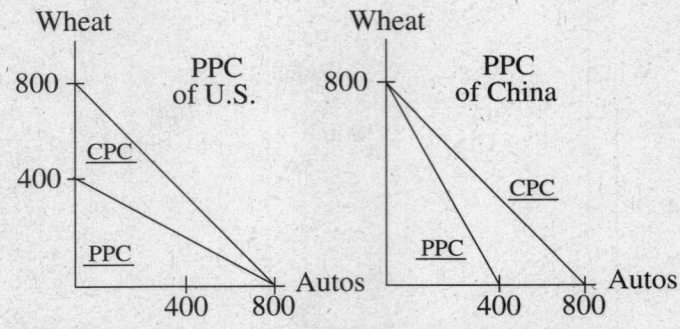

```
Wheat                           Wheat
 |                               |
800┤\  PPC                    800┤\  PPC
 |  \ of U.S.                  |  \ of China
 |   \                         |   \
 | CPC\                        |    \
400┤----\                      |  CPC\
 |      \                      |------\
 |  PPC  \                     | PPC   \
 |--------\___ Autos           |--------\___ Autos
          400  800                      400  800
```

Note: Both nations can consume more with free trade than without free trade.

    In a sense, by freely and fairly trading, nations can pool their abilities to produce. It's as if the U.S. area of comparative advantage is linked, or has full access, to the utmost capabilities of China. Similarly, China's relatively most efficient area of production is linked to that of the U.S. We see in the illustration above that by using comparative advantage, each nation has a new and greater **consumption possibilities curve**.

    This curve is farther out and to the right of the PPC in each case, indicating that greater levels of consumption and higher standards of living are possible for both nations as a result of trade. Following comparative advantage has allowed the nations of the world to use their resources more effectively, and thus act as an engine of growth for the world. The enhanced growth, and resulting higher standard of living, in nations that trade freely is the true gain from trade, and it is made possible by adhering to comparative advantage.

PROTECTIONISM

Then what is all this talk about obstructing free trade, and keeping *our markets* for *our producers*? This is called **protectionism**. Any and all measures taken to secure domestic markets for domestic producers is said to be protectionist. At face value, the arguments can seem persuasive, because after all, when you import goods from another nation, do you not stimulate their economy at the expense of your own? It's certainly a bit more complex than this narrow opinion might suggest. To appreciate how overly simplistic this opinion is, let's first examine some motivations for protectionist measures.

Trust

In the real world, there's no such thing as the perfect trust that we described in our hypothetical examples above. Nations worry about maintaining some degree of self-sufficiency, especially in particular areas that may be crucial to a nation's growth or security. No nation wants to be completely dependent on a foreign power for its entire supply of modern semi-conductors, as long as the economic cost of avoiding such dependence is not extremely prohibitive. Domestic producers of cars, for example, may lobby Congress for, and receive, some protection from foreign encroachment.

Additionally, because of the real world's lack of trust, some degree of protection may be used as a threat to keep the game of trade sufficiently fair. Remember that we assumed trade would be free and fair. But as with any other enterprise, if you play by the rules, and the other team takes advantage of this blind allegiance, they may be the only one to gain from the situation. Nations use obstructions to trade—or the threat of such measures—to keep each other honest.

Infant Industry

You will often hear certain industries ask for protection so that they can recover from hard times or get started in the first place. This is the so-called **infant industry argument**. Although it is possible for protection to give an industry breathing space to recover or grow, it's unlikely. A good illustration may be to contrast the two most-adhered-to strategies for growth in the developing world—**import substitution** and **export led growth**.

With import substitution, a nation protects its markets from more established foreign competition in the hope that domestic citizens will then patronize domestic producers, in effect substituting domestic production for a product that may have been imported formerly. In this way, growth of domestic industries, employment, and the standard of living should be enhanced. But this strategy has generally been ineffective, because it robs the domestic producer of the pressure to compete. It no longer has to produce a better product sooner or with greater efficiency. To survive, they usually become dependent on government subsidy and protection into the indefinite future.

On the other hand, export led growth is a strategy dependent on following the principle of comparative advantage. Nations with absolute disadvantages across the board do have comparative advantages. By focusing on those areas of the economy that the rest of the world will gladly foster through trade, the disadvantaged nation's economy will grow. At first growth occurs in sectors most directly affected by the trade, but with time, the increased wealth forms the basis for investment and growth of other sectors of the nation's economy. This strategy works. In fact, most of the Pacific Rim economies are prime examples of success stories. Protection more often weakens than enhances the prospects of a nation and the industries it hopes to help because export-led growth depends on comparative advantage, not protection.

Special Interest Groups
Probably the most significant motivation for protectionism depends on the goals of special interest groups. Unions and corporations have an obvious incentive in maintaining the status quo, which they dominate. Realize that as a nation begins to follow its comparative advantage in a number of areas, it will transform the mix of goods it produces. New skills and different labor attributes will be necessary to produce this different mix of goods. However more efficient the new combination of goods makes the nation, and despite how many more jobs it creates and how much the standard of living rises, it will threaten the status quo—the existing order of things—of the jobs and the businesses that now compose the nation's economy.

Recognize that the power and money concentrated in the hands of big business and big labor will be brought to bear on Congress. These powerful entities choose whether to make political contributions or withdraw them. No matter how greatly the benefits of free trade outweigh the costs, there will always be some outcry from special interest groups for protectionism. Understanding this, let's now look at the most common forms of protectionist obstruction to free international markets.

PROTECTIONIST MEASURES
Although there are a variety of different ways to hinder trade, the most direct is by using **quotas**, or their less formal counterparts **voluntary restriction agreements** (VRAs). A quota sets a strict and binding limit on the absolute amount of imports that can enter a nation and, by doing so, hopes to secure domestic demand for domestic producers. Setting limits on goods entering a market does not make those goods any less desirable to consumers. As a consequence of restricted supply and sustained high demand, prices for the imported goods often rise precipitously, as do foreign corporate profits. Similarly, domestic producers who now face less competition than before, usually raise their prices to nearly match the price of the costly imported goods that have been restricted. They are inclined to do this in an attempt to raise short-run profits, but they lose the opportunity to gain market share in the process.

The net effect of quotas generally is the following:
- a less-competitive domestic producer,
- foreign competitors with increased profits, and
- domestic consumers paying enormously more for the same goods as before.

Such a policy can do little more than secure a few jobs in a particular area of the present economy, however, without long-run advantages, as domestic production suffers from the lack of competitive discipline in markets.

A second technique for restricting trade is through the application of tariffs. Tariffs are taxes placed on imports, which make those imports more expensive for domestic consumers. As a result, consumers will buy fewer imports and substitute domestic production for them. In most respects, the tariff has a similar effect as a quota. For instance, you could effectively raise tariffs as high as is necessary to choke off any desired level of domestic demand for imported goods. This will reduce competition and efficiency domestically. Thus, as with quotas, tariffs usually lead to less-efficient domestic industries and higher domestic prices. And, as with quotas, the negative effect on consumers always outweighs any short-term benefit that may be enjoyed by a particular business interest.

The tariff is only superior to the quota in that it can lead the domestic government to collect some revenue; however, these funds are hardly sufficient to compensate for the losses of economic efficiency and the ensuing consumer costs associated with the application of tariffs.

Lastly, any other measure to obstruct trade, which is neither a tariff nor quota, is grouped under the title **nontariff barrier** (NTB). NTBs to trade include subsidies to certain businesses that then make the businesses artificially appear more efficient and make their goods more appealing in international markets. Another NTB might be the extra licensing or certification that many nations require of foreigners who wish to do business within their borders. If such regulation is not required of the domestic producers, it's clear that this would give domestic producers a cost advantage in their own markets, not due to efficiency, but because of differential regulation.

The same could be said of varying pollution standards. Every nation has a right to establish its own norms; however, some nations will extend or expand on these differences solely to gain advantage in trade negotiations. Many instances of such differing standards were issues in the **North American Free Trade Agreement** (NAFTA) negotiations.

Even though there is a great variety of NTBs, they—just like quotas and tariffs—obstruct free trade and deny a nation the ability to follow its areas of comparative advantage, which means that:

- the world will be using its resources less efficiently,
- world output will suffer, and
- nations will not grow as well as they would have in a world of free trade.

In the final analysis, this is the bane of protectionism.

Even without factoring in lost efficiency, many studies have indicated that it costs the economy hundreds of thousands of dollars per job saved in a particular industry in the short run. If it costs $500,000 to preserve a job for which a competitive labor market pays only a $50,000 salary, it is equally absurd to hand someone $10 for every single dollar bill they hand to you. If any of you would like to send us $10, we would be glad to send $1 back to you. An address will be provided at the end of this chapter! Of course, we're joking, but that's what protectionism amounts to: an extremely expensive, impractical joke played on the consumer and the growth of a nation.

This is why obstructions to trade are at historically low levels, especially among the dominant players in this world. Despite the lobbying of special interest groups, whose interest lies with maintaining the current structure of our economy as opposed to transforming it for maximum growth, tariffs, quotas, and the like are not even placed on most products. In addition, their average impact on the cost of imported goods is measured in the small single digits. This is equally true for our major trading partners because all nations are aware of the stimulating effect that free trade can exert on an economy.

International institutions like the World Trade Organization (WTO) have worked since the end of World War II to negotiate barriers to trade downward multilaterally for a majority of the world's nations because the prosperity of the world depends on an efficient use of its resources.

In a world with less than complete trust, there may be a need for the threat of tariffs and quotas to keep free trade sufficiently fair. But all well-informed parties resist the outbreak of a full-scale trade war, because like real wars, in the end, few if any interests are served.

Chapter 16

INTERNATIONAL FINANCE

Money reduces transaction costs for the exchange of goods and services. By doing so, it facilitates this exchange and encourages expansion. This is true domestically, but it is no less true internationally. Nations use money to facilitate and expand their international trade. The study of international flows of money and their effect on economies involved is known as international finance. A detailed analysis of this study would be exhaustive, but luckily, the basics are very straightforward, and that is what we will emphasize.

BALANCE OF PAYMENTS

Any time a respectable foreign currency, so-called foreign exchange, enters or leaves a nation, a system of accounts known as the balance of payments (BOP) tracks it. When money flows into a nation, it is recorded as a credit to the nation's balance of payments. When money flows out of a nation, it is recorded as a debit to the nation's balance of payments. Essentially, the balance of payments consists of two accounts. The upper half of the balance of payments focuses primarily on the flow of money into and out of a nation, which is associated with the export or import of goods and services. This upper half is called the current account. The lower half of the balance of payments focuses primarily on the flow of money into and out of a nation, which is associated with investment. This lower half is called the capital account.

A Simplified Balance of Payments

Current Account
Exports +
Imports –
―――――――
if Trade Deficit –

Capital Account
K– inflows +
K– outflows –
―――――――
then K-surplus +

Note: Buying more GDS from foreigners provides
them with the $'s to invest in our nation's growth

In a particular year, it is possible to have a balance of trade in the current account, whereby imports and exports are equal in value. It is also possible to experience an imbalance in this upper half of the BOP. One possibility is that the value of exports outweighs the value of imports, creating a trade surplus. In recent years, more often than not, the reverse has been true—imports have outweighed exports, yielding a trade deficit for the U.S. When the U.S. experiences a trade deficit, more money flows out of the U.S. to pay for imports than flows into the U.S. to pay for the exports. In other words, the negatives outweigh the positives and the current account experiences a net negative effect, which defines the size of the trade deficit.

Remember, the GDP of a nation can be calculated by adding all types of spending together:

$$\text{Consumption} + \text{Investment} + \text{Government} + \text{Net Exports} = \text{GDP}$$

If a country were experiencing a trade deficit (X < IM), a negative amount is added in the place for net exports, thus reducing GDP. This trade deficit is often criticized for reducing our GDP, job creation, and growth. After all, net exports is merely the difference between a nation's exports and imports, and as we have already pointed out, this is a net negative when a nation runs a trade deficit. Critics of free trade often make assertions like "importing goods is like exporting jobs," the logic being that when consumers buy foreign products, they stimulate a foreign nation's economy at the expense of our own. But this is a simplistic argument at best. Indeed, it borders on misleading. Let's see why:

1. The absolute difference in exports and imports may seem large. Yearly trade deficits in the U.S. sometimes exceed 100 billion dollars, but even in such cases, this amounts to 1 or 2 percent of the nation's GDP, which is approaching 9 trillion dollars a year. This amounts to dropping a penny or two out of every dollar, which is hardly intolerable.

2. The real gains from trade are due to nations following their comparative advantage and using their resources better. To state the situation more accurately, our nation is significantly better off for having traded freely in the first place, and then—out of a much enlarged pie—we must drop a penny or two in the worst years. If I told you I would give you an extra dollar, but then sometimes I'd want a couple of nickels back from you, you'd be a fool not to jump at this offer. And if our nation did not have free trade, but did have a wonderfully balanced current account, we'd all notice the difference because our nation would be poorer as a result. The real gains from trade are realized through a more efficient use of resources, not an occasional trade surplus as opposed to a trade deficit. Moreover, the trade statistic is significantly flawed, as there tends to be a significant undercounting of the exports that are never taxed. This means that a nation could appear to have a trade deficit but actually be balanced or even in surplus. In fact, our nation seems biased toward running trade deficits, without an equal number of counterbalancing trade surpluses. This is implied proof that there is something wrong with the way these data are collected and accounted for, since one additional thing now needs to be made clear: In the long run, a nation pays for its imports with its exports. No one keeps delivering goods to your doorstep without being paid for them. This is obvious when money does not exist, but it is no less true when nations operate in a monetized environment. Money just aids in increasing the volume of trade, and in stretching payments between years in much the same way that it does domestically. But eventually, goods must be paid for with other goods. In the long run, trade deficits should be matched with corresponding trade surpluses. If they are not, something must be wrong with the statistic you are using. And as was already noted, there is.

3. The combined upper and lower halves of this account are known as a balance of payments, not an imbalance of payments. To understand the significance of this, let's use an illustration. Suppose there is a Mercedes dealer in New York. Her showroom is filled with German-made cars. How did they get there? They were produced in Germany and shipped to America. But how did she pay for them? She couldn't use dollars in Germany to buy a hot dog, a banana, or a shipment of cars. First, she has to convert her dollars to German money—the Deutsche mark—then she can buy German goods. Thus, to import goods to the U.S., people like our Mercedes dealer must dump American money, dollars, into foreign banks in exchange for the currencies of those other nations.

Note that these dollars are no more use to the German bank than they were to the American Mercedes dealer, because dollars buy American goods. So, the German bank may turn right around and help finance a deal for American goods, which would help transform a U.S. trade deficit into a trade surplus, or they could facilitate Germans and other foreigners who wish to invest in dollar-denominated U.S. properties, like American stocks, bonds, Treasury bills, real estate, etc. As we import goods from abroad, we supply foreigners with the raw material to invest in our nation, thus bringing the capital account into play.

The **capital account** keeps track of money flowing into or out of our nation because of investment. If an American invests abroad, it is called a **capital outflow** and shows up as a debit in the capital account. When a foreigner invests in America, it is called a capital inflow, and shows up as a credit in the capital account. With all those imports coming into the U.S., much American money is being provided to foreigners. If they don't buy our goods, the money will come back to us in the form of foreign investment. Thus, if we are running a deficit in the current account, it is the basis for our running a surplus in the capital account. Foreigners will be investing more in our economy than we will in theirs.

As we pointed out previously, in the long run, this cannot logically be sustained; however, in the short run, it will help keep our domestic property values high, our interest rates low, our taxes low, and our growth rate high. This is the upside of running a trade deficit: it is the capital surplus or net inflow of funds from abroad. Now you can see why the statement that importing goods leads to a loss of jobs domestically is more than simplistic, it is inaccurate.

FOREIGN EXCHANGE MARKETS

There was something interesting that we glossed over in our example of the Mercedes dealer. Remember she dumped dollars to get marks. How did they know how many marks to give her for her dollars? The answer is by knowing the price of one currency in terms of another. This is the **exchange rate**.

In Germany, and other nations, one may purchase fruit, vegetables, cars, healthcare, or any other such thing for a price denominated in the domestic currency. In Germany that is marks. The price of fruit is denominated in marks. The price of vegetables is denominated in marks, and so on. You can also buy foreign exchange in Germany. Foreign exchange is any respectable, internationally traded currency. In Germany, one such foreign currency is the American dollar. There is a price of dollars in terms of marks called the exchange rate, which determines how many marks one would receive for depositing a certain pile of dollars in a German bank.

Broadly speaking, there are two systems for establishing exchange rates. One is called a **fixed exchange rate system** and the other is known as a **flexible (or floating) exchange rate system**.

Fixed exchange rate systems involve establishing and maintaining the relative values of currencies within a narrow band of fluctuation via the obligation of central banks buying and selling FOREX (foreign exchange). So, if the U.S. was following fixed exchange rates and suddenly the dollar started to rise in value, the Federal Reserve would be obligated to buy FOREX with dollars. Because of the Fed's actions, foreign currencies would increase in value and the dollars, which were sold in large amounts on the foreign exchange market, would be devalued. The fixed relative values would be reestablished.

The virtue of such a system rests on its ability to assure traders that they will not face any increased risk due to fluctuations in exchange rates. For instance, if one was to be paid a month from now in British pounds, but in the interim, the pound declined in value, the businessman would, in effect, not be paid as much as he had anticipated. The same amount of pounds would not translate into as many dollars as before. It is clear that this will reduce profit, and possibly even turn a profitable deal into a losing proposition. Such uncertainty could only discourage trade flows and the gains associated with it.

You should, however, understand that today the dominant nations in the world's economy follow floating exchange rate systems or slight variations on them. With such systems, the relative values of currencies are established—as in any other free market—on the basis of supply and demand. But what of the uncertainty involved? Flows of trade, and more importantly, flows of speculative capital are so large at present, that if the major economies of the world tried to establish a fixed exchange rate system, they would squelch the game itself. Thus, central banks must also recognize their limited ability to even nudge markets that trade up to 2 trillion dollars in FOREX per business day. This is one reason for the emergence and popularity of derivative financial assets like futures and options. They provide some insurance against the fluctuations inherent in a flexible rate regime. Now, let's look at a flexible or floating system.

Flexible Exchange Rates

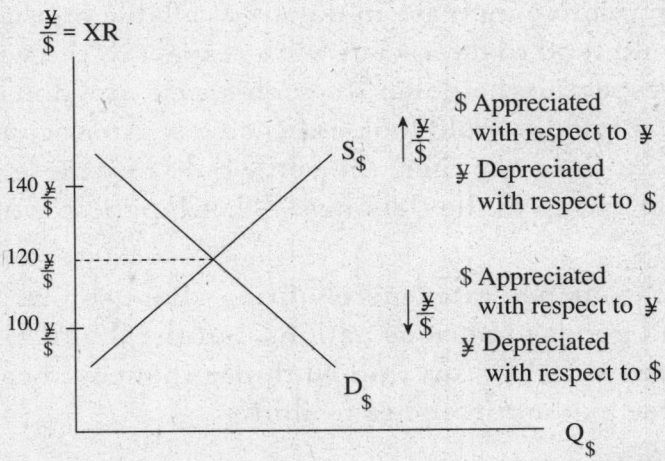

The operation of such a flexible system is merely a special case of free markets. Above, we have the market for dollars with respect to its yen (Japanese currency) price. The supply of dollars is generated any time Americans dump dollars on the FOREX market to finance importation or foreign investment. Like in any other market, as the reward for providing goods rises, so does the inclination to supply. In this case, you are more willing and able to provide dollars as the reward, in terms of yen you received, rises. The demand for dollars is generated when someone wishes to buy American goods or properties. If a Japanese businessperson had to give up more yen to receive dollars, he'd be less willing and able to do so.

What we have described is simply the laws of supply and demand as they apply to the case of the FOREX markets. Where the demand and supply intersect the market forms an equilibrium price, or in this case, exchange rate. Suppose, as in this example, the exchange rate was 120 yen to the dollar. It means that for every dollar dumped on the market, one would receive 120 yen. In other words, the yen is worth a little less than a penny.

But isn't it conceivable that the demand for dollars could rise? Of course, if people wish to use dollars to purchase American goods or properties. And isn't it conceivable that the supply of dollars could fall? Of course, if Americans stop importing as much or investing abroad. Well, if the demand for dollars rose and/or the supply of dollars fell, then the inevitable result would be dollar appreciation. The dollar may buy something closer to 140 yen, which also means that the yen has depreciated with respect to the dollar. Suddenly, Americans could sacrifice fewer dollars and still receive the yen they wanted for the purchase of Japanese goods. This should stimulate American imports, and worsen the U.S. trade deficit with Japan.

By the same token, the dollar is now more expensive for the Japanese. They must sacrifice larger amounts of yen to receive the same dollars as before. This will discourage their importation of our goods, and should add to any trade surplus they may have with us. You should recognize that the supply of dollars could just as easily rise, and the demand for dollars could just as easily fall. If there was a sudden relative increase in dollars available on the FOREX market, then the dollar would tend to depreciate with respect to the yen, as the yen appreciated with respect to the dollar. In such a case, the dollar wouldn't buy as much yen. Japanese goods would look expensive to Americans. Americans would import less. At the same time, the yen would buy more dollars. American goods would appear cheap to the Japanese. The Japanese would buy more American goods.

In the long run, exchange rates merely bring about similarity among the differentially priced goods of various nations, but the fluctuations, which occur in the short run, are caused by any and all things that could cause the supply and demand of these major currencies to shift.

CAUSES OF FLUX IN EXCHANGE RATES

Before we jump into a brief discussion of what causes these fluctuations in exchange rates, keep in mind that the reason one wants the money of a particular nation is because one wants that nation's goods and services. Only if you wish to buy goods or invest in Germany will you need marks. Only if you wish to buy goods or invest in Japan will you need yen. Only if you wish to buy goods or invest in the United Kingdom will you need pounds, and so on, for any nation. You only want and need their currency because you want to buy their goods and services. Note: trading in international currencies accounts for only a very small part of the international currency market.

If suddenly Americans developed an unquenchable thirst for French wine, then our demand for French francs would rise. And to buy those French francs, we would have to provide dollars. Thus, if a nation's relative tastes rise for another nation's goods, the buying nation's currency will depreciate and the selling nation's currency will appreciate. In this case, the dollar will depreciate with respect to the franc, while the franc will appreciate with respect to the dollar.

What if the prices of Italian goods were going through the roof? Would anyone want to buy them? A nation with runaway inflation will not only see a domestic devaluation of its currency, but a relative depreciation of its currency as compared to the currencies of its major trading partners. If no one wants Italian goods, then no one wants Italian lira, and the Italian lira will fall, relative to other currencies, which are being withheld from Italian FOREX markets.

Another factor could be growth. A nation that grows faster than its major trading partners becomes a very good customer for the goods of those slower growing nations. In the 1990s the U.S. has generally outperformed the economies of the other major nations of the world. This makes the U.S. more inclined to import, dump dollars on FOREX markets, and see the dollar depreciate as a result.

We can't forget about expectations. Everyone wants to buy an appreciating asset. If we told you the value of the homes in a certain neighborhood was rising rapidly, you would be that much more inclined to buy a house there, believing that if you ever had to resell, you would make a profit on the appreciated asset. Currencies operate in much the same fashion. If international bankers and speculators believe the dollar will appreciate, then they will buy dollars, which causes the expected appreciation to occur. If the fundamentals are askew, the dollar may eventually plunge. If this widely held expectation of appreciation was well-founded, the dollar will remain high. Such is the peril of the self-fulfilling prophecy, and the contrast of destabilizing with stabilizing speculation.

Finally, and most importantly, the force that usually dominates short-term fluctuation in the exchange markets is the difference in real interest rates. Where would you want to keep your money, in a safe bank with a 10 percent return or in an equally safe bank with a 5 percent return? Of course, you would go for the higher return. Currencies flow in search of the highest rate of return for their investment, often ignoring political differences.

Similarly, speculative capital, which represents the lion's share of all FOREX flows, follows the best return adjusted for risk and the inflation rate of the different nations involved. Speculators want the currency of a nation whose real return is higher than others. Thus, nations with safe, sound economies and high rates of return are predisposed toward appreciation of their currencies. If a central bank tightens the money supply, and as a result interest rates rise in that nation, that nation's currency is likely to appreciate with respect to most others.

For a quick review of exchange rates, their changes, and implications, consult the chart below.

Summary:

$	Means	Could Have Been Caused By
Appreciates	– $ Buys More Foreign Exchange – Foreign goods Seem Cheaper – Encourages U.S. Imports	– ↑ Taste for U.S. goods – ↓ U.S. Price Level – ↓ U.S. Growth – Expection that $ Would ↑ – ↑ U.S. i -Rates
Depreciates	– $ Buys Less Foreign Exchange – Foreign goods Seem Costly – Encourages U.S. Exports	– ↓ Taste for U.S. goods – ↑ U.S. Price Level – ↑ U.S. Growth – Expection that $ Would ↓ – ↓ U.S. i -Rates

Chapter 17

IDEOLOGY

Economics is not a hard science. Many of its assertions cannot be tested repeatedly under precisely the same conditions until the absolute truth is apparent. In fact, it would probably not be stretching things to say that economics is as much an art as a science. And having recognized this, it is clear that philosophy, ideology, even opinion can motivate how we apply what we do know about economics. In every age, there are a number of ideological currents and undercurrents; however, there is often a single ideology, or set of widely held beliefs, which motivates policy within the dominant nations of the day.

MERCANTILISM

Throughout the seventeenth and most of the eighteenth centuries, mercantilism and neo-mercantilism operated as the dominant economic force within the major powers of that time. Mercantilism stressed the importance of maintaining the power of the state by keeping a large army and navy, and financing it through huge trade surpluses, which would cause a large influx of gold. In those times, major economies were on a gold standard, and so this influx of gold was tantamount to having an enhanced availability of money, a sort of expansionary monetary policy. With more gold, the wealth of the nation would be enhanced too.

Colonialism, and later imperialism, tied into such mercantilist sentiments well. Outlying regions known as colonies were under the power of the state and subject to having their resources plundered to bring wealth back to the more developed nations. That is why even today nations that perpetuate the following characteristics are known as mercantilist or neo-mercantilist:

- they favor policies that perpetuate consistent trade surpluses,
- they stress a great interdependence between state and business, and
- they allow smaller, less developed nations to act as suppliers of raw materials for the more developed trading partner.

Mercantilism, which measures a nation's wealth by its trade surpluses and the strength of its military, has missed a crucial point: a nation is truly better off when its people enjoy a higher material standard of living. Mercantilism does not guarantee this result.

CLASSICAL ECONOMICS

The school of thought that emphasized that a nation's wealth should be measured on the basis of its citizens enjoying a higher standard of living was the **classical school of economic thought. Adam Smith** was the first economist to most clearly express these classical beliefs. Smith's book, ***The Wealth of Nations***, predominantly espoused and promoted free market economies, the competition that arises in them, and the ensuing efficiency that they bring about. *The Wealth of Nations* was published in 1776, a time when mercantilist sentiment dominated the world. Within a couple of generations of its publication every major nation that was engaged in the incipient Industrial Revolution was moving toward a free market system. As we have seen, with fits and starts, this trend continues throughout the world to this day.

J.B. Say, a French writer and economist who was impressed by Smith's logic, deserves much of the credit for promoting Smith's work to a larger, continental audience in the early years of the nineteenth century. Unfortunately, Say had a way with words, a turn of phrase that could be persuasive, but could be imprecise and not necessarily as subtle as the original. A case in point is Say's Law.

Say's Law states that "supply creates its own demand," meaning that by producing goods of a certain value, you also generate an equal stream of payments or income. If output equals income, then you can never have over- or underproduction in the long run, because the income is always out there to buy whatever output has been produced. Naturally, particular markets could be uncoordinated in the short run, but this too would abate in time. For example, a manufacturer would never deliberately produce more bicycles than it could profitably sell; however, without having a crystal ball at his disposal, it's a possibility that the manufacturer would produce too many bicycles. Ah, but free markets dictate that this surplus will not last as pressure on price is downward, and a signal is sent not to produce as much in the future. Similarly, the manufacturer would not deliberately produce fewer bicycles than it could profitably sell, but it is possible that this may occur briefly. Of course, with too few bicycles available, the price will rise to ration them, and a signal is sent to increase production in the future, as the reward is now higher. Knowing Say's Law and the assumption of free and fair markets, a nation could never experience an imbalance in the long run. If there were bad times, with much unemployment, they would soon pass, as the wage paid to labor would moderate, and employment would recover. There's no need to adjust the economy; it adjusts itself. This self-adjustment is often referred to as the "invisible hand," a term coined by Smith.

Additionally, classical economists tended to believe strictly in the **interest mechanism**, which is really just a special case of the price mechanism.

The Interest Mechanism

$$\text{Savings} = \text{Supply of Loanable Funds} = F(\text{interest rate})$$

$$\text{Investment} = \text{Demand for Loanable Funds} = F(\text{interest rate})$$

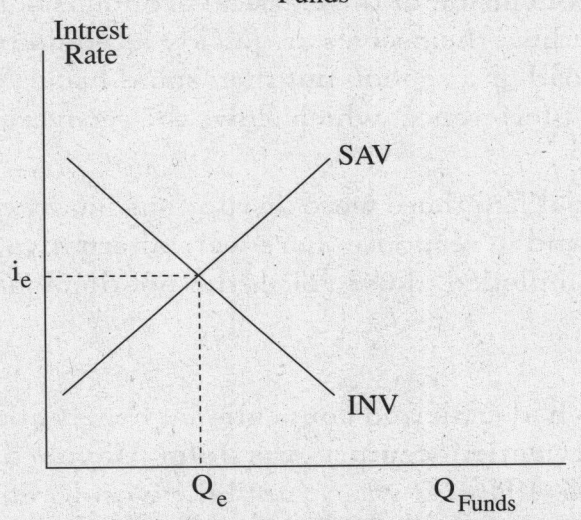

– Balance of savings and productive investment is automaticlly achieved through negotiation in Free Markets

If savings were not balanced with the productive investments of society, then the economy would fail to grow optimally, and might experience short-run disruptions. But the classical economists weren't afraid this would last because of the interest mechanism. Look at the graph above and see that savings is just the supply of loanable funds. This is sensitive to the price paid for those funds, which is the interest rate. As the interest rate rises, it promotes savings. Like most other supply curves, it has a positive slope. Also note that the investment is the demand for the use of those loanable funds, and it, too, is sensitive to the price of those funds, which is the interest rate. As the interest rate rises, it becomes more expensive to borrow funds for starting or growing a business. Thus, less will be borrowed. Like most other demand curves, it has a negative slope. Taken together, we have supply and demand negotiating their differences. If a surplus of funds exists, it won't for long because the interest rate will fall in response to this abundance. If there is a shortage of funds, it won't exist for long because the interest rate will rise to ration the few funds available.

If the predisposition of savers or investors was to change, and there was a resulting shift in the supply or demand of these funds, no problem would exist for long, as the interest rate would automatically adjust to the new conditions of this free market. Although it may be possible for the savings/investment market to cause disruptions of the economy, again, they will not in the long run, as the interest mechanism in this free market for loanable funds will automatically adapt. The inevitable conclusion of the classical economists: as long as markets are free and fair, they adjust themselves as quickly as could be hoped. Have an army, a navy, build a road or a school, but then stand back. Most government intervention is merely interference, which slows the recovery of a free market economy.

In the early Industrial Era there were disruptions, many of them quite large by modern standards, and in response there were alternative voices to be heard, but until things really imploded, those voices did not dominate the debate.

KEYNESIANISM

One talented man who had criticized conventional beliefs about the market system since the early twentieth century was **John Maynard Keynes** (pronounced "canes") (1883–1946). It wasn't until the world went into the Great Depression that a greater number of influential persons were willing to listen to his remonstrations. The essence of his work in this area is captured in his book, ***The General Theory of Employment, Interest, and Money***, or as it is popularly referred to, simply *The General Theory*. It is a complex work, but it started with a simple criticism of Say's Law. Keynes stated that Say was correct but irrelevant, since he never clearly defined what is meant by the long run. Keynes felt that economic systems are tools designed by men, for the benefit of men, and that it is an obligation, even a duty, to understand these systems, to fine tune them, and to promote maximum employment and efficiency in each successive short-run period. As Keynes put it, "in the long run, we are all dead." Essentially, forget the long run and intervene.

Further, Keynes asserted that savers and investors are different people. Although interest rates may be a prime concern of investors, as it represents their cost, it is only one concern for savers, who first must have the means to save. Keynes felt that disposable income was at least as important in determining savings as were interest rates. Naturally, this means that a perfect coordination of available savings for productive, or planned, investments would be an exception in any short period of time. In other words, with respect to the short run, balance between savings and planned investment is unlikely, and a balanced economy is a special and unusual case in reality. It's more likely that some imbalance would be suffered with respect to the short run, thus necessitating the intervention of government.

Because he constantly emphasized intervention to adjust the economy, and he influenced beliefs about this throughout the developed world, Keynes can be considered the "Father of Modern Fiscal Policy." Any economist profoundly influenced by him is called a Keynesian. Indeed, half a century after his death, it's been said more than once that "today, we're all Keynesians." This is true to the extent that we are dominated by free markets, but believe they need significantly more government regulation to work well.

MONETARISM

Although Keynesianism may be the dominant ideology of the most successful market economies of the twentieth century, it is not without its critics, most of whom find their inspiration from the more strictly free-market classical ideology of the past. The most successful alternative approach is known as **monetarism**. Monetarists believe that fiscal policy, so favored by Keynesians, is usually quite weak and ineffective. They contend that with balanced budgets, even a Keynesian would recognize that one is working against one's self. But, nations with deficits do even worse, as public spending tends to "crowd out" more directly productive private spending. Monetarists might say a welfare state is necessary because government hinders the natural growth of a market economy so much. It would be better to leave business alone, and have a minimally invasive government, with a nearly dormant, stripped down fiscal policy.

As for monetary policy, monetarists believe that it can have great impact with respect to the short run, but that this impact is variably lagged. If one does not know the precise timing of the effect of policy, it is possible, even statistically likely, that one will cause greater destabilization as opposed to stabilization in the economy. Based on such logic, and studies to support this claim, the monetarists would suggest that discretionary changes in the money supply do more harm than good. They would argue for a decreased policy-making role of the central bank. They would recommend following a **monetary rule**.

A monetary rule would involve strict adherence to a certain growth rate in the money supply. This rate would be set in coordination with the estimated potential for real growth in a nation's economy. For example, a 2–3 percent increase in the nation's money supply should generate a 2–3 percent increase in the nation's GDP. In this way, there would be sufficient money and credit available to sustain maximum growth over the long run, without increasing the average tendency to destabilize the economy in the short run. All fluctuations of the economy should be ignored by the central bank because it needs to focus its attention on strict control of the money supply. Monetarists want a minimal fiscal policy and an automatic, nondiscretionary monetary policy. The seeds of classicism are sown deep.

SUPPLY-SIDE ECONOMICS

Another influential approach, which has a long lineage, is called supply-side economics. Prior to the Keynesian Revolution in economic thought, economists routinely emphasized the supply side of the marketplace. Recall, "supply creates its own demand." But with Keynes came an appreciation of the demand side, and how raising or lowering spending might play a dynamic role in economic adjustment. After a couple of generations of Keynesian economists, some believed there was an overemphasis on demand and a distinct lack of appreciation for some effective policies of old, especially those dealing with the nation's productive capacity—its supply-side.

Supply-side economics usually refers to any and all measures the government takes that can enhance the productive powers of a nation. More often than not, these are policies of lowered taxes on business, or deregulation. It can be argued that although some taxes are necessary and some regulations are vital, to the degree we are overtaxed or over-regulated, we are discouraged from maximum effort and the incentive to produce and grow economically. By reducing such burdens, the government offers back these incentives, and in so doing encourages private economic ventures, along with the creation of jobs and wealth.

To understand how this ideology may motivate policy, refer to the Laffer Curve below:

The Laffer Curve

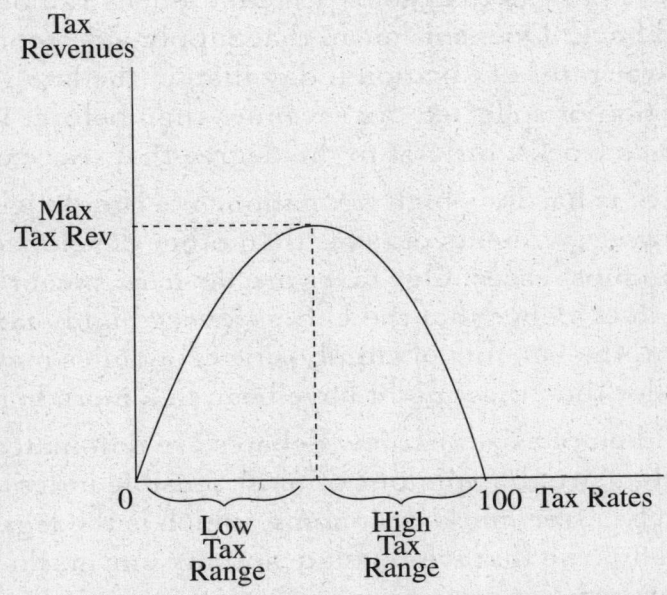

— Demonstrates how it is possible to lower Tax Rates and raise Tax Revenues, given you are operating in High Tax Range

The Laffer curve shows the simplest logical relation between tax revenues and the tax rate.

$$\text{Tax Revenue} = (\text{Tax Base})(\text{Tax Rate})$$

As tax rates rise, the tax base falls. In other words, when you are punished for generating income, you are less inclined to generate it. On our graph, as the tax rate rises through the low tax range, the tax revenues rise. This is true because the tax base will barely shrink when taxes are still only pennies out of a dollar. Eventually, a best tax rate is reached somewhere between 0 and 100 percent. At this rate, the maximum tax revenues are collected. But past this point, we enter the high tax range. In the high tax range, as rates rise, revenues fall, because a government may be taking a large share, but it is a large share of a shrinking pie. The tax base begins to collapse in the high tax range.

If you assume that a nation is already operating in the high tax range, then reducing taxes could raise tax revenues, while at the same time promoting private economic activity. It was just such a proposition that helped elect President Reagan back in 1980. He said he'd balance the budget, expand the navy, and modernize the nuclear armaments, while lowering taxes. He assumed we were a high tax nation, and by lowering the tax rate, he would so stimulate the base of economic activity that revenues would rise.

All did not come to pass as Reagan expected. Deficits ran out of control, even as goals were scaled back. Does this mean that supply-side economics is untrue? No. In fact, with lower rates of taxation today than in the late 1970s, the rich pay a higher proportion of collected tax revenues than before. In other words, supply-side economics works, but not to the degree that was expected.

In reality, the U.S. is hardly a high tax nation. We run deficits more often that not. We have lower payments of taxes than other developed nations — significantly lower in most cases. Our taxes are far from recent historical highs. No, there is not much evidence that the U.S. is a very highly taxed nation. In such an environment, the benefits of supply-side economics may be real, even significant, but smaller than they might have been in a more highly taxed nation.

Finally, we should emphasize that few debates are dominated by extremes in ideology, anymore than are the opinions of most sensible individuals. It is fair to say that we are largely a free market economy, which is the legacy of Adam Smith. But it is equally true that we regulate and tax our markets more in the late-twentieth century than at earlier times. Our interventionist fiscal and monetary policies are the legacy of Keynes.

Having inspected the past, we can recognize that there are many other voices to be heard and that the debate regarding the structure and maintenance of our economy is ongoing and perpetual.

The summary that follows can be used as a guide to studying economic ideologies. In today's complex world, the lines between the ideologies are not as closely drawn as we would like. Groups associated with certain ideologies change often and cross-overs are prevalent on certain issues.

Summary:

Ideology	Propositions	Associated With:
Mercantilists & Neo-Mercantilists	− Protectionist Trade Policies − Government & Business Cooperate	− Trade Unionist Liberals & Some Conservatives
Neo-Classical & Classical	− Free Markets − Little Regulation By Government	− Libertarians
Keynesians	− Free Markets But Significant Short Run Regulations, Especially Fiscal Policy	− Pervasive Influence on All especially Associated with Democrats
Monetarists	− Free Markets − Limit Government Intervention − Follow Monetary Rule	− Conservative Republicans
Supply Side	− Free Markets − ↓Taxes & Regulation on Business, & Economy will grow	− Conservative and Progressive Republicans

Chapter 18

MARKET STRUCTURE

Markets are configured in different ways—some are more competitive, some are less. Economists usually make the distinction between an extreme known as **perfect competition** (or pure competition) and three other models of **imperfect competition: monopolistic competition, oligopoly**, and **monopoly**.

Spectrum of Market Structures

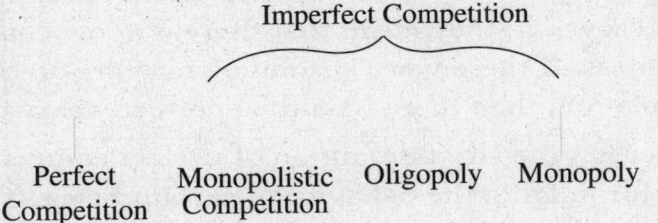

Imperfect Competition

Perfect Competition | Monopolistic Competition | Oligopoly | Monopoly

The diagram above should help you visualize these different models as a spectrum ranging from the more competitive to the less competitive ends of a scale. As useful as each model of competition may be in understanding the behavior of a particular firm, it's rare that you can absolutely pigeon-hole a real-world case into any particular model. Today's firms often have characteristics associated with different market structures. Our analysis is of models only.

Let's now contrast the extreme of perfect competition with the other cases, all of which are imperfectly competitive.

PERFECT COMPETITION

The model for perfect competition is defined by certain characteristics including the following:

- large number of firms in the industry
- homogeneous good
- easy entry into the market
- individual firms as price takers

Large Number of Firms

There should be an extremely large number of firms that make up the industry. Firms are the individual companies, and the industry represents the collective of all firms manufacturing a similar product. For example, there might be hundreds or thousands of apple growers, which taken together make up the apple growing industry. In such a case, any single grower would provide only a small fraction of all the apples that are produced in the industry as a whole. In this way, the individual firm would be insignificant in terms of its effect on the aggregate market.

Homogeneous Good

The good produced by a perfectly competitive firm should be homogeneous, meaning that there should not be any noticeable differences in the product, no matter which firm produced it. Apples are a good example because a bushel of apples is a bushel of apples, no matter where it may have originated.

Easy Entry

Entry into the market should be easy. When economists refer to easy entry, which also implies easy exit, they mean that there is a low cost and few obstacles to start such a business. If there were absolutely no start-up cost and absolutely no red tape or regulation, then there would be perfectly easy entry.

No business ever fits the strict definition of perfect competition, as it's really only a benchmark for judging the behavior of certain firms. Many firms—for example, American agriculture in its incipient stages—do, however, go through a stage in their development where they adhere to the above characteristics fairly closely. Cases like those are a good fit for this model.

Individual Firm as Price Taker

**The D-Curve Facing
A Perfectly Competitive Firm**

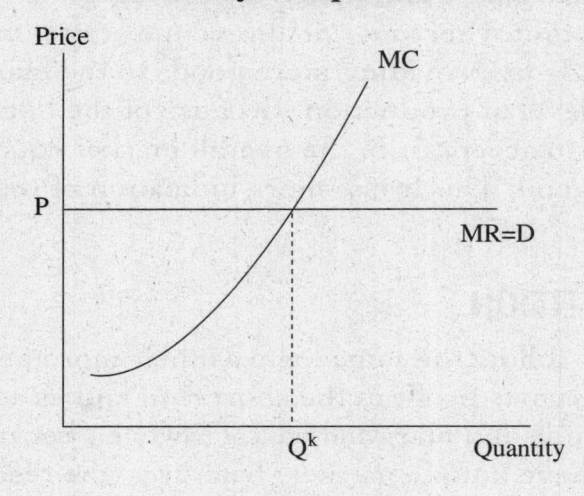

[Graph: Price on vertical axis, Quantity on horizontal axis. A horizontal line at price P labeled MR=D intersects an upward-curving MC curve at quantity Q^k.]

Because of the insignificance in size of the individual firm that produces the homogeneous good, it is said to be a price taker. The graph above illustrates the implications of being a price taker. Such a small firm has no influence over establishing the price in a market. It is merely one small voice trying to outbid its equally fit competition for one more customer. In this way, the aggregate market establishes the price for the good, on the industry level. The individual firms then accept that established price, and it's as if each firm faces a flat demand curve for its goods. Effectively, the firm can sell as many or as few units at the price that has been established in the overall market.

In the short run, this price may fluctuate up or down based on the conditions of supply and demand in the overall market. If it rises, firms may make a profit, and if it falls, firms may lose in the short run; however, the price will hover around a level where firms break even in the long run. Easy entry ensures this. Easy entry makes it so that if firms profit, other firms will enter, diluting the market and lowering price and profitability. Conversely, if firms lose money, then some will exit, leaving more for the fewer remaining firms and price and profitability will rebound.

In the short run, perfectly competitive firms may gain or lose. In the long run, they break even—covering the costs of production and rewarding their workers sufficiently—but never getting so enriched as to grow and dominate a market.

One other thing to note: because the perfectly competitive firm faces a flat demand curve for the good it produces, the marginal (extra) revenue it receives from selling an additional unit of the good will be constant and equal to the price it accepted. In the short run, the firm will decide how much to produce on the basis of whether this marginal revenue covers the marginal cost of providing another good. At the point where marginal revenue equals marginal cost, no more profit can be made by providing more goods to the marketplace, and so this will be the firm's level of production. Because of the flat demand the firm faced, the price it had to accept from the overall market equals the additional cost of providing the good. This is one more indication of the efficiency of perfect competition.

IMPERFECT COMPETITION

Imperfect competitors follow the same logic as their more perfect counterparts. They, too, wish to maximize profit in the short run, and as a result pay attention to their marginal revenue and marginal cost. However, because they are imperfect competitors that have unique market structures, the results differ from perfect competition in some significant ways.

Below is an illustration of the basic structure of an imperfectly competitive producer.

The D-Curve Facing An Imperfectly Competitive Firm

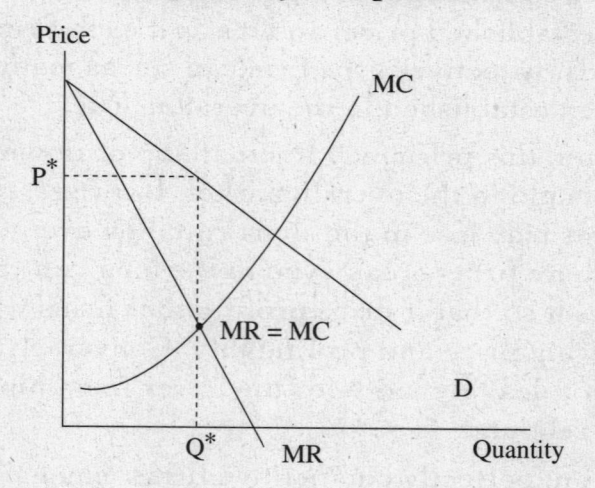

Because an imperfectly competitive firm is a significant player—sometimes the only player—on the supply side of the market, it faces a negatively sloped demand for its goods. To sell another good, it must lower price. This also reduces marginal revenue at a faster rate than price because the firm must drop the price on all goods—up to and including the last one sold. In this way, there is a magnified effect on the marginal revenue reduction. So if, as with imperfect competition, the demand curve has a negative slope, then the marginal revenue also has a negative and steeper slope, as it falls that much more quickly than price.

It's easy to determine the implications of this: the marginal revenue and marginal cost will cross earlier than with perfect competition. Because the price is set in accordance with what consumers are willing and able to pay for goods, it will be set on the demand curve, above the added cost of providing those goods. Simply, all other things being equal, there will be less produced and at a higher price under imperfectly competitive conditions than under perfectly competitive conditions. In the real world, conditions are seldom strictly comparable; however, to the extent that they are, you will get less and pay more for it when dealing with a less competitive producer.

TYPES OF IMPERFECT COMPETITION

Monopolistic Competition

As the name implies, monopolistic competition has elements of more and less competitive market structures. It has many firms and entry is fairly costless and easy, similar to perfect competition. But monopolistic competitors also exhibit some heterogeneity in their products, which differ somewhat depending on the producer. This product differentiation establishes each firm's niche in the total market, and thus gives the firm some singular control over a small subsection of the consuming population. Considering that whatever power one firm has in the marketplace is derived from this distinction between goods, it's beneficial for the monopolistic competitor to accentuate the perception of these differences by advertising.

Advertising is a form of nonprice competition. It does not try to increase sales by lowering price, but instead by appealing to consumers' tastes and perceived needs. It can be very informative, aiding consumers in making better decisions as to satisfy their needs. But often, it merely titillates and tempts and sometimes even misleads. Either way, advertising is a technique a firm uses to raise the demand for its goods to increase market share, price, and profitability.

Monopolistic competitors operate under fairly competitive conditions, but if they can convince consumers of the unique and vital nature of their goods, they will profit more consistently. Some examples of goods produced by monopolistic competitors include most retail items, from toothpaste to soap. How different is one soap from another? Yet, the small differences, and the allegiance they attract, are what allow a particular producer of a particular soap to profit.

Oligopoly

Oligopoly is a market structure characterized by a few large producers that has very significant cost and other barriers to entry. The products the oligopolist produces may be homogeneous, in which case this is a **pure oligopoly**. If there is significant heterogeneity in the goods produced, the market structure is a **differentiated oligopoly**.

Interdependence is a unique attribute of oligopoly. Because there are so few firms, all of which have significant shares of the market, no single firm can do anything without it affecting the fortunes and choices of other firms. This presents two interesting possibilities that are peculiar to oligopoly—ruinous competition and collusion.

One possibility is ruinous competition, which involves actions like price wars, where businesses set prices successively lower and absorb enormous short-run losses with the prospect of eliminating the competition and gaining market share. Once they've gained the market share, businesses are then in a position to profit in the long run, which would far outstrip any losses that resulted from the "war" in which they had engaged.

Our own domestic airline industry often competes in this game of ruinous competition. However, the U.S. government has intervened consistently to keep any single airline from winning the war. In the 1990s, the consumer has experienced bargain prices at times, but because of government intervention still does not face the prospect of being treated poorly by a single provider of airline service in the long run.

The other possible outcome of interdependence is **collusion**. This occurs when businesses combine their efforts in an attempt to raise prices and profitability at the expense of consumers. The most overt forms of collusion occur when groups, which are usually known as cartels, explicitly set territories, production quotas, and prices. Cartels, such as OPEC, are illegal in the U.S. However, they continue to operate outside the jurisdiction of the U.S. legal system and get away with subjecting American consumers to their practices.

Moreover, there are many subtler ways to fix markets in order for firms to profit. The most common, and a difficult one to detect in many instances, is **price leadership**. An oligopolistic industry is comprised of a few big firms, but there is often a biggest firm, which may set the tone for others. Because similar firms may have similarities in cost, it is difficult to prove that smaller firms raise prices merely because they are taking a signal from a larger firm, but this is often the case. By doing so, the individual firms reduce competition and raise profit.

Many of our largest industrial producers are oligopolists, including producers of cars, steel, and oil, as well as airlines. It would be wrong to imply that the size and scope of these enterprises has not benefited America, but it would be equally wrong to neglect the attendant dangers of having a few, large, interdependent providers of a good. In fact, when a single firm becomes big enough, even more dangerous consequences may attend, and that leads us to a brief discussion of monopoly.

Monopoly

A monopoly exists when there is only one producer of a unique good in a market, and entry into that market is impossible. The firm is the industry. There is no need to coordinate the actions of a few large producers to ration goods and raise price. The single firm can do so on its own, often to the detriment of consumption and employment. The U.S. government has established legal safeguards against such activity, but litigation can be costly, and instances of market restriction can be difficult to prove. Because it stifles competition and the incentive to innovate and provide, beware of monopoly.

Simply recognizing the dangers of monopoly does not mean that it can always be avoided. There are several reasons why a monopoly may have arisen in the first place. One reason is the exclusive control of an input. If someone has legal claim to a vital input—a raw material for the production of a unique good—then he will control its output. Years ago, this was the case with aluminum production.

Another reason why monopoly arises is an extension of the first. In order to give incentives for innovation, we must protect the right of the inventor to market her product. Nations grant **patents** for this purpose; however, this gives one person exclusive control of a vital input—a particular technology—that may not be easily replaced or replicated in a different form. This results in industries like computer software, which start under very competitive circumstances, evolving into something approaching monopoly.

A last reason for the advent of monopoly involves simple productive efficiency. Some businesses get better as they get bigger. More precisely, their average cost of production falls as their level of production rises. This is known as **economies of scale**. Some businesses by their very nature experience significant economies of scale. Businesses that require large investments in research and in capital are likely to become significantly more technically efficient as they grow larger. This means a start-up business wouldn't stand a chance if it entered this market. It just couldn't be large enough to experience those same cost savings as the larger firm. Of course, there is no guarantee that the cost savings of the larger firm will be passed along to consumers. It's likely that the larger firm would keep prices just low enough to make its market uncontestable by smaller firms. Then, being the only producer, it could ration output and keep prices significantly higher than the cost of providing goods.

Monopolies are illegal in the U.S., but certain companies, such as public utilities, are allowed to operate as a type of monopoly because they have achieved economies of scale. The government regulates the prices these monopolies charge for goods and services. A monopoly that is allowed to exist with government supervision is known as a **natural monopoly**.

In closing, if all things are equal—which is rare—then imperfectly competitive markets tend to provide less employment, fewer goods, and goods at higher prices than more competitive markets.

Carefully review the tables below so that you can recognize and understand the ramifications of different market structures.

Characteristics of Different Market Structures

Market Structure	# of Firms	Nature of Good	Entry
Perfect Competition	Many	Homogeneous	Cost Less = No Cost & Easy
Monopolistic Competition	Many	Heterogeneous	Low Cost Fairly Easy
Oligopoly	Few	Pure -Homogeneous Differentiated -Heterogeneous	Expensive & Difficult
Monopoly	One	Unique	Prohibitive & Impossible

Comparison of :

Perfect Competition	Imperfect Competition
Lower Prices	Higher Prices
More Output	Less Output
Greater Employment	Less Employment
Efficient Use of Capacity	Inefficient Use of Capacity
Self-Regulating	Requires Government Oversight

Chapter 19

LABOR MARKETS

There are two types of markets—output and input. The output market is where goods and services are exchanged. The input market is where resources, including land, labor, and capital, are exchanged. Much of what can be said of markets in general can be said of either of these types of markets. Further, what can be said specifically about a particular resource market can usually be equally applied to other resource markets. With this in mind, let's turn our attention to the labor market, where labor is exchanged for a price we call the wage or wage rate.

DEMAND FOR LABOR

Like any other market, the labor market has two sides, one of which is the demand side.

The demand for labor is affected significantly by several factors. One of these factors is the demand for the product that labor is helping to produce. It is often said that the demand for any resource, labor being no exception, is a derived demand. Its demand is derived from the demand for some other good. Simply, if autoworkers are in demand, it is because people want the autos that they help produce. If that demand for autos is high, then so will the demand for autoworkers. But if consumers can take or leave autos, then they will be just as easily inclined to take or leave autoworkers.

The outcry of various unions to "buy American" is given impetus by their recognition that the demand for American labor, which they supply, depends on the sale of American goods. By encouraging domestic consumers to patronize domestic producers, they hope to maintain a high demand for American labor, and with it a high wage. Of course, to the extent that this is viewed as protectionist and incites retaliation of a similar kind by other trading partners, this could lead down a path where no one will benefit, as we discussed in the chapter on international trade.

A second factor that affects the demand for labor is cost. Quite obviously, if all other things were the same, one would prefer to employ cheaper labor rather than expensive labor. This is one of those mantras that are recited by protectionists as they warn of the impending doom if the U.S. deals with "cheap labor" nations, the logic being that all our jobs will be lost to those nations because of their inexpensive labor. This is a simplistic argument, as things in the real world are seldom equal. There is a good reason why an autoworker in one country gets paid more handsomely than his counterpart in a less-developed nation. One worker is often many times more productive, and is worth the added expense. If nation A has workers that cost twice as much as nation B, but at the same time, nation A's workers are four times as productive as those in nation B, then only a fool would move his production facilities to nation B. If we do not consider differences in productivity with the same care that we apply to differences in cost, then we will have an incomplete and often misleading understanding of the situation.

Education, training, and experience are important aspects of the labor market because they raise a worker's productivity, and rewards in the form of wages will rise along with it. Productive labor is worth the price you pay for it. This is just one more reflection of how rising productivity is crucial to a nation's enhanced standard of living.

Marginal Revenue Product

The essence of why labor is demanded at all rests with its ability to generate products that can be sold to enhance revenue. Thus, the demand for labor is proportional to its marginal revenue product, which is the extra revenue generated from sales of the additional production from hiring one last unit of labor. In short, it is the extra revenue received from selling the extra product that the extra labor produced.

The marginal revenue product (MRP) can be calculated as the product of labor's marginal product (MP) and the marginal revenue (MR) associated with it.

$$\text{MRP of labor} = (\text{MP of labor})(\text{MR})$$

**The Marginal Revenue
Product of Labor**

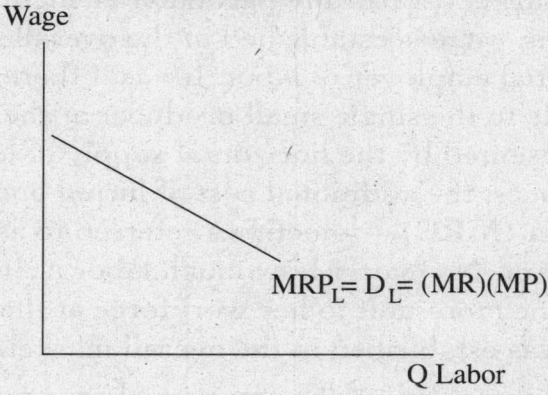

Graph: Wage vs Q Labor, showing downward-sloping line labeled $MRP_L = D_L = (MR)(MP)$

Notice that the MRP, or demand for labor, has a negative slope, as do most demand curves. The reason for this is easy to determine: mathematically, we understand that there is a Law of Diminishing Marginal Returns, which means that the marginal product of labor will sooner or later, and inexorably, fall. Even if marginal revenue were maintained, and in reality it too will fall, the falling MP would pull the MRP down as you hired more labor. Intuitively, as you hire more labor, the additional benefit associated with doing so falls, and with it, your willingness and ability to pay for labor. So wages must fall to entice you to buy more labor. As the wage drops, you are willing and able to buy more labor. As the wage rises, you are less willing and able to buy labor.

SUPPLY OF LABOR

As with most supply curves, the supply of labor has a positive slope with respect to the entire labor market, indicating that as wages rise, the willingness and ability to provide labor rises as well. However, if we look at the supply of labor with respect to a specific firm, there are some crucial differences in perspective, which largely hinge on just how competitive the labor market itself is.

**The Supply of Labor
In a Competitive Labor Market**

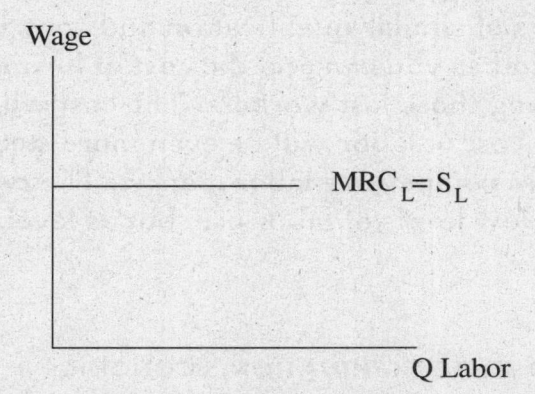

Graph: Wage vs Q Labor, showing horizontal line labeled $MRC_L = S_L$

In a competitive labor market, there are many firms bidding for the services of labor. The overall market dwarfs any particular element that composes it. Thus, when a prevailing wage is established in the overall market, it is then applied to every potential employer of labor. It's as if there is an infinite abundance of labor available to the single small producer at the established, prevailing wage. This is represented by the horizontal supply of labor above. Note that under such circumstances, the additional cost of hiring one last unit of labor, the **marginal resource cost (MRC)**—sometimes referred to as the marginal factor cost (MFC)—is constant. No matter how much labor a single producer employs, she could add one more unit to her workforce at the same cost as the prevailing wage that was established in the overall market.

Of course, in a less competitive labor market, there are only a few buyers of labor, and each is a significant player in the market. Because of this, if one company wishes to add labor, it must entice it away from others via a higher wage. Thus, the supply of labor with respect to such a significant buyer of labor has a positive slope.

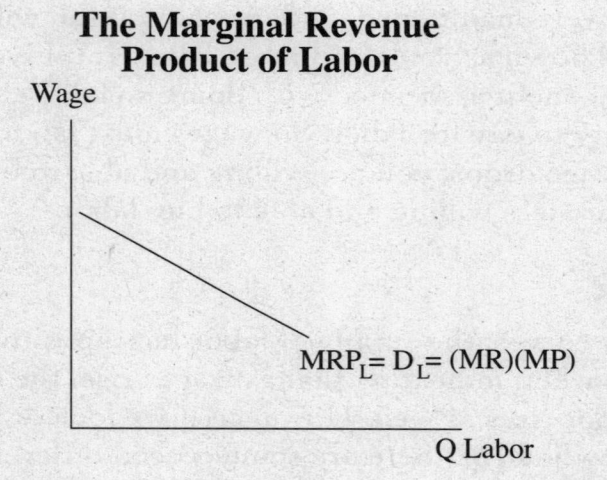

The Marginal Revenue Product of Labor

$MRP_L = D_L = (MR)(MP)$

But a positively sloped supply of labor also has repercussions for the marginal cost of hiring a laborer. If the wage must be raised to attract more labor, as contracts come due, then a multiple effect on the cost of having hired that last bit of labor occurs. Others of similar qualification and contribution will demand a similar higher wage, and as you can see, the cost of hiring more labor will exceed the simple cost of paying those last workers. The cost will be magnified, and so the marginal resource cost of labor will be even more steeply sloped than the supply of labor in a less competitive labor market. The two curves will start close together at very low levels of labor use, but as levels increase, they will diverge significantly.

COMPARISON OF COMPETITIVE AND IMPERFECTLY COMPETITIVE LABOR MARKETS

Any market has two sides, and if we bring them together, we will understand the solution to why and how much is provided. Because of some distinct differences discussed above, competitive and less competitive labor markets will tend toward different results, even while following the same logic.

The Supply of Labor in an Imperfectly Competitive Labor Market

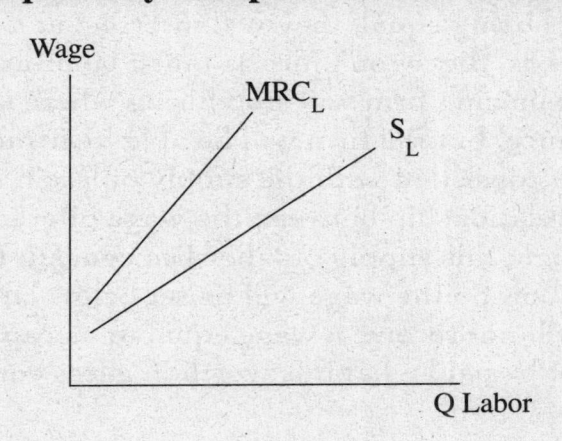

Above, you see two diagrams. On the left is a competitive labor market with respect to the individual buying firm. This is obvious, because of the essentially flat, infinite availability of labor at the prevailing wage. On the right is an imperfectly competitive labor market with respect to a significant buying firm. This is clear because of the divergence between the supply curve of labor and the marginal resource cost of labor. In either case, the same simple logic is applied. A firm will want to hire any labor that generates more revenue than cost. This means that any labor unit whose marginal revenue product exceeds its **marginal resource cost** is one that contributes to the profitability of the firm. The labor unit is therefore desirable.

Because the marginal revenue product declines as more labor is hired, eventually it reaches a point where the marginal revenue product equals the marginal resource cost. This is the point where the profit-maximizing firm will cease hiring because to go any farther, additional labor becomes more costly than revenue producing and in turn reduces profits. This is the logic of any profit-maximizing firm, whether it bids for labor in a more or less competitive market.

If we focus our attention on the competitive scenario on the left, two things become apparent. One is that with a flat supply of labor, any given demand for labor will have to decline if there are greater levels of labor utilization to reach the balance we discussed above. In simple terms, by the time the extra revenue and extra cost equal each other, the firm will have hired a lot more labor than under a different circumstance.

The second thing to note is that since the supply and marginal cost of hiring more labor are the same in a competitive case, at the point of balance, a wage is set equal to the marginal revenue product of labor. Simply, the wage will be set in accord with the revenue-generating capacity of labor. Even more succinctly, labor will be paid what it is worth.

On the other hand, a less competitive case is shown above at right. Because the marginal resource cost rises to meet the declining marginal revenue product of labor, all other things being equal, they will intersect at a lower level of labor utilization. In other words, they won't hire as much labor as in a competitive market. The profit-maximizing firm will stop hiring where the extra revenue and extra cost of labor balance, but the firm will be able to attract that amount of labor by paying a wage consistent with the supply of labor. After all, the supply of labor expresses the relationship between the wage offered and the provision of labor. Crucially though, this supply of labor lies beneath the marginal resource cost of hiring labor. So the wage will be set below labor's marginal revenue product. Labor will not receive a wage equal to its capacity to generate revenue. Labor will not be paid what it is worth in a less competitive labor market.

A good example of such labor market imperfection is the baseball players' market prior to the mid-1970s. At that time, if a team drafted a player, the team could trade him, but he could never negotiate with any other team, even when his contract expired. The team had a reserve clause, which gave it exclusive rights to deal with its players until it was no longer interested in them.

Free-agency came about in the mid-1970s and established a loosening of these former restrictions for baseball players. Now, with certain minor impediments, a player can market his skills fairly and freely. Free agency has led to enormous salary increases. For decades ballplayers made millions for the team owners and were compensated only barely enough to keep them from venturing into an alternative trade. This was possible because of the imperfection of their labor market. As that imperfection was reduced, these players, with their rare and valued skills, suddenly were compensated with the revenue they helped to generate.

To summarize, if all things are equal, a competitive labor market will lead to more jobs and higher pay that corresponds to the value of the employee to the business. Less competitive labor markets will lead to fewer jobs and lower pay that is below the value of the employee to the business.

Part III

THE PRINCETON REVIEW GSE ECONOMICS PRACTICE TESTS

Chapter 20

THE PRINCETON REVIEW GSE ECONOMICS PRACTICE TEST I

PART I: MULTIPLE-CHOICE QUESTIONS

You will have 45 minutes to complete the multiple-choice section of this exam. For each question, please indicate the best response out of the four provided.

1. Economics is best defined as the study of
   A. money.
   B. banking systems.
   C. scarcity and choice.
   D. profit and consumption.

2. Having a high price is most likely to indicate that a good
   A. is scarce.
   B. is of little value to consumers.
   C. has a demand that exceeds its supply.
   D. has a supply that exceeds its demand.

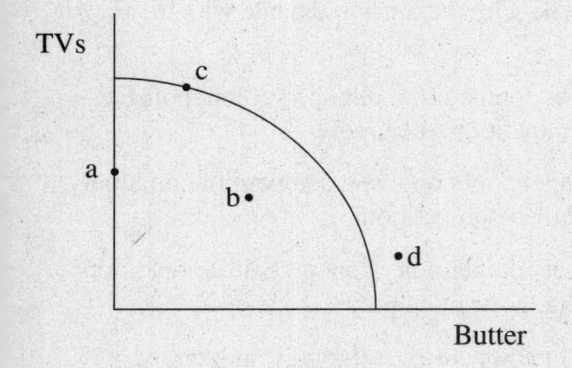

3. At which point is the economy using its resources efficiently?
   A. a
   B. b
   C. c
   D. d

4. Gains from specialization are a primary reason for
   A. diminishing marginal returns.
   B. increasing marginal cost.
   C. decreasing returns to scale.
   D. increasing marginal returns.

5. Which of the following is best classified as a factor of production?
   A. A refrigerator
   B. Inflation
   C. A loaf of bread
   D. A worker

6. For a given good or service and within a given period, the demand curve indicates the relationship between
   A. income and quantity consumed.
   B. price and availability.
   C. price and quantity demanded.
   D. quantity demanded and quantity supplied.

7. As more spinach is produced, the opportunity cost of spinach production most likely
   A. decreases.
   B. increases.
   C. remains constant.
   D. becomes negative.

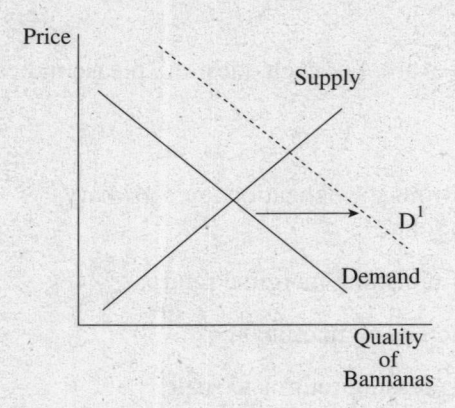

[Graph: Price vs. Quality of Bannanas, showing Supply curve, Demand curve, and a shifted demand curve D¹ to the left of Demand]

8. The shift in the demand curve for bananas above is most likely the result of
   A. successful advertising.
   B. a drought.
   C. a reduction in harvesting costs due to new technology.
   D. a report that bananas cause poor health.

9. Externalities are most frequently a source of
   A. pride and joy.
   B. monopoly power.
   C. efficiency.
   D. market failure.

10. Which type of business organization receives a large majority of total sales in the U.S.?
    A. Partnerships
    B. Sole Proprietorships
    C. Corporations
    D. Perfectly competitive firms

11. Marginal revenue product is
    A. the additional revenue gained by selling one more unit of a product.
    B. the additional revenue gained by hiring one more unit of an input.
    C. the government's measure of the increase in total business revenue over the past 12 months.
    D. the smallest increment in revenue that makes it worthwhile to make one more unit of a product.

12. If income is distributed evenly among all families, the Lorenz curve will be
    A. straight, on a diagonal.
    B. horizontal.
    C. vertical.
    D. circular.

13. Which of the following lists market structures in order from the one with the most to the one with the fewest firms?
    A. perfect competition, oligopoly, monopolistic competition, monopoly
    B. monopoly, monopolistic competition, oligopoly, perfect competition
    C. perfect competition, monopolistic competition, oligopoly, monopoly
    D. perfect competition, oligopoly, monopoly, monopolistic competition

14. The U.S. gross domestic product is the total value of all final goods and services produced within a year
    A. by U.S. citizens.
    B. for U.S. citizens.
    C. within the U.S.
    D. for export.

15. An increase in the GDP is most likely to correspond with which of the following?

    A. A decrease in unemployment

    B. An increase in inflation

    C. A decrease in the CPI

    D. An increase in unemployment

16. An increase in exports will directly result in a(n)

    A. increase in aggregate supply.

    B. decrease in aggregate supply.

    C. increase in aggregate demand.

    D. decrease in aggregate demand.

17. The direct effect of fiscal policy is a shift in which of the following curves?

    A. Production Function

    B. Aggregate Supply

    C. Marginal Cost

    D. Aggregate Demand

18. The federal budget deficit is

    A. the difference between federal government spending and tax collections for a given year.

    B. the accumulation of past national debts.

    C. the total amount that the federal government owes foreigners at a given time.

    D. the difference between exports and imports in a given year.

19. Which of the following constitutes monetary policy?

    A. An increase in government transfer payments

    B. An increase in government spending

    C. A decrease in income taxes

    D. A decrease in the discount rate

20. Which of the following statements about the Federal Reserve System is true?

    A. There are 52 member banks, one in each state.

    B. It began operating in 1776 as designated by the U.S. Constitution.

    C. It has considerable control over the availability of money and credit in the U.S.

    D. The vice president of the United States serves as its chairperson.

21. In a command economy, decisions of what, how, and for whom to produce are made by

    A. a central planning bureau.

    B. the market mechanism.

    C. the chairperson of the Federal Reserve.

    D. the interaction of demand and supply.

22. Which of the following promotes growth in the money supply?

    A. An increase in the discount rate

    B. A fractional reserve banking system

    C. The sale of bonds by the Fed

    D. An increase in the required reserve ratio

23. Unemployment resulting from a skills mismatch is called

    A. seasonal unemployment.

    B. structural unemployment.

    C. frictional unemployment.

    D. cyclical unemployment.

24. By definition, the act of carrying out intranational trade involves

    A. one country.

    B. two countries.

    C. at least three countries.

    D. individuals with two different nationalities.

25. If the Fed wants to increase the value of the dollar relative to the yen, it should

    A. sell yen for dollars.

    B. supply dollars on the open market.

    C. sell dollars for yen.

    D. demand yen on the open market.

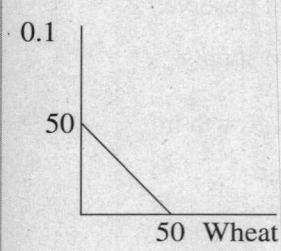

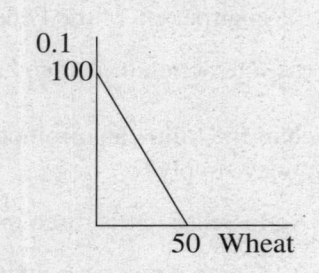

```
      Country A              Country B
  0.1 |                  0.1 |
      |\                 100\
   50 | \                    |\
      |  \                   | \
      |___\_                 |__\_
        50  Wheat              50  Wheat
```

26. Countries A and B have the same resources and their simplified production possibilities curves are illustrated above. Which of the following statements is true?

    A. Country A has a comparative advantage in wheat production.

    B. Country B has an absolute advantage in wheat production.

    C. Only Country A would benefit from international trade.

    D. Only Country B would benefit from international trade.

27. Price is determined by

    A. supply only.

    B. demand only.

    C. marginal cost only.

    D. supply and demand.

28. Which of the following is the most likely to result from the introduction of a trade tariff?

    A. Retaliatory trade restrictions

    B. Lower domestic prices for the good on which the tariff is imposed

    C. An increase in the competition faced by domestic producers

    D. A decrease in short-run profits earned by domestic producers

29. A firm in which of the following market structures faces a horizontal marginal revenue curve?

    A. Monopoly

    B. Oligopoly

    C. Monopolistic competition

    D. Perfect competition

30. If aggregate demand increases and aggregate supply decreases, it is certain that

    A. the price level will decrease.

    B. the price level will increase.

    C. real output will increase.

    D. real output will decrease.

PART II: ESSAY QUESTIONS

The essay questions will allow you to demonstrate your graphing and analytical skills. You will have 45 minutes in which to write two essays. Your teacher will notify you when 20 minutes have passed.

Directions:

1. Read each of the essay topics carefully.

2. Organize your thoughts before you start writing. You may want to outline your essays or experiment with a few graphs first. You may write notes and practice diagrams on the test booklet. Only writing on the lined pages of the answer sheet will be scored.

3. Write your essays on the appropriate pages of the answer sheet.

4. The two essays receive equal credit, and you must write both essays to receive full credit. Allow yourself sufficient time to write each essay—an equal division of time would give you 22.5 minutes for each one.

5. Be sure to draw the relevant graphs, be specific, and use economic concepts, terms, and policies to reinforce your reasoning.

6. Don't waste time going off on tangents. Rather, address the given topic with well-supported responses.

1) Topic:

The growing popularity of e-mail cuts paper use

Answer the questions below in an essay that employs economic concepts, reasoning, and supply and demand graphs.

A. Using a graph, explain how this will affect the market for paper.

B. Who benefits and loses as the result of the changes in price, quantity, and employment in the paper market that accompany the transition from paper correspondence to e-mail?

C. If logs can either be used to make paper or lumber, what affect will the shift to e-mail have on the markets for lumber and for nails? Use graphs to explain your answer.

2) Topic:

Expansionary fiscal policy hits
while economy enjoys full employment

Answer the questions below in an essay that employs economic concepts, reasoning, and an aggregate supply/aggregate demand graph.

A. Using a graph, explain the short run and long run effects of this fiscal policy.

B. What are the likely short run and long run affects on real GDP, employment, and the price level?

C. Give examples of those who would be harmed and helped by the resulting change in the price level.

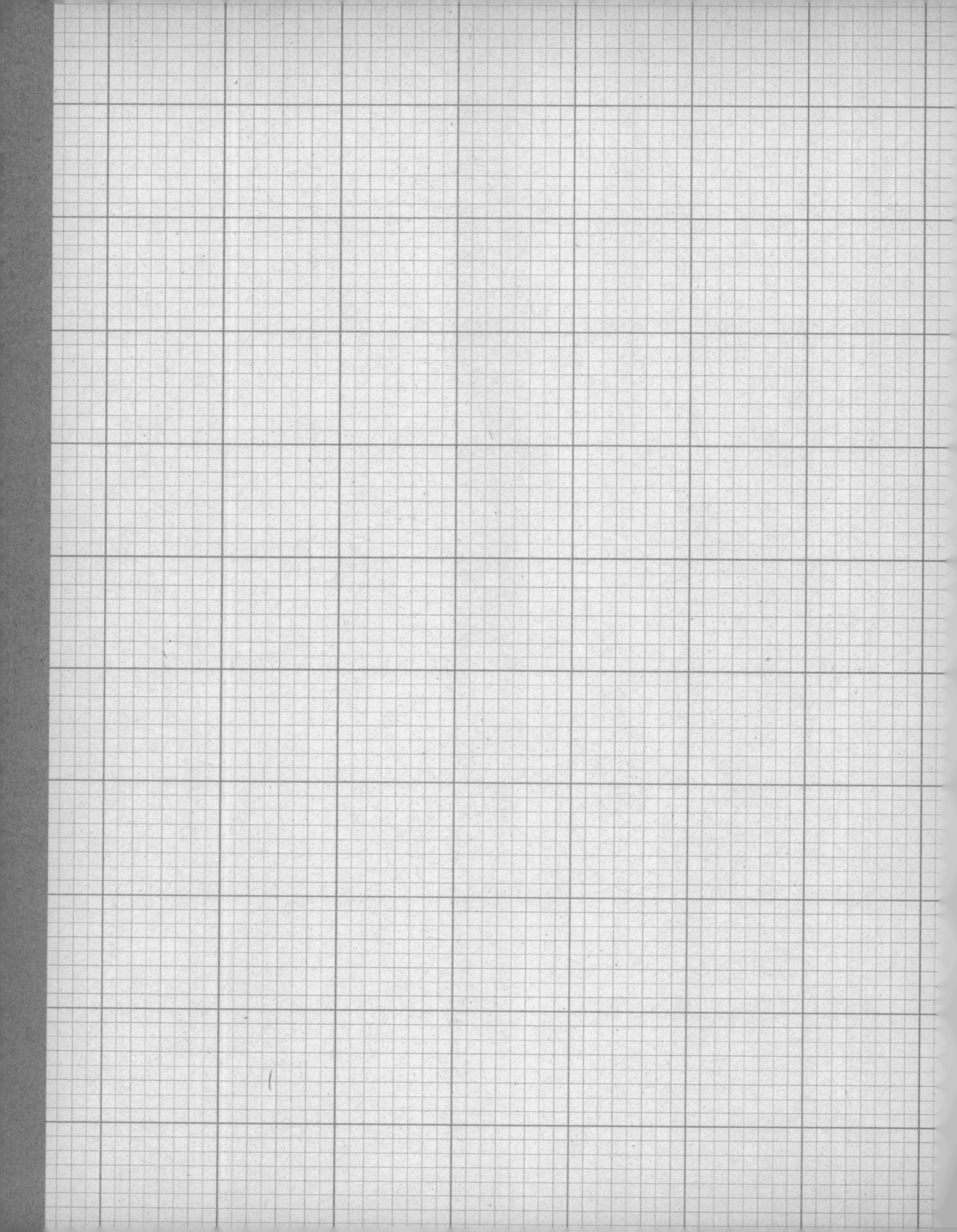

THE PRINCETON REVIEW

YOUR NAME: _____
(Print)   Last   First   M.I.

SIGNATURE: _____ **DATE:** ___/___/___

HOME ADDRESS: _____
(Print)   Number and Street

_____
City   State   Zip Code

PHONE NO.: _____
(Print)

Completely darken bubbles with a No. 2 pencil. If you make a mistake, be sure to erase mark completely. Erase all stray marks.

Practice Test 1

1. Ⓐ Ⓑ Ⓒ Ⓓ
2. Ⓐ Ⓑ Ⓒ Ⓓ
3. Ⓐ Ⓑ Ⓒ Ⓓ
4. Ⓐ Ⓑ Ⓒ Ⓓ
5. Ⓐ Ⓑ Ⓒ Ⓓ
6. Ⓐ Ⓑ Ⓒ Ⓓ
7. Ⓐ Ⓑ Ⓒ Ⓓ
8. Ⓐ Ⓑ Ⓒ Ⓓ
9. Ⓐ Ⓑ Ⓒ Ⓓ
10. Ⓐ Ⓑ Ⓒ Ⓓ
11. Ⓐ Ⓑ Ⓒ Ⓓ
12. Ⓐ Ⓑ Ⓒ Ⓓ
13. Ⓐ Ⓑ Ⓒ Ⓓ
14. Ⓐ Ⓑ Ⓒ Ⓓ
15. Ⓐ Ⓑ Ⓒ Ⓓ

16. Ⓐ Ⓑ Ⓒ Ⓓ
17. Ⓐ Ⓑ Ⓒ Ⓓ
18. Ⓐ Ⓑ Ⓒ Ⓓ
19. Ⓐ Ⓑ Ⓒ Ⓓ
20. Ⓐ Ⓑ Ⓒ Ⓓ
21. Ⓐ Ⓑ Ⓒ Ⓓ
22. Ⓐ Ⓑ Ⓒ Ⓓ
23. Ⓐ Ⓑ Ⓒ Ⓓ
24. Ⓐ Ⓑ Ⓒ Ⓓ
25. Ⓐ Ⓑ Ⓒ Ⓓ
26. Ⓐ Ⓑ Ⓒ Ⓓ
27. Ⓐ Ⓑ Ⓒ Ⓓ
28. Ⓐ Ⓑ Ⓒ Ⓓ
29. Ⓐ Ⓑ Ⓒ Ⓓ
30. Ⓐ Ⓑ Ⓒ Ⓓ

THE PRINCETON REVIEW GSE ECONOMICS PRACTICE TEST I

Multiple-Choice Answer Key

1	C	9	D	17	D	25	A
2	A	10	C	18	A	26	A
3	C	11	B	19	D	27	D
4	D	12	A	20	C	28	A
5	D	13	C	21	A	29	D
6	C	14	C	22	B	30	B
7	B	15	A	23	B		
8	A	16	C	24	A		

Part I: Multiple-Choice Explanations

1. **C** Although economics is sometimes thought to be all about money, banking systems, or profit and consumption, it is much broader than any of these. Economics is about making the necessary choices when allocating scarce resources among competing ends.

2. **A** Prices are determined by the interaction of supply and demand. A high price can indicate that a good is in short supply (scarce) and/or in great demand. There is no reason to think that there is a shortage or surplus of a good on the basis of its price. Shortages and surpluses result from prices that differ from the equilibrium price, however low or high that might be.

3. **C** The production possibilities curve is a collection of points at which resources are used efficiently. Operation at points below the PPC indicates the inefficient use of resources, thus eliminating choices (A) and (B). Points outside the PPC are unobtainable with the current resources, thus eliminating (D). This leaves (C) as the best choice.

4. **D** Diminishing marginal returns means the firm gets less additional output from added units of an input, holding other inputs constant, so (A) is wrong. Increasing marginal cost means the cost of additional units of output increases, so you can eliminate (B). Decreasing returns to scale means that output increases less than in proportion to an increase in all inputs, so (C) is wrong. Since all of these involve getting less output or spending more money, they do not reflect the gains from specialization. Increasing marginal returns means that

additional units of an input (such as labor) produce more output than the units before them; specialization can be the source of these gains — choice (D) is best.

5. **D** Factors of production are the inputs that are used to create outputs like refrigerators and bread. Inflation may or may not influence output levels, but it is not considered an input into the production process.

6. **C** The demand curve displays the relationship between price and the quantity demanded of a good within a given period.

7. **B** The opportunity cost of making another unit of spinach is the value of the next best alternative forgone in order to make that spinach. The opportunity cost of production typically increases as more is produced for several reasons. For example, workers must forgo more and more valuable alternative uses for their time, and inputs that are less and less specialized for the production of spinach must be used to further spinach production, rather than for the uses where they are more valuable.

8. **A** A drought would shift the supply curve to the left, so (B) is wrong. A decrease in harvesting costs would shift the supply curve to the right, so you can eliminate (C). A report that bananas cause poor health would shift the demand curve to the left, making (D) wrong. A shift to the right in the demand curve means that consumers would pay more for any given quantity of bananas and could be the result of successful advertising. Choice (A) is best.

9. **D** Externalities are effects felt beyond or "external to" those factors creating them. Some are positive, like nice smells wafting from bakeries, but many are negative, like noise and pollution from cars. It is possible that some cause pride and joy, but this is not the rule, so you can eliminate choice (A). They do not cause monopoly power, choice (B), or efficiency, choice (C). Rather, they are a source of market failure because whether they are positive or negative, the difference between private and social costs or benefits results in an outcome that is not the best outcome for society. That is, activities or goods that cause negative externalities are overconsumed and those that cause positive externalities are underconsumed.

10. **C** Although corporations represent less than 20 percent of all firms, they account for about 90 percent of total sales. Proprietorships and partnerships divide the other 10 percent fairly equally—(A) and (B) are wrong. Perfect competition is a type of market structure, not a type of business organization, so you can eliminate (D).

11. **B** Marginal revenue product is the additional revenue gained from hiring one more unit of an input. Answer choice (A) describes marginal revenue, which is multiplied by the marginal product of an input to determine its marginal revenue product.

12. **A** The Lorenz curve indicates the cumulative percentage of income held by each percentage of families, starting with the poorest and ending with the richest. With equality, the percentage of income and the percentage of families would always be the same; for example, the poorest 39 percent of families would hold 39 percent of the income and so forth. This would result in a Lorenz curve that is straight and on a diagonal from the origin (zero percent of families making zero percent of the income) to 100 percent, 100 percent.

13. **C** A perfect competitive market has a nearly infinite number of firms. Monopolistic competition involves many firms. Oligopoly involves a few firms. Monopoly involves one firm.

14. **C** The U.S. gross domestic product (GDP) is the total value of all final goods and services produced within the U.S. in a given year. Our gross national product (GNP) is the total value of all final goods and services produced within a year by factors of production owned by U.S. citizens. For GNP, it doesn't matter in what country the output is actually produced. Use of the expression *"final goods and services"* means that intermediate goods like lumber and steel that go into the production of other goods like homes and cars are omitted to avoid double counting.

15. **A** An increase in gross domestic product (GDP) could correspond with an increase, decrease, or no change in inflation, depending on the relative increases in aggregate demand and aggregate supply. On the other hand, increasing GDP is very likely to decrease unemployment because it will take more workers to produce the additional output.

16. **C** Exports are a component of aggregate demand. When they increase, so does AD.

17. **D** Fiscal policy involves changes in government purchases, taxes, and transfer payments. Each of these changes will shift the aggregate demand curve.

18. **A** The federal budget deficit is the difference between federal government spending and tax collections in a given year. The **national debt** is the accumulation of past deficits—the total amount that the federal government owes at a given time.

19. **D** Monetary policy is the use of money and credit controls to influence interest rates, inflation, exchange rates, unemployment, and real GDP. The Fed can change the money supply by adjusting the discount rate or the reserve requirement, or through open market operations. Answer choices (A), (B), and (C) constitute fiscal policy.

20. **C** There are 12 regional banks; get rid of (A). The Federal Reserve System started operating in 1914; eliminate (B). Its chairperson is not the vice president; get rid of (D). The Fed does have considerable control over the availability of money and credit in the U.S.

21. **A** In a command economy, rather than allowing the market mechanism of supply and demand determine what, how, and for whom to produce, these decisions are made by a central planning bureau within the government.

22. **B** An increase in the discount rate or the required reserve ratio will inhibit money creation. Banks will borrow fewer reserves from the Fed when the discount rate they have to pay for them increases, and they will be forced to hold on to more of their deposits when the required reserve ratio increases. Both of these effects will result in fewer loans and inhibit the process of money creation, so choices (A) and (D) are incorrect. The sale of bonds by the Fed decreases the money supply because the Fed exchanges bond certificates for money, which it holds, so choice (C) is wrong. The fractional reserve banking system promotes the growth of money because it allows banks to lend out most of their deposits, which become new money holdings by those receiving the loans; choice (B) is correct.

23. **B** Structural unemployment is caused by a skills mismatch. For example, when pro football players become too old to play ball, they may experience structural unemployment because their football skills do not match other needs in the labor market.

24. **A** Intranational trade is trade within a single country.

25. **A** By selling yen in exchange for dollars, the Fed is effectively supplying yen and demanding dollars. This increase in the supply of yen and the demand for dollars will increase the equilibrium price of dollars in terms of yen, increasing the value of the dollar relative to the yen.

26. **A** A country is said to have an absolute advantage in the production of a good when it can produce that good using fewer resources per unit of output than another country. A country is said to have a comparative advantage in the production of a good when it can produce that good at a lower opportunity cost (a smaller loss in terms of the production of another good) than another country. Country A gives up 1 unit of oil for 1 unit of wheat, whereas country B gives up 2 units of oil per unit of wheat (for example, starting from making only oil, B must give up 100 units of oil to make 50 units of wheat). Thus, country A has a lower opportunity cost and a comparative advantage in producing wheat. Neither country has an absolute advantage in wheat production because they can both produce the same amount with the same resources, so choice (B) is wrong. Since A has a comparative advantage in producing wheat, *both* countries could benefit from international trade of some of A's wheat for some of B's oil, making choices (C) and (D) incorrect.

27. **D** Price is determined by the intersection of supply and demand. Just as it takes two blades on a pair of scissors to make a cut, it takes both supply and demand to establish a price.

28. **A** Trade restrictions on the part of one country often provoke similar actions by other countries. They also result in higher prices, decreased competition, and increased short-run profits.

29. **D** A perfectly competitive firm faces a horizontal marginal revenue curve because it can sell all that it wants at the market price. Firms in all of the other market structures face downward sloping marginal revenue curves because they must lower their price to sell more output.

30. **B** An increase in aggregate demand increases the price level and real output. A decrease in aggregate supply increases the price level and decreases output. Since both of these shifts increase the price level, it is certain that the price level increases. The opposing effects of these shifts on real output make the net effect on real output uncertain.

Part II: Essay Explanations

Topic 1

Figure 1

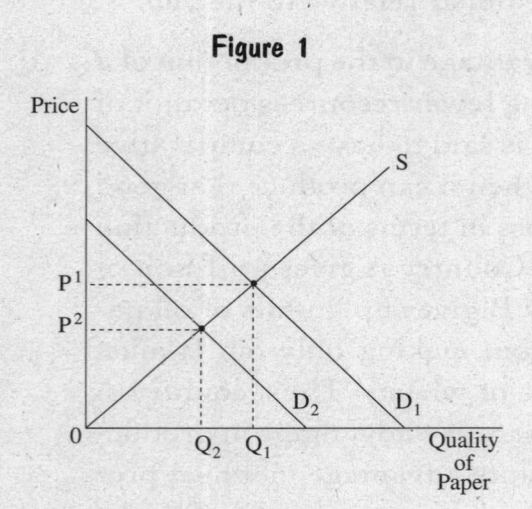

[Graph showing Price vs. Quality of Paper with supply curve S, demand curves D₁ and D₂ (D₂ shifted left), equilibrium moving from (Q₁, P¹) to (Q₂, P²)]

Figure 2

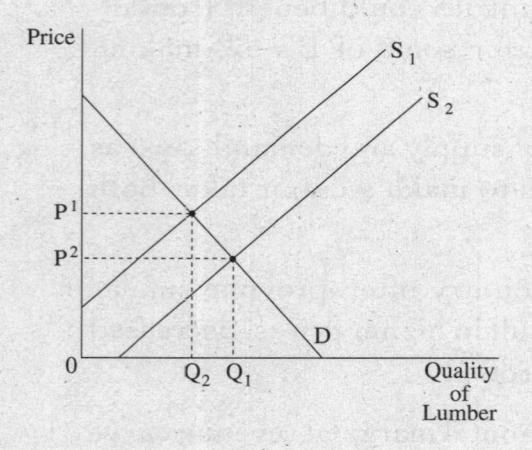

[Graph showing Price vs. Quality of Lumber with demand curve D, supply curves S₁ and S₂ (S₂ shifted right), equilibrium moving from (Q₁, P¹) to (Q₂, P²)]

An excellent response:

A. As e-mail replaces paper use, the demand for paper will decrease. As illustrated in Figure 1, consumers will purchase less paper at any given price, and the demand curve for paper will shift to the left. At the beginning price of P_1, a surplus of paper will exist after the demand shift, bringing producers to lower their prices. As the price falls, the quantity demanded will increase and the quantity supplied will decrease. This process will continue until the quantity demanded equals the quantity supplied at a new equilibrium price of P_2 and a new quantity of Q_2.

B. The transition to e-mail will cause prices and quantities to fall in the paper industry. Those who still use paper will benefit from a lower price. However, as the quantity produced decreases, so will employment in paper making jobs, so some employees of paper companies will become unemployed.

C. As fewer logs are used to make paper, more of this resource will be available for lumber production. This increase in the supply of logs for lumber will lower the price of logs and shift the supply curve of lumber to the right as in Figure 2. The equilibrium price of lumber will decrease from P_1 to P_2, and the quantity of lumber will increase from Q_1 to Q_2.

Since nails and lumber are complementary goods, when the price of lumber goes down, the demand for nails increases. Thus, the demand curve for nails will increase as in Figure 3, leading to a higher equilibrium price and quantity in the nail market.

Figure 3

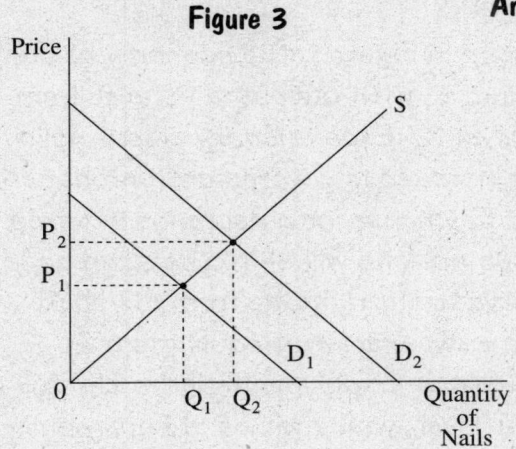

[Graph showing Price vs Quantity of Nails, with supply curve S, demand curves D₁ and D₂ shifting right, equilibrium moving from (Q₁, P₁) to (Q₂, P₂)]

An average response:

A. As e-mail replaces paper use, the demand for paper will decrease as illustrated in Figure 1. This leads to a new equilibrium price of P_2 and a new quantity of Q_2.

B. The transition to e-mail will cause prices and quantities to fall in the paper industry. Those who still use paper will benefit from a lower price. However, as the quantity produced decreases, so will employment in paper making jobs, so some employees of paper companies will become unemployed.

C. As fewer logs are used to make paper, the supply curve of lumber shifts to the right as in Figure 2. The equilibrium price of lumber will decrease from P_1 to P_2, and the quantity of lumber will increase from Q_1 to Q_2.

When the price of lumber goes down, the demand for nails increases. Thus, the demand curve for nails will increase as in Figure 3.

A poor response:

A. Less paper will be used. See Figure 1. I have a paper due in my English class that I wish I were writing instead of this test.

B. Paper makers will be hurt. They will lose their jobs when the price changes. Prices increase and decrease with fluctuations in the market. The market is a useful tool according to Adam Smith. He had an invisible hand.

C. People will make more lumber. They will probably make more nails too. They will need the nails to attach the lumber together and build things. This will probably affect supply and demand in significant ways.

Topic 2

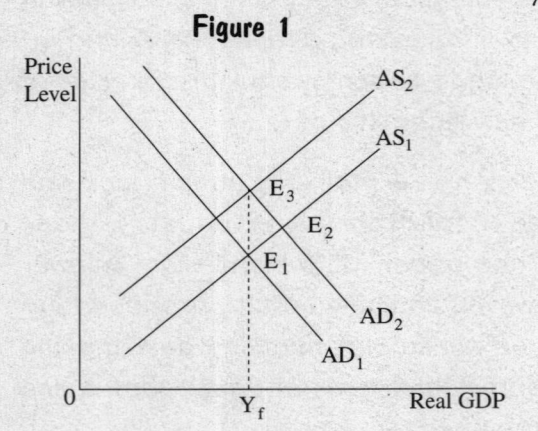

Figure 1

[Figure 1: AS-AD diagram showing Price Level on vertical axis and Real GDP on horizontal axis. Curves AS₁ and AS₂ slope upward, AD₁ and AD₂ slope downward. Equilibria E₁, E₂, E₃ are shown, with E₁ and E₃ at full-employment output Y_f.]

An excellent response:

A. As illustrated in Figure 1, the economy begins at equilibrium E_1 with output at the full-employment level Y_f. Expansionary fiscal policy involves an increase in government purchases or transfer payments, or a decrease in taxes. Any of these actions will shift the aggregate demand curve to the right, as from AD_1 to AD_2, achieving a new short-run equilibrium at E_2. Since this brings employment above the full-employment level, wages will be bid up, resulting in a leftward shift in the aggregate supply curve from AS_1 to AS_2. The new long-run equilibrium is E_3, again at the full-employment level of output.

B. In the short run, both the price level and real output increase. After wages adjust to the increase in the price level and the aggregate supply shifts back to AS_2, real output returns to its original level of Y_f. However, the price level remains elevated because both the increase in AD and the decrease in AS result in an increase in the price level. Employment will exceed the full-employment level in the short run, meaning that unemployment will fall below its "natural" rate. Since real output is unchanged in the long run, there is no long-run effect on employment.

C. Since the price level rises, the purchasing power of currency and forthcoming fixed amounts of money falls. This hurts anyone holding significant amounts of cash, receiving a fixed income, or receiving fixed interest on loans or savings. Any change in prices also hurts businesses that must adjust price lists, menus, and the like. The increase in the price level helps those who must pay fixed amounts of money as interest, salary, or loan repayment because the value of these payments in terms of purchasing power has decreased.

An average response:

A. As illustrated in Figure 1, the economy begins at equilibrium E_1. Expansionary fiscal policy will shift the aggregate demand curve to the right, as from AD_1 to AD_2, achieving a new short-run equilibrium at E_2. Low unemployment will cause wages to increase and shift the aggregate supply curve from AS_1 to AS_2. The new long-run equilibrium is E_3.

B. The price level certainly increases because both the increase in AD and the decrease in AS increase the price level. Employment will increase in the short run, but since real output is unchanged in the long run, there is no long-run effect on employment.

C. An increase in prices hurts those holding cash or earning fixed incomes or interest rates. An increase in prices helps those who must make fixed interest payments.

A poor response:

A. The demand curve shifts as in Figure 1. The long run will be different from the short run because the effects set in more.

B. Output will increase, prices will increase, and employment will increase. In the long run these effects will be the same but larger.

C. When the price goes up, people have to pay more so they are hurt, while businesses get more so they like it.

Chapter 21

THE PRINCETON REVIEW
GSE ECONOMICS
PRACTICE TEST II

PART I: MULTIPLE-CHOICE QUESTIONS

You will have 45 minutes to complete the multiple-choice section of this exam. For each question, please indicate the best response out of the four provided.

1. Which of the following is dealt with primarily in macroeconomics?

   I. Individual decision making

   II. The determinants of real GDP

   III. The pricing decision of a firm

   IV. The causes of inflation

   V. Solutions to unemployment

   A. I and III only

   B. II, IV, and V only

   C. II only

   D. IV and V only

2. Which of the following schools of thought most favors active fiscal and monetary policy to bring about desired economic goals?

   A. Classical

   B. Laissez-faire

   C. Keynesian

   D. Monetarist

3. Which of the following provides the strongest incentive to conserve and improve scarce resources?

   A. Public ownership of waterways

   B. Private property ownership

   C. Permits for the commercial removal of lumber from national parks

   D. The tragedy of the commons

4. Suppose Clark's income went from $50,000 to $100,000 and at the same time the average price level tripled. Which of the following statements is correct?

   A. Clark's real income increased and his nominal income decreased.

   B. Clark's real income and nominal income both decreased.

   C. Clark's real income and nominal income both increased.

   D. Clark's nominal income increased and his real income decreased.

5. Capital is a

   A. factor of production.

   B. final good.

   C. unit of account.

   D. resource used mostly in capitalist economic systems.

6. If supply increases and price stays the same, the result is

   A. a surplus.

   B. a price ceiling.

   C. deflation.

   D. a shortage.

Wallets

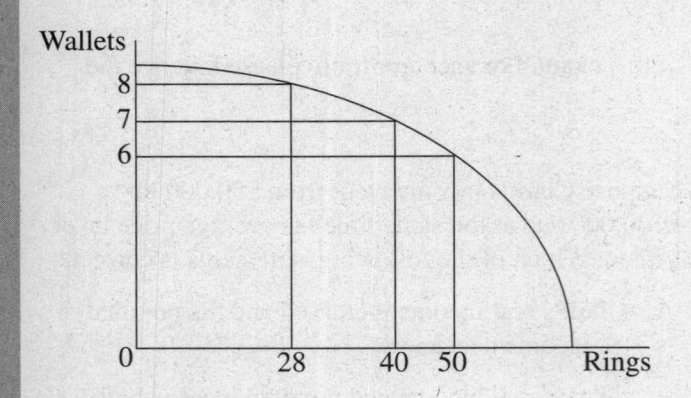

[graph showing PPC with values 8, 7, 6 on wallets axis and 28, 40, 50 on Rings axis]

7. On the basis of the diagram above, the opportunity cost of producing the seventh wallet is

   A. 50 rings.
   B. 40 rings.
   C. 12 rings.
   D. 10 rings.

8. Suppose that in the same period the incomes of Frisbee purchasers increase and there is improvement in the technology for their production? Which of the following statements most accurately summarizes the effect on equilibrium price and quantity?

   A. The price of Frisbees might increase or decrease and the quantity will certainly increase.
   B. The price and quantity of Frisbees will both increase with certainty.
   C. The price of Frisbees will increase and the quantity might increase or decrease.
   D. The price will increase and the quantity will decrease with certainty.

9. Assuming perfect information, perfect competition, no externalities, and no public goods, a market system filled with individuals acting in their own self-interest will most likely lead to

   A. famine.
   B. excess production.
   C. socially optimal outcomes.
   D. excess consumption.

10. The least complex and most common form of business organization is a

    A. partnership.
    B. sole proprietorship.
    C. corporation.
    D. industry.

11. If the labor supply curve facing a firm is horizontal and the price of the good that the firm produces increases, which of the following will result?

    A. Wages paid by the firm will increase.
    B. The number of workers hired by the firm will increase.
    C. Wages paid by the firm will decrease.
    D. The number of workers hired by the firm will decrease.

12. If Bill Gates received all of the income in the U.S., the Gini coefficient would be

    A. 0.
    B. −1.
    C. 1.
    D. 100.

13. An oligopoly is a market structure involving

    A. a large number of firms selling a homogeneous product.
    B. a single seller selling a unique product.
    C. many firms selling differentiated products.
    D. a small number of firms selling a standardized or differentiated product

14. The market basket of goods and services used to compute the consumer price index is based on

    A. base year quantities of goods and services purchased.
    B. current year quantities of goods and services purchased.
    C. the quantities of goods and services purchased in 1970.
    D. an estimate of the goods and services that will be purchased in the year 2002.

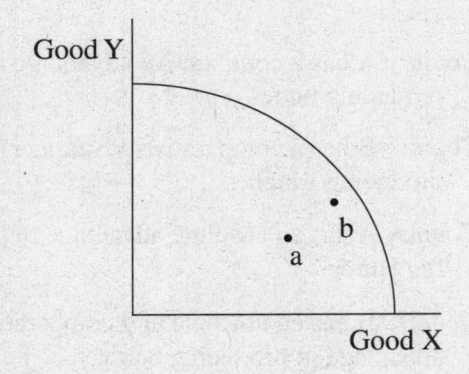

15. Movement from point a to point b in the above graph represents

    A. a decrease in the GDP.
    B. a decrease in the CPI.
    C. a decrease in efficiency.
    D. economic growth.

16. The direct effect of an improvement in technology that decreases the cost of producing many types of goods will be a(n)

    A. increase in aggregate demand.
    B. increase in aggregate supply.
    C. decrease in aggregate demand.
    D. decrease in aggregate supply.

17. Expansionary fiscal policy is most likely to reduce which of the following?

    A. Unemployment
    B. Inflation
    C. Interest rates
    D. Real output

18. The national debt is

    A. the same thing as the federal budget deficit.
    B. smaller than the federal budget deficit.
    C. the total amount that the federal government owes at a given time.
    D. between $1,000,000,000 and $25,000,000,000.

19. The discount rate and the reserve requirement are manipulated by

    A. entrepreneurs.
    B. firms.
    C. the Fed.
    D. corporate bankers.

20. Which of the following is not a function of the Federal Reserve System?

    A. It backs all U.S. currency with gold.
    B. It is a lender of last resort for banks.
    C. It sets the discount rate.
    D. It sets the required reserve ratio.

21. Which of the following types of economic systems has the most centralized decision making?

    A. Traditional
    B. Command
    C. Free Market
    D. Laissez-faire

22. Workers who are temporarily between jobs because they are moving to a new location or occupation where they will be more productive are considered

    A. seasonally unemployed.
    B. structurally unemployed.
    C. frictionally unemployed.
    D. cyclically unemployed.

23. Inflation helps those

    A. with fixed incomes.
    B. who lend at fixed interest rates.
    C. who borrow at fixed interest rates.
    D. who lend at variable interest rates.

24. Which of the following is the least likely to be included among arguments for protectionism?

    A. Competition promotes efficiency and innovation.
    B. Infant industries need a boost in the beginning.
    C. Excess dependence on other nations can be a problem.
    D. Intranational trade leads to a loss of jobs domestically.

25. Which of the following would cause the U.S. dollar to appreciate relative to the French franc?

    A. An increase in U.S. imports of French goods
    B. A decrease in U.S. exports to France
    C. An increase in the supply of dollars
    D. Expectations that the dollar will appreciate

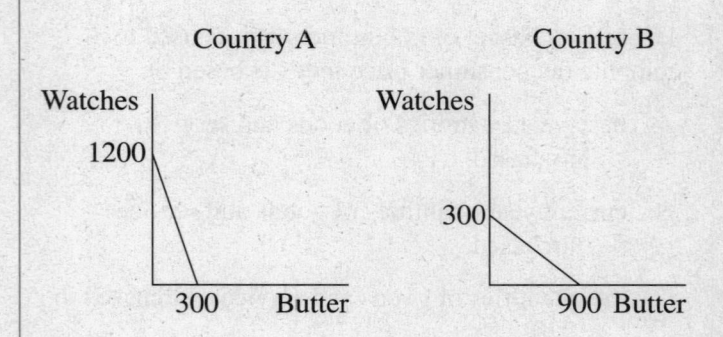

26. Countries A and B have the same resources and their simplified production possibilities curves are illustrated above. Which of the following statements is true?

    A. Country A has a comparative advantage in producing butter.
    B. Country B has a comparative advantage in producing watches.
    C. Country A has an absolute advantage in producing butter.
    D. Country B has an absolute and comparative advantage in producing butter.

27. Trade between two countries

    A. always helps one country and hurts the other.
    B. is often beneficial to both countries.
    C. is never necessary to maximize the welfare of the societies involved.
    D. improves the standard of living in the smaller country at the expense of the larger country.

28. A quota is

    A. another name for a tariff.

    B. a limit on the imports that can enter a nation.

    C. a unit of currency in Western Europe.

    D. what economists call an equilibrium in the labor market.

29. The term "price taker" refers to firms in which of the following types of market structures?

    A. Monopoly

    B. Oligopoly

    C. Monopolistic competition

    D. Perfect competition

30. Inflation is most likely to be caused by

    A. an increase in aggregate supply.

    B. a decrease in aggregate demand.

    C. a decrease in aggregate supply.

    D. a decrease in government spending.

PART II: ESSAY QUESTIONS

The essay questions will allow you to demonstrate your graphing and analytical skills. You will have 45 minutes in which to write two essays. Your teacher will notify you when 20 minutes have passed.

Directions:

1. Read each of the essay topics carefully.

2. Organize your thoughts before you start writing. You may want to outline your essays or experiment with a few graphs first. You may write notes and practice diagrams on the test booklet. Only writing on the lined pages of the answer sheet will be scored.

3. Write your essays on the appropriate pages of the answer sheet.

4. The two essays receive equal credit, and you must write both essays to receive full credit. Allow yourself sufficient time to write each essay—an equal division of time would give you 22.5 minutes for each one.

5. Be sure to draw the relevant graphs, be specific, and use economic concepts, terms, and policies to reinforce your reasoning.

6. Don't waste time going off on tangents. Rather, address the given topic with well-supported responses.

1) Topic:

Popularity of Ally Mcbeal boosts the number of lawyers

Answer the questions below in an essay that employs economic concepts, reasoning, and supply and demand graphs.

A. Using a supply and demand graph, explain how the increase in the number of lawyers will affect the market for legal services immediately and in the longer term.

B. What impact will this popularity have on law school tuition and enrollment?

C. Explain how some groups benefit and some groups are harmed by the popularity of the show.

2) Topic:

Global warming takes a permanent bite out of natural resource availability

Answer the questions below in an essay that employs economic concepts, reasoning, and an aggregate supply/aggregate demand graph.

A. Using an aggregate supply/aggregate demand graph, explain the short run and long run effects of this problem.

B. What are the likely short run and long run effects on real GDP, employment, and the price level?

C. Explain what policies could help counteract the problems with global warming.

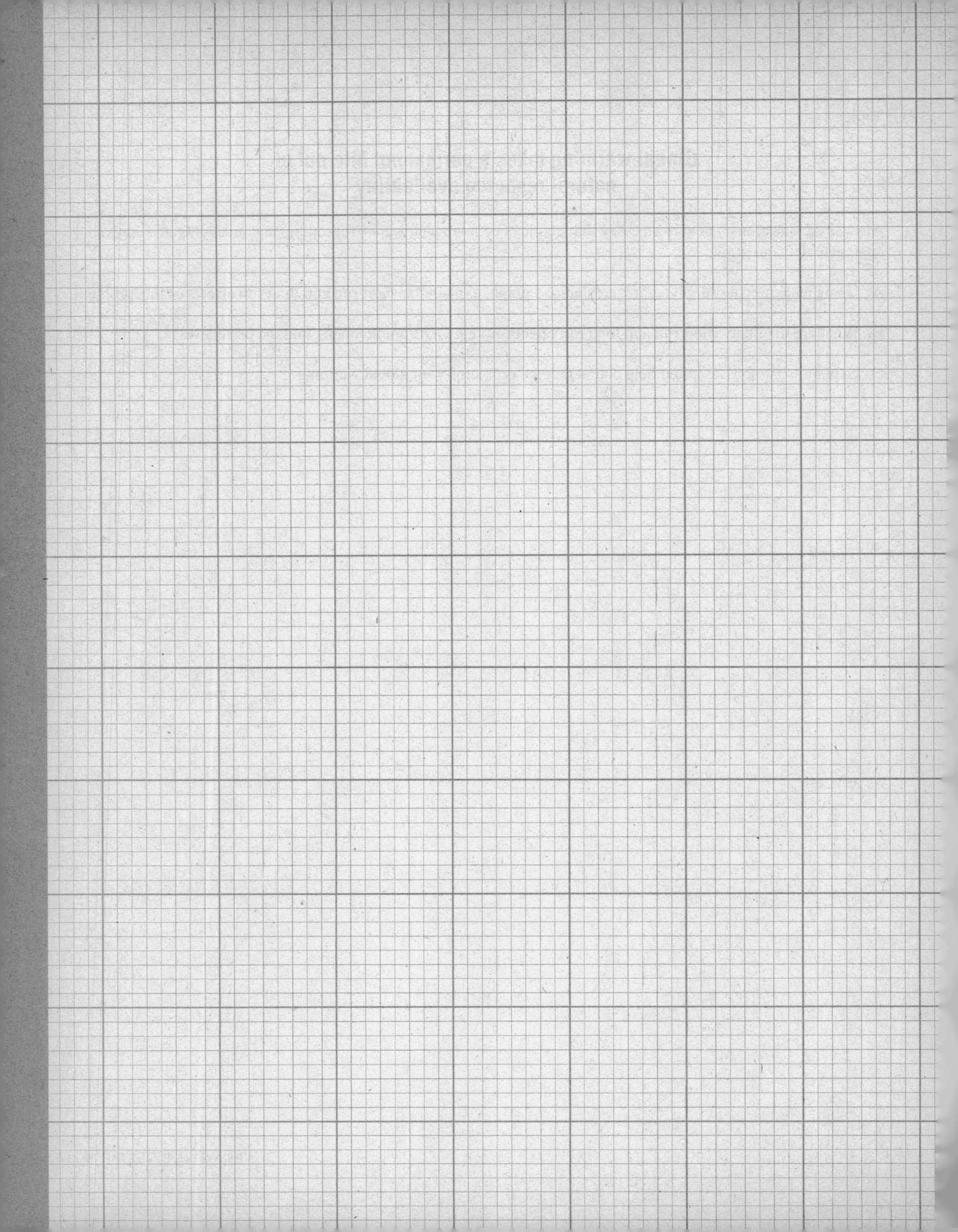

The Princeton Review

YOUR NAME: _____
(Print)   Last   First   M.I.

SIGNATURE: _____ DATE: __/__/__

HOME ADDRESS: _____
(Print)   Number and Street

_____
City   State   Zip Code

PHONE NO.: _____
(Print)

Completely darken bubbles with a No. 2 pencil. If you make a mistake, be sure to erase mark completely. Erase all stray marks.

Practice Test II

1. Ⓐ Ⓑ Ⓒ Ⓓ   16. Ⓐ Ⓑ Ⓒ Ⓓ
2. Ⓐ Ⓑ Ⓒ Ⓓ   17. Ⓐ Ⓑ Ⓒ Ⓓ
3. Ⓐ Ⓑ Ⓒ Ⓓ   18. Ⓐ Ⓑ Ⓒ Ⓓ
4. Ⓐ Ⓑ Ⓒ Ⓓ   19. Ⓐ Ⓑ Ⓒ Ⓓ
5. Ⓐ Ⓑ Ⓒ Ⓓ   20. Ⓐ Ⓑ Ⓒ Ⓓ
6. Ⓐ Ⓑ Ⓒ Ⓓ   21. Ⓐ Ⓑ Ⓒ Ⓓ
7. Ⓐ Ⓑ Ⓒ Ⓓ   22. Ⓐ Ⓑ Ⓒ Ⓓ
8. Ⓐ Ⓑ Ⓒ Ⓓ   23. Ⓐ Ⓑ Ⓒ Ⓓ
9. Ⓐ Ⓑ Ⓒ Ⓓ   24. Ⓐ Ⓑ Ⓒ Ⓓ
10. Ⓐ Ⓑ Ⓒ Ⓓ   25. Ⓐ Ⓑ Ⓒ Ⓓ
11. Ⓐ Ⓑ Ⓒ Ⓓ   26. Ⓐ Ⓑ Ⓒ Ⓓ
12. Ⓐ Ⓑ Ⓒ Ⓓ   27. Ⓐ Ⓑ Ⓒ Ⓓ
13. Ⓐ Ⓑ Ⓒ Ⓓ   28. Ⓐ Ⓑ Ⓒ Ⓓ
14. Ⓐ Ⓑ Ⓒ Ⓓ   29. Ⓐ Ⓑ Ⓒ Ⓓ
15. Ⓐ Ⓑ Ⓒ Ⓓ   30. Ⓐ Ⓑ Ⓒ Ⓓ

The Princeton Review

THE PRINCETON REVIEW GSE ECONOMICS PRACTICE TEST II

Multiple-Choice Answer Key

1	B	9	C	17	A	25	D
2	C	10	B	18	C	26	D
3	B	11	B	19	C	27	B
4	D	12	C	20	A	28	B
5	A	13	D	21	B	29	D
6	A	14	A	22	C	30	C
7	D	15	D	23	C		
8	A	16	B	24	A		

Part I: Multiple-Choice Explanations

1. B   Macroeconomics looks at the big picture and considers larger-scale economic phenomena, including the determinants of real GDP, inflation, unemployment, and interest rates. Microeconomics focuses on the behavior of individuals and firms.

2. C   Classical, laissez-faire, and monetarist schools generally criticize active government policy, whereas Keynesians advocate government assistance when the economy is misbehaving.

3. B   Private property ownership provides an incentive to conserve and improve scarce resources, including renewable and nonrenewable resources. This is because when an individual owns property, he or she is hurt by any actions that diminish the resources on that property. Thus, the individual has a personal interest in preserving and protecting the property. When resources are publicly owned, individuals can destroy resources with excessive mining, hunting, fishing, and so on, and then move on with no personal loss. This is sometimes called the tragedy of the commons.

4. D   Nominal income is the actual number of dollars received and real income is the purchasing power of those dollars. Clark is receiving twice as many dollars as before, so his nominal income increased. Since the number of dollars that he receives increased by less than the price level, he can now buy less with his money, so his real income decreased.

5. A   Capital is a factor of production, along with labor, land/natural resources, entrepreneurship and human capital. Capital includes equip-

ment, buildings, and other manufactured goods that can be used in the production process.

6. **A** A price ceiling prevents prices from rising, whereas in this case the price should fall. Also, a price ceiling is the reason, not the result, of price rigidity, so choice (B) is wrong. Deflation is the result of a sustained decrease in the overall price level, so even if the price for a particular good or service did decrease (which it did not here), this alone would not constitute deflation—eliminate (C). If supply increases and the price does not change, a surplus will result, as producers want to supply more than consumers want to purchase at the current price. So choice (A) is best.

7. **D** When wallet production increases from 6 to 7 units, ring production must decrease from 50 to 40 units. Production of the seventh wallet thus forces the society to forgo 10 rings.

8. **A** An increase in the income of Frisbee purchasers will shift the demand curve to the right, increasing the equilibrium price and quantity. Improvement in the technology for Frisbee production will shift the supply curve to the right, decreasing the equilibrium price and increasing the equilibrium quantity. Since each of these shifts increases the equilibrium quantity, the change in quantity is clearly positive. However, with the supply shift decreasing the equilibruim price and the demand shift increasing it, it is uncertain what will happen to price.

9. **C** One of the virtues of the market system is that in the absence of the sources of market failure (imperfect information, imperfect competition, public goods, and externalities), actions based on individual self interest are likely to result in socially optimal outcomes.

10. **B** In a proprietorship, one person owns and in a sense is the firm. This is the simplest and most common form of business organization.

11. **B** The demand for labor is derived from the demand for whatever labor produces. If the price of a firm's output increases, as would result from an increase in the demand for their good or service, the value of workers' contributions (their marginal revenue product) increases. This increases the demand for labor. With a horizontal labor supply curve, wages are unaffected by shifts in the labor demand curve. However, an increase in the output price will increase the labor demand (shift it to the right) and thereby increase the number of workers hired.

12. **C** The Gini coefficient is the ratio (a)/(a + b) where (a) is the area above the Lorenz curve and below the line of equality and (a + b) is all of the area below the line of equality. With one individual receiving all of the income, the Lorenz curve lies on the horizontal axis and there is no difference between (a) and (a + b). Since anything over the same thing is one, and the Gini coefficient in this case is the ratio of two equivalent areas, the Gini coefficient's value is one.

13. **D** An oligopoly is a market structure involving a small number of firms selling a standardized or differentiated product. Choices (A), (B), and (C) describe competitive, monopolistic, and monopolistically competitive market structures respectively.

14. **A** The current year's CPI is calculated as the cost of a market basket of goods and services in the current year divided by the cost of the same market basket of goods and services in a "base year." The quantities of goods and services included in the market basket are those purchased in the base year (currently an average of 1982–84).

15. **D** A movement outward toward the production possibilities curve represents an *increase* in GDP and efficiency, making choices (A) and (C) wrong. There is not a clear effect on the CPI, so you can eliminate (B). This graph shows one type of economic growth; the other is an expansion of the PPC.

16. **B** Widespread changes in the cost of production are reflected in the aggregate supply curve, which increases (shifts to the right) when production costs decrease and decreases when production costs increase.

17. **A** Expansionary fiscal policy will shift the aggregate demand curve to the right, thus increasing the price level and real output, so choices (B) and (D) are wrong. As the increase in purchases increases the demand for money, interest rates are also likely to rise—you can eliminate choice (C). The only thing among those listed that is likely to fall is unemployment, choice (A), as more workers are needed to produce the extra goods.

18. **C** The national debt is the accumulation of past federal budget deficits, and the total amount that the federal government owes at a given time. As of late 1999, the national debt was approaching $6,000,000,000,000.

19. **C** The discount rate and the reserve requirement are tools the Fed uses to make changes in the money supply and interest rates.

20. **A** Currency in the U.S. is no longer backed by gold as it was until 1933 when we had a "gold standard." Trust in our money is now based on faith in the stability of our government and economic system.

21. **B** A traditional economy is one in which economic and political power are determined by tradition. This would imply that it is neither market based nor centrally organized, so choice (A) is wrong. A free market or laissez-faire economy also has no centralized planning, which eliminates (C) and (D). At the other end of the spectrum, decisions for a command economy are made by a central planning bureau, making choice (B) the best answer.

22. **C** Since there is no indication that these workers lost or will gain employment with the change of the season, seasonal unemployment, choice (A), is not the best answer. Frictional unemployment occurs as workers and employers search for the optimal worker-job pairings, which is what the question described.

23. **C** Inflation makes the purchasing power of any fixed amount of money decrease. Thus, those with fixed incomes or lenders receiving fixed interest rates are hurt by inflation because the value of what they receive goes down—get rid of (A) and (B). Variable interest rates can be adjusted for inflation, thus keeping the purchasing power of the payments constant, so choice (D) is wrong. Inflation helps those who borrow at fixed interest rates because the value of the interest payments they make goes down, choice (C).

24. **A** Protectionism removes competition, and thus can deter efficiency and innovation. The infant industry, choice (B), and excess dependence, choice (C), arguments are common. Intranational trade is trade within a country, so it would not challenge jobs domestically, and you can eliminate choice (D).

25. **D** The first three choices will cause the dollar to depreciate. Expectations that the dollar will appreciate will lead people to demand more dollars, which increases the value of the dollar in terms of other currencies.

26. **D** A country is said to have an absolute advantage in the production of a good when it can produce that good using fewer resources per unit of output than another country. A country is said to have a comparative advantage in the production of a good when it can produce that good at a lower opportunity cost (a smaller loss in terms of the production

of another good) than another country. Since country B can produce more butter than country A with the same resources, and country B can produce butter at an opportunity cost of 1/3 watch per unit of butter as opposed to A's cost of 4 watches per unit of butter, B has both a comparative and an absolute advantage in butter production.

27. **B** Trade between two countries often benefits both countries involved. By each country producing what it makes most efficiently and trading for what it makes relatively inefficiently, everyone involved can come out better off. This is true regardless of size and other differences between the countries.

28. **B** A quota sets a strict and binding limit on the absolute amount of imports that can enter a nation.

29. **D** A perfectly competitive firm faces a horizontal demand curve, meaning that it can sell all that it wants at the market price. Since perfectly competitive firms are too small to affect the price themselves, they are called price takers. Firms in all of the other market structures face downward sloping demand curves and cannot sell all of the output they want at the market price.

30. **C** A decrease in aggregate supply will increase the price level and decrease real output. A sustained increase in the price level constitutes inflation. Each of the other possible answers would decrease the price level.

Part II: Essay Explanations

Topic I

Figure 1

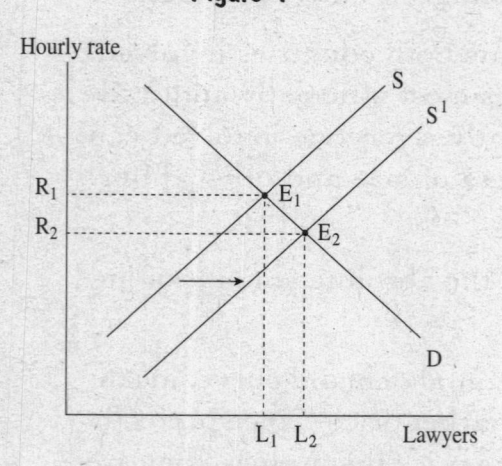

Hourly rate vs Lawyers; supply curve S shifts right to S¹, equilibrium moves from E₁ (R₁, L₁) down to E₂ (R₂, L₂).

Figure 2

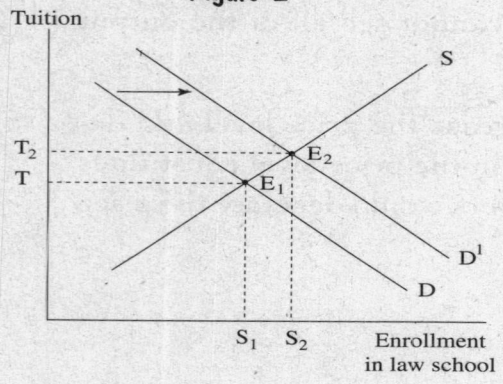

Tuition vs Enrollment in law school; demand curve D shifts right to D¹, equilibrium moves from E₁ (T₁, S₁) up to E₂ (T₂, S₂).

An excellent response:

A. The increased number of lawyers will result in more legal services being available at any given hourly rate. This shifts the supply curve for legal services to the right as illustrated in Figure 1. At the beginning hourly rate of R_1, a surplus of legal services will exist, leading to a decrease in the hourly rate. As the rate falls, the quantity demanded will increase and the quantity supplied will decrease. This process will continue until the quantity demanded equals the quantity supplied at a new equilibrium rate of R_2 and a new quantity of L_2.

B. The influx of new lawyers is likely to begin with an influx of new law students. The demand for legal education will increase, as students would like to purchase more education at any given tuition level. This shifts the demand curve for law school to the right as in Figure 2. The equilibrium tuition level will increase from T_1 to T_2, and the number of students enrolled will increase from S_1 to S_2.

C. Beneficiaries of the popularity of Ally McBeal include those seeking legal services and the employees of law schools. The increase in the supply of lawyers lowers the hourly rate paid by purchasers of legal services. Those who would have purchased them at the higher rate now enjoy a lower rate, and the rate cut enables some additional consumers to benefit, for whom legal services would not have been worthwhile at the higher rate. The consumer surplus for users of legal services increases by the area $R_1 R_2 E_2 E_1$ on Figure 1. At the same time, law schools enjoy higher enrollments and tuitions. They can hire more employees and their revenues will increase. Producer surplus for law schools increases by the area $T_2T_1E_1E_2$ in Figure 2.

Those harmed by Ally's appeal include lawyers previously working for R_1 and law students who would otherwise pay T_1. With the increase in the number of lawyers, those previously earning R_1 experience a rate cut of R_1 minus R_2 per hour of services provided. Students who would have paid T_1 experience a tuition hike of T_2 minus T_1.

An average response:

A. The increased number of lawyers will result in more legal services being available at any given hourly rate. This shifts the supply curve for legal services to the right as illustrated in Figure 1. The result is a new equilibrium rate of R_2 and a new quantity of L_2.

B. The demand for legal education will increase as the result of Ally's popularity. This shifts the demand curve for law school to the right as in Figure 2. The equilibrium tuition level will increase from T_1 to T_2, and the number of students enrolled will increase from S_1 to S_2.

C. Beneficiaries of the popularity of Ally McBeal include those seeking legal services and the employees of law schools. The increase in the supply of lawyers lowers the hourly rate paid by purchasers of legal services, while law schools enjoy higher enrollments and can charge higher tuition.

Those harmed by Ally's appeal include lawyers and law students. With the increase in the number of lawyers, lawyers now receive R_2 instead of R_1 per hour of services provided. Students who would have paid T_1 experience a tuition hike to T_2 instead.

A poor response:

A. This shifts the supply curve for legal services as illustrated in Figure 1. There are more lawyers around and there are probably too many. Some can't find work.

B. Schools will get more students, making tuition more expensive. Law schools are already pretty expensive. All my friends want to go to law school and it just makes it hard to get in.

C. The advertisers like it but people who want to watch sports and things on TV miss out. Lawyers don't like the competition but they like the attention. My mom likes Ally McBeal and my sister would rather watch something else so my mom's helped and my sister is hurt. The people helped also include people working at law schools.

Topic 2

Figure 1

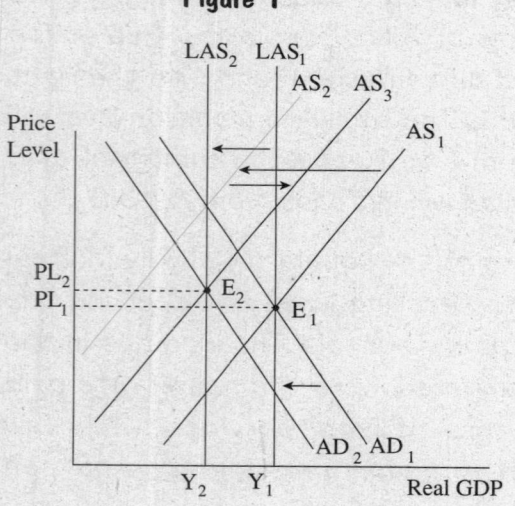

An excellent response:

A. As illustrated in Figure 1, the economy begins at equilibrium E_1 with output at the full-employment level Y_1. A decrease in resource availability will shift the short-run aggregate supply curve to the left, as from AS_1 to AS_2, as resources become more costly and difficult to obtain. The excessive heat will lower the incomes and wealth of a substantial number of resource providers and users, lowering aggregate demand from D_1 to D_2. Both the decrease in aggregate demand and the decrease in short-run aggregate supply result in employment levels below the full-employment level of output. The excess supply of labor will eventually lead to lower wages, shifting short-run aggregate supply out from S_2 to S_3 as labor costs fall. Since the decrease in resource availability is permanent, the long-run aggregate supply curve will shift to the left as from LAS_1 to LAS_2.

B. Both the net decrease in aggregate supply and the decrease in aggregate demand result in a lower real GDP in the short and long run. Employment will fall with real GDP in the short and long run, although it is somewhat unclear what happens to unemployment because the global warming might eliminate some of the labor force at the same time that employment is decreasing. (Indeed, even relatively short heat waves often result in the loss of human life.) The decrease in aggregate supply increases the price level, while the decrease in aggregate demand lowers the price level. The net effect depends on the relative sizes of the AS and AD shifts. As I have drawn it, the price level increases, but a relatively large AD shift would have the price level decreasing. With the second shift in aggregate supply, from AS_2 to AS_3, the price level comes down a bit to PL_2.

C. There are a number of possibilities here. Policies that tax or regulate pollution might reduce the global warming itself. For example, the government could impose strict guidelines on emissions and support international efforts to educate people about the long-term repercussions of their behaviors. Although it does not appear to be the primary problem, the government could counter the increased price level with contractionary monetary or fiscal policy. The long-run problem of decreased resource availability could be addressed with policies to invest in education and training, productivity-enhancing capital, and new, resource-saving technologies, all of which could improve real output levels in the long run.

An average response:

A. A decrease in resource availability will shift the short-run aggregate supply curve to the left, as from AS_1 to AS_2. Demand may also fall from D_1 to D_2. Both the decrease in aggregate demand and the decrease in short-run aggregate supply help bring employment levels below the full-employment level of output. The excess supply of labor will eventually lead to lower wages, shifting short-run aggregate supply out from S_2 to S_3. Since the decrease in resource availability is permanent, the long-run aggregate supply will remain low in the long run.

B. Employment will fall with real GDP in the short and long run as a result of the decreases in AS and AD. The decrease in aggregate supply increases the price level, while the decrease in aggregate demand lowers the price level. As I have drawn it, the price level increases.

C. Policies that tax or regulate pollution might reduce the global warming itself. The long-run problem of decreased resource availability could be addressed with policies to improve real output levels in the long run, like better technology.

A poor response:

A. The supply curve shifts as in Figure 1. The long-run effect will be worse than the short-run effect.

B. Output will decrease, prices will increase, and employment will decrease. With fewer resources there is little we can do and productivity is damaged.

C. We would need to try to boost the economy. Tax cuts or encouragement are some of the incentives we could give people to make more.

Chapter 22

THE PRINCETON REVIEW GSE ECONOMICS PRACTICE TEST III

PART I: MULTIPLE-CHOICE QUESTIONS

You will have 45 minutes to complete the multiple-choice section of this exam. For each question, please indicate the best response out of the four provided.

1. Economics focuses on reconciling
   A. limited wants with unlimited resources.
   B. abundant supply with adequate demand.
   C. scarce resources with unlimited desires.
   D. low prices with inadequate interest.

2. The opening of a new business involves a great deal of risk. For this reason, new businesses require
   A. labor.
   B. capital.
   C. entrepreneurs.
   D. human capital.

3. Efficiency is achieved when production is continued until
   A. the marginal cost equals the marginal benefit.
   B. the total cost equals the total benefit.
   C. the average cost equals the average benefit.
   D. the total variable cost equals the total benefit.

4. Since the third employee hired at Buy-A-Bagel allows the workers to become proficient at specialized tasks, she increases the bagel output by more than the second worker does. However, the fourth worker mostly gets in the way and increases bagel output by less than the third worker. With the third and fourth worker, respectively, Buy-A-Bagel experiences
   A. increasing and then decreasing total product.
   B. increasing and then decreasing marginal returns.
   C. the law of diminishing marginal returns in both cases.
   D. positive and then negative marginal returns.

5. Which of the following is best classified as an output?
   A. Entrepreneurship
   B. Land
   C. Labor
   D. Luggage

6. The law of supply says that
   A. as price increases, fewer consumers will want to buy a good.
   B. as price decreases, shortages are inevitable.
   C. as price increases, the quantity supplied will increase.
   D. as price decreases, firms will be asked to supply more.

7. Opportunity cost is
   A. the cost premium placed on new opportunities such as space travel or debut albums.
   B. the value of the best alternative to what actually takes place.
   C. the cost of materials used in the production process.
   D. the cost of the inputs that need not increase as output increases.

8. Which of the following is most likely to shift the supply curve for grapes to the left?
   A. an infestation of grape-eating insects.
   B. a boycott of grapes.
   C. good weather for growing grapes throughout the season.
   D. a successful advertising campaign for grapes.

9. The sources of market failure include all of the following except

   A. imperfect competition.
   B. diminishing marginal utility.
   C. public goods.
   D. externalities.

10. Which form of business organization rests on a legal charter and establishes the business as an entity separate from the owners?

    A. Proprietorship
    B. Industry
    C. Partnership
    D. Corporation

11. A firm's labor demand curve is the same as its

    A. marginal cost curve.
    B. marginal product curve.
    C. marginal revenue curve.
    D. marginal revenue product curve.

12. What is the value of the Gini coefficient if all income is distributed equally?

    A. 0
    B. 1
    C. 1/2
    D. 100

13. Under perfect competition, long-run economic profits are

    A. zero.
    B. positive.
    C. negative.
    D. zero or positive.

14. If Martha Stewart (a U.S. citizen) makes a cake in England and sells it to the queen, the sale of her cake would be included in

    A. U.S. GDP.
    B. England's GDP.
    C. the U.S. CPI.
    D. England's Lorenz curve.

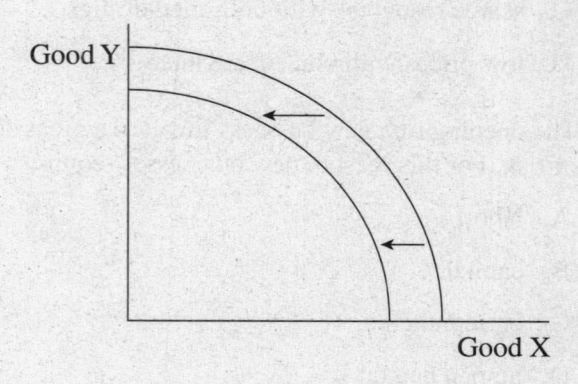

15. A shift in the PPC as indicated in the above graph is most likely to result from

    A. an increase in inflation.
    B. expansionary fiscal policy.
    C. a previous decline in investment in capital goods.
    D. a less efficient use of existing resources.

16. An increase in the price level combined with a decrease in real output can result from which of the following?

    A. A shift in the aggregate supply curve to the right
    B. A shift in the aggregate demand curve to the right
    C. A shift in the aggregate supply curve to the left
    D. A shift in the aggregate demand curve to the left

17. Fiscal policy is carried out by changing any of the following except:

    A. The money supply
    B. Transfer payments
    C. Taxes
    D. Government purchases

18. Which of the following is not a drawback to balancing the federal budget on a yearly basis?

    A. It is procyclical.
    B. It makes economic fluctuations worse.
    C. It limits fiscal policy.
    D. It increases the national debt.

19. Which of the following constitutes expansionary monetary policy?

    A. The Fed sells bonds.
    B. The Fed lowers the discount rate.
    C. The government raises taxes.
    D. The government increases its purchases of goods and services.

20. A U.S. dollar is all of the following except:

    A. Commodity money
    B. A store of value
    C. A medium of exchange
    D. A standard unit of value

21. Socialism is an example of which of the following types of economies?

    A. Traditional
    B. Command
    C. Free Market
    D. Laissez-faire

22. Autoworkers who lose their jobs during a recession experience

    A. seasonal unemployment.
    B. structural unemployment.
    C. frictional unemployment.
    D. cyclical unemployment.

23. A decrease in the discount rate will

    A. increase the interest rate.
    B. increase the money supply.
    C. decrease lending by banks.
    D. decrease the required reserve ratio.

24. Tariffs and quotas are most likely to

    A. limit intranational trade.
    B. avoid protectionism.
    C. increase domestic prices.
    D. increase the efficiency of domestic industries.

25. If the international demand for U.S. goods increases,

    A. the value of foreign currencies will appreciate.
    B. the price level in the U.S. will decrease.
    C. the dollar will appreciate in value relative to other currencies.
    D. import quotas should be set in place by the U.S.

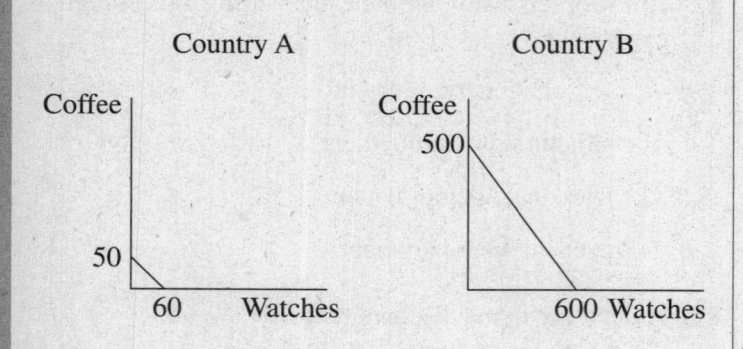

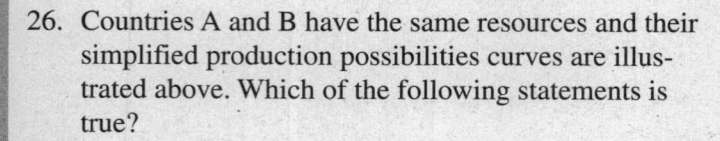

26. Countries A and B have the same resources and their simplified production possibilities curves are illustrated above. Which of the following statements is true?

   A. Country A gives up 6 watches for every 5 units of coffee it produces.

   B. Country B gives up 6 units of coffee for every 5 watches it produces.

   C. Country A has an absolute advantage in making coffee.

   D. Country B has a comparative advantage in making watches.

27. When the value of the merchandise we import exceeds the value of the merchandise we export, the difference between these two values constitutes a(n)

   A. trade surplus.

   B. budget deficit.

   C. trade deficit.

   D. increase in the national debt.

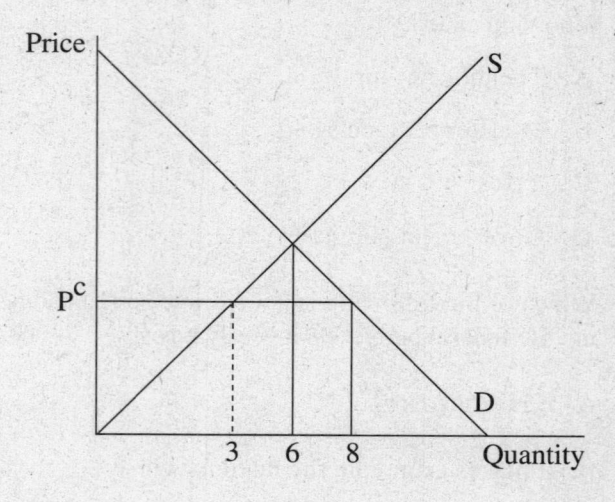

28. If the government imposes a price ceiling of P_c as illustrated in the above graph, the result would be

   A. a shortage of 2.

   B. a surplus of 5.

   C. a shortage of 3.

   D. a shortage of 5.

29. An oligopoly

   A. has eight firms.

   B. involves substantial barriers to entry and market power.

   C. has one firm.

   D. is governed by a political oligarchy.

30. Which of the following is the most likely to increase as the quantity of widgets produced and consumed increases?

   A. The marginal utility derived from widgets

   B. The opportunity cost of producing widgets

   C. The marginal revenue received from widget sales

   D. The average fixed cost of widget production

PART II: ESSAY QUESTIONS

The essay questions will allow you to demonstrate your graphing and analytical skills. You will have 45 minutes in which to write two essays. Your teacher will notify you when 20 minutes have passed.

Directions:

1. Read each of the essay topics carefully.

2. Organize your thoughts before you start writing. You may want to outline your essays or experiment with a few graphs first. You may write notes and practice diagrams on the test booklet. Only writing on the lined pages of the answer sheet will be scored.

3. Write your essays on the appropriate pages of the answer sheet.

4. The two essays receive equal credit, and you must write both essays to receive full credit. Allow yourself sufficient time to write each essay—an equal division of time would give you 22.5 minutes for each one.

5. Be sure to draw the relevant graphs, be specific, and use economic concepts, terms, and policies to reinforce your reasoning.

6. Don't waste time going off on tangents. Rather, address the given topic with well-supported responses.

1) Topic:

Surfer music increases surfboard sales

Answer the questions below in an essay that employs economic concepts, reasoning, and supply and demand graphs.

A. Using a supply and demand graph, explain how consumers' new interest in surfing will affect the surfboard market.

B. What other markets might be helped by the increase in surfboard sales? Explain.

C. What other markets might be hurt by the increase in surfboard sales? Explain.

2) Topic:

Dollar stronger, domestic sales hard hit

Answer the questions below in an essay that employs economic concepts, reasoning, and an aggregate supply/aggregate demand graph. For simplicity, please ignore the effects the stronger dollar might have on *inputs* purchased abroad.

A. Using an aggregate demand/aggregate supply graph, explain the short-run and long-run effects of this decrease in the purchase of U.S. goods and services.

B. What are the likely short-run and long-run effects on real GDP, employment, and the price level?

C. Give examples of those who would be harmed and helped by the resulting change in the price level.

The Princeton Review

YOUR NAME: _____
(Print)   Last   First   M.I.

SIGNATURE: _____ **DATE:** ___/___/___

HOME ADDRESS: _____
(Print)   Number and Street

_____
City   State   Zip Code

PHONE NO.: _____
(Print)

Completely darken bubbles with a No. 2 pencil. If you make a mistake, be sure to erase mark completely. Erase all stray marks.

Practice Test III

1. Ⓐ Ⓑ Ⓒ Ⓓ
2. Ⓐ Ⓑ Ⓒ Ⓓ
3. Ⓐ Ⓑ Ⓒ Ⓓ
4. Ⓐ Ⓑ Ⓒ Ⓓ
5. Ⓐ Ⓑ Ⓒ Ⓓ
6. Ⓐ Ⓑ Ⓒ Ⓓ
7. Ⓐ Ⓑ Ⓒ Ⓓ
8. Ⓐ Ⓑ Ⓒ Ⓓ
9. Ⓐ Ⓑ Ⓒ Ⓓ
10. Ⓐ Ⓑ Ⓒ Ⓓ
11. Ⓐ Ⓑ Ⓒ Ⓓ
12. Ⓐ Ⓑ Ⓒ Ⓓ
13. Ⓐ Ⓑ Ⓒ Ⓓ
14. Ⓐ Ⓑ Ⓒ Ⓓ
15. Ⓐ Ⓑ Ⓒ Ⓓ
16. Ⓐ Ⓑ Ⓒ Ⓓ
17. Ⓐ Ⓑ Ⓒ Ⓓ
18. Ⓐ Ⓑ Ⓒ Ⓓ
19. Ⓐ Ⓑ Ⓒ Ⓓ
20. Ⓐ Ⓑ Ⓒ Ⓓ
21. Ⓐ Ⓑ Ⓒ Ⓓ
22. Ⓐ Ⓑ Ⓒ Ⓓ
23. Ⓐ Ⓑ Ⓒ Ⓓ
24. Ⓐ Ⓑ Ⓒ Ⓓ
25. Ⓐ Ⓑ Ⓒ Ⓓ
26. Ⓐ Ⓑ Ⓒ Ⓓ
27. Ⓐ Ⓑ Ⓒ Ⓓ
28. Ⓐ Ⓑ Ⓒ Ⓓ
29. Ⓐ Ⓑ Ⓒ Ⓓ
30. Ⓐ Ⓑ Ⓒ Ⓓ

THE PRINCETON REVIEW GSE ECONOMICS PRACTICE TEST III

Multiple-Choice Answer Key

1	C	9	B	17	A	25	C
2	C	10	D	18	D	26	A
3	A	11	D	19	B	27	C
4	B	12	A	20	A	28	D
5	D	13	A	21	B	29	B
6	C	14	B	22	D	30	B
7	B	15	C	23	B		
8	A	16	C	24	C		

Part I: Multiple-Choice Explanations

1. **C** Economics is the allocation of scarce resources in the presence of unlimited desires.

2. **C** It is entrepreneurs who bring the willingness to accept risk in the pursuit of rewards. Without entrepreneurs, there would not be opportunities for the other inputs—labor, capital, land, and human capital—to come together to form output.

3. **A** Efficiency is achieved when production (like any other activity) is continued until the marginal cost equals the marginal benefit. Lower production levels would fail to take advantage of opportunities to produce units for which the added cost is less than the added benefit; higher production levels necessitate the production of units that add more to costs than to benefits.

4. **B** The law of diminishing marginal returns states that as the amount of one input is increased, holding the amounts of all other inputs constant, the incremental gains in output ("marginal returns") will eventually decrease. Buy-A-Bagel experiences increasing marginal returns with the third worker, but then the law of diminishing marginal returns sets in with the fourth worker. Since both the third and the fourth worker increase total output, there are neither negative marginal returns nor (equivalently) a decrease in total product.

5. **D** The typical inputs are entrepreneurship, land, labor, capital, and human capital. These would be used to make outputs like luggage.

6. **C** The law of supply says that as price increases, the quantity supplied will increase (and vice versa). The other answer choices all involve the demand of consumers, which is separate from the law of supply.

7. **B** Opportunity cost is the value of the best alternative to what actually takes place. The opportunity cost of your reading this book might be that you can't watch TV instead. (You made a good choice.)

8. **A** If insects eat some of the grape supply, fewer grapes will be supplied at any given price, shifting the supply curve to the left. A grape boycott would shift the demand curve to the left. Good growing weather would shift the supply curve to the right. A successful advertising campaign would shift the demand curve to the right.

9. **B** The sources of market failure are imperfect competition, imperfect information, public goods, and externalities. Diminishing marginal utility will exist even in a successful market.

10. **D** This describes a corporation. The separation between the owners and the corporation limits the liability of the owners to the amounts of their own investments. In partnerships and proprietorships, the owners are liable for all of the firm's debts. An industry is a collection of firms.

11. **D** The marginal revenue product curve indicates the additional revenue gained from each additional worker's contribution to output. Thus, it indicates the most a firm would be willing to pay for each additional worker. This is also the definition of the firm's labor demand curve.

12. **A** The Gini coefficient is the ratio (a)/(a + b) where (a) is the area above the Lorenz curve and below the line of equality and (a + b) is all of the area below the line of equality. With perfect equality, the Lorenz curve is directly over the line of equality, so (a) is zero. Since the area under the line of equality is not zero, the Gini coefficient in this case will be zero over a non-zero number, which is always zero

13. **A** Under perfect competition, the lack of barriers to entry mean that new firms will enter until economic profits are competed away. In the long run, competitive firms will earn zero economic profits.

14. **B** The gross domestic product (GDP) for a country includes the value of all final goods and services produced within that country. Since Martha made the cake in England, it would be part of England's GDP,

not that of the U.S., so choice (A) is wrong. The U.S. consumer price index (CPI), choice (C), is a measure of prices in the U.S., and England's Lorenz curve, choice (D), is a measure of the income dispersion among English families, so neither applies to Martha's sale.

15. **C** An increase in inflation has no real effects on the economy in the long run, and can have positive or negative effects on output in the short run, so choice (A) is wrong. Expansionary fiscal policy should increase output if anything; eliminate choice (B). A less efficient use of existing resources would result in a movement toward the origin within a given PPC, so you can get rid of (D). The correct answer is that a previous decline in investment in capital goods is likely shift the PPC inward because with less capital, other inputs such as labor will be less productive.

16. **C** When the aggregate supply curve shifts to the left, the new equilibrium occurs at a higher price level and a lower level of real GDP.

17. **A** Fiscal policy involves changes in transfer payments, taxes, or government purchases. Changes in the money supply constitute monetary policy.

18. **D** Although a balanced budget is often a good thing, there are drawbacks to balancing the budget every year. Because tax revenues increase in years when the economy is strong, a balanced budget would imply increases in government expenditures to balance the increased tax revenues. This pro-cyclical practice of the government spending more when the economy is strong and spending less when the economy is weak will exaggerate peaks and troughs in the business cycle. Limiting government spending to the amount of taxes collected also places undesirable constraints on fiscal policy. Since the national debt is an accumulation of past deficits, to balance the budget is to curtail growth in the debt.

19. **B** Selling bonds is a form of contractionary monetary policy because when the bonds are sold, money is taken in by the Fed, thus contracting the money supply, so you can eliminate choice (A). By lowering the discount rate, the Fed makes it easier for banks to borrow funds and in turn lend them out—increasing the money supply. Changes in taxes, choice (C), and government spending, choice (D), constitute fiscal policy.

20. **A** Commodity money has value beyond its usefulness as money. Examples of commodity money include coins made of precious metals, cigarettes used as money in prisons, and shells and arrowheads used as money in the past. Today, most of our money is fiat money, meaning that it has no intrinsic value.

21. **B** Under socialism, the state owns capital and natural resources, and central planners answer the questions of what, how, and for whom to produce by command.

22. **D** A recession is a downturn in the business cycle during which aggregate output declines for two consecutive quarters. Unemployment caused by downturns in the business cycle is called cyclical unemployment.

23. **B** The discount rate is the interest rate the Fed charges when it loans money to banks. When the discount rate goes down, banks tend to decrease their interest rates and increase their lending. An increase in lending promotes the money creation process and increases the money supply. Changes in the discount rate do not result in changes in the required reserve ratio.

24. **C** Tariffs and quotas are typically used to hinder international trade. They are a form of protectionism. By reducing competition from other countries, tariffs and quotas increase domestic prices and decrease the efficiency of domestic industries.

25. **C** To purchase more U.S. goods, consumers from other nations will demand more U.S. dollars. An increase in the demand for dollars will increase the dollar's value relative to other currencies. The value of foreign currencies will thus depreciate, so choice (A) is incorrect. If the increase in exports is large enough to have any effect on the U.S. price level, it will *increase* the price level—get rid of choice (B). Import quotas would not be appropriate when exports of U.S. goods are increasing because they do not apply to exports, and exports are generally considered to be a good thing, so you know that choice (D) is wrong.

26. **A** A country is said to have an absolute advantage in the production of a good when it can produce that good using fewer resources per unit of output than another country. A country is said to have a comparative advantage in the production of a good when it can produce that good at a lower opportunity cost (a smaller loss in terms of the production

of another good) than another country. Since both countries give up six watches for every five units of coffee they produce, neither country has a comparative advantage in either good. Country B can produce more of both using the same resources, so it has an absolute advantage in both goods.

27. **C** A trade deficit exists when merchandise imports exceed exports. When exports exceed imports, this is a trade surplus, choice (A). Budget deficits, choice (B), and the national debt, choice (D), are determined by the size of government expenditures relative to tax collections.

28. **D** At price P_c, the quantity demanded would be 8 and the quantity supplied would be 3, resulting in a shortage of 5.

29. **B** An oligopoly involves a small number of firms selling a standardized or differentiated product. Barriers to entry are high and market power (the ability of an individual firm to influence price) is substantial.

30. **B** As more widgets are produced, the opportunity cost of producing widgets increases. Initially resources that are the most productive for creating widgets are employed for that purpose, but as more and more widgets are produced, resources less and less specialized for widget production must be employed. As resources that are better for making other goods are used to make widgets, we must forgo increasing amounts of other goods for every incremental change in widget production. This represents an increasing opportunity cost for widgets. The other answer choices can be expected to decrease or remain the same as production and consumption increases.

Part II: Essay Explanations

Topic 1

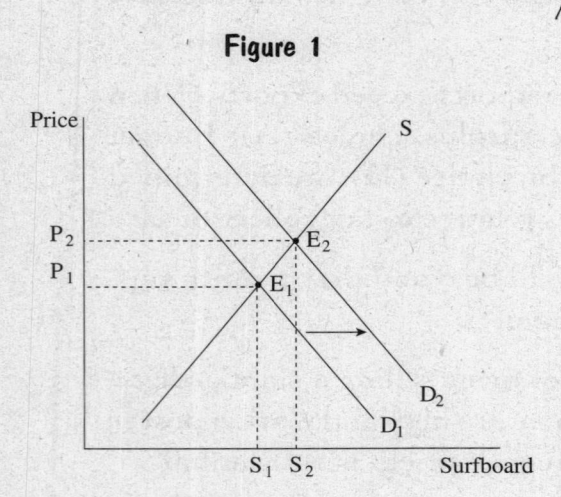

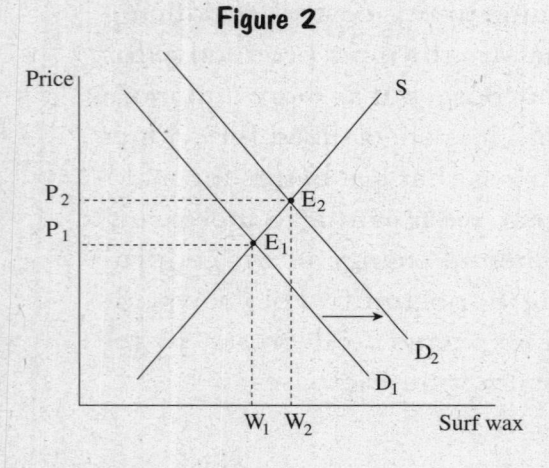

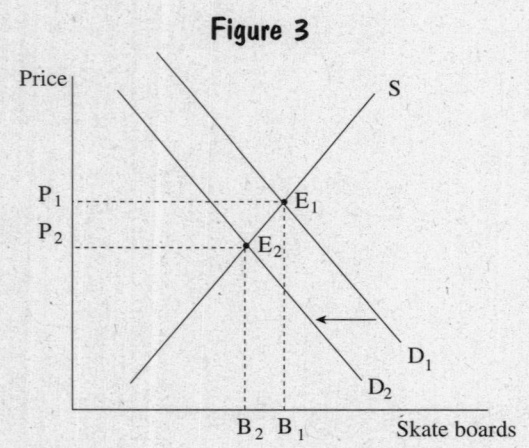

Figure 1

Figure 2

Figure 3

An excellent response:

A. As surfing becomes the "in" thing, surfers will buy more surfboards at any given price, thus shifting the demand curve for surfboards to the right from D_1 to D_2 as illustrated in Figure 1. At the beginning price of P_1, a shortage of surfboards will exist after the demand shift, bringing producers to raise their prices. As the price rises, the quantity demanded will decrease and the quantity supplied will increase. This process will continue until the quantity demanded equals the quantity supplied at a new equilibrium price of P_2 and a new quantity of Q_2. At the new equilibrium E_2, price and quantity are higher than at the old equilibrium E_1.

B. Complementary goods will experience an increase in demand as surfboard sales increase. For example, as the popularity of surfing increases, more surf wax will be needed. Surfers will buy more surf wax at any given price, thus shifting the demand curve for surf wax to the right as in Figure 2. This increases the equilibrium price and quantity of surf wax. Sellers of surf wax sell more at a higher price, and are likely to employ more workers.

C. Substitutes for surfboards are likely to be hurt by the increase in surfboard popularity. The market for skateboards, for example, may take a plunge as board riders take to the waters. If fewer skateboards are purchased at any given price, the demand curve will shift to the left as in Figure 3. Equilibrium price, quantity, and employment in the skateboard market will all fall.

An average response:

A. The new zest for surfing will shift the demand curve for surfboards to the right as illustrated in Figure 1. At the new equilibrium E_2, price and quantity are higher than at the old equilibrium E_1.

B. Complementary goods will experience an increase in demand as surfboard sales increase. For example, surfers will buy more surf wax, thus shifting the demand curve for surf wax to the right as in Figure 2. This increases the equilibrium price and quantity of surf wax.

C. Substitutes for surfboards are likely to be hurt by the increase in surfboard popularity. The market for skateboards, for example, may take a plunge as board riders take to the waters. Equilibrium price, quantity, and employment in the skateboard market will all fall.

A poor response:

A. People will buy more surfboards as in Figure 1. They like them more so they'll pay more for them.

B. People will probably buy more surf wax and watch more beach movies.

C. With more people surfing, fewer people will be in school, so teachers will be hurt. People might also buy fewer skateboards.

Topic 2

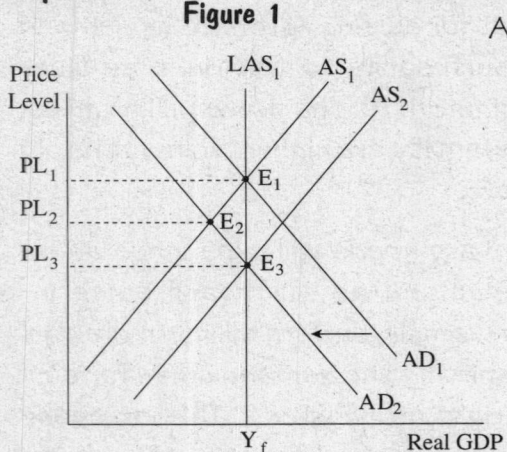

Figure 1

[Figure 1: AD-AS diagram showing Price Level vs Real GDP, with curves LAS₁, AS₁, AS₂, AD₁, AD₂, equilibria E₁, E₂, E₃ at price levels PL₁, PL₂, PL₃, and full-employment output Y_f. AD shifts leftward.]

An excellent response:

A. As illustrated in Figure 1, the economy begins at equilibrium E_1 with output at the full-employment level Y_1. A stronger dollar results in an increase in imports and a decrease in exports. Both of these changes have a negative effect on aggregate demand, shifting it from AD_1 to AD_2. The result is a new short-run equilibrium at E_2. Since this brings employment below the full-employment level, wages will be bid down, resulting in a rightward shift in the aggregate supply curve from AS_1 to AS_2 as labor costs decrease. The new long-run equilibrium is E_3, again at the full-employment level of output.

B. In the short run, both the price level and real output decrease. After wages adjust to the decrease in prices and employment and the aggregate supply shifts out to AS_2, real output returns to its original level of Y_f. However, the price level remains depressed because both the decrease in AD and the increase in AS result in a decrease in the price level. Employment will fall short of the full-employment level in the short run, meaning that unemployment will exceed its "natural" rate. Since real output is unchanged in the long run, there is no long-run effect on employment.

C. Since the price level falls, the purchasing power of currency and forthcoming fixed amounts of money increases. This helps anyone holding significant amounts of cash, receiving a fixed income, or receiving fixed interest on loans or savings. The decrease in the price level hurts those who must pay fixed amounts of money as interest, salary, or loan repayment because the value of these payments in terms of purchasing power has increased. Any change in prices also hurts businesses that must adjust price lists, menus, and the like to reflect the price changes.

An average response:

A. A stronger dollar results in an increase in imports and a decrease in exports, shifting aggregate demand from AD_1 to AD_2. Since this brings employment below the full-employment level, wages will be bid down, resulting in a rightward shift in the aggregate supply curve from AS_1 to AS_2 as labor costs decrease.

B. In the short run, both the price level and real output decrease. After wages adjust to the decrease in prices and employment, the aggregate supply shifts out to AS_2. However, the price level remains depressed. Employment will fall short of the full-employment level in the short run, but rebound in the long run.

C. Since the price level falls, this helps anyone holding significant amounts of cash, receiving a fixed income, or receiving fixed interest. The decrease in the price level hurts those who must pay fixed interest or salaries because what they pay is worth more at lower prices.

A poor response:

A. Demand will shift to the left as in Figure 1.

B. Prices and output fall, and fall even more in the long run. People will be out of work due to this problem unless the government does something.

C. People who like to spend money are better off. Those taking in the money are bothered by the lower prices.

Chapter 23

THE PRINCETON REVIEW GSE ECONOMICS PRACTICE TEST IV

PART I: MULTIPLE-CHOICE QUESTIONS

You will have 45 minutes to complete the multiple-choice section of this exam. For each question, please indicate the best response out of the four provided.

1. The imposition of an effective price floor will have which of the following results?

    A. The price will rise and the quantity sold will fall.

    B. The price and quantity sold will both rise.

    C. The price and quantity sold will both fall.

    D. The price will fall and the quantity sold will rise.

2. If the average cost of law school increases, what is likely to happen to the equilibrium wage and employment of lawyers?

    A. Wage increases and employment decreases.

    B. Wage and employment both decrease.

    C. Wage and employment both increase.

    D. Wage decreases and employment increases.

3. The unemployment rate is calculated as

    A. the number unemployed divided by the number in the population.

    B. the number in the population minus the number employed, divided by the number in the population.

    C. the labor force participation rate divided by the number in the population.

    D. the number unemployed divided by the number in the labor force.

4. Land is best classified as a(n)

    A. form of capital.

    B. factor of production.

    C. output.

    D. inferior good.

5. Which of the following is an advisable role for government?

    A. To subsidize activities that create negative externalities

    B. To tax activities that create positive externalities

    C. To provide public goods using tax dollars

    D. To avoid intervention when dealing with public goods and externalities

6. At equilibrium in the market for telephones, which of the following is true?

    A. The price at which producers want to sell equals the price at which consumers want to buy.

    B. The quantity that producers want to sell at the market price equals the quantity that consumers want to buy.

    C. Producers would sell more at the market price if consumers would buy them.

    D. Consumers would buy more telephones at the market price if they were available.

7. The opportunity cost of going to the prom with Chris might be

    A. that you can't go with Pat.

    B. the price of dinner and a tux/dress.

    C. the emotional loss because you may never see Chris and some of your other friends again.

    D. the risk that participants will drink and drive multiplied by the damages that could result from such stupidity.

8. If supply increases and demand decreases, which of the following will occur with certainty as the market reaches its new equilibrium?

    A. Price will increase.

    B. Quantity will increase.

    C. Price will decrease.

    D. Quantity will decrease.

9. When positive externalities are created by a good or service, relative to the socially optimal situation, it is likely to be

    A. underpriced.

    B. underconsumed.

    C. overconsumed.

    D. a good candidate for extra taxation.

10. Mamma Donna's Pizzeria installs a windmill on the roof that helps power the oven and lowers the restaurant's cost of cooking each pizza. Which of the following is the most certain to result?

    A. Mamma Donna's demand curve will shift to the left.

    B. Mamma Donna's demand curve will shift to the right.

    C. Mamma Donna's supply curve will shift to the left.

    D. Mamma Donna's supply curve will shift to the right.

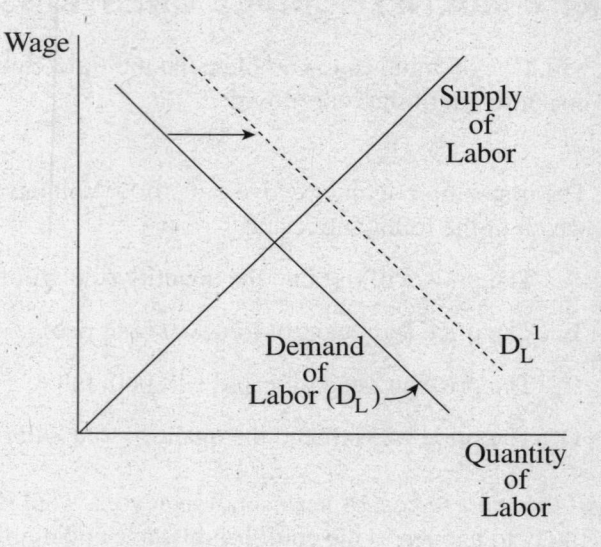

11. The shift depicted in the graph above most likely resulted from

    A. an increase in the workforce.

    B. a decrease in the retirement age.

    C. an increase in the demand for the output produced by workers.

    D. a decrease in the marginal product of workers.

12. Which of the following is the most likely to correct for excessive income inequality?

    A. A reduction in property and inheritance taxes

    B. A reduction in the highest marginal tax rates

    C. An increase in transfer payments such as welfare and unemployment insurance

    D. A decrease in capital gains taxes

13. Under perfect competition, long-run economic profits are

    A. zero.

    B. negative.

    C. positive.

    D. zero or positive.

14. Which of the following most accurately represents the components that can be added up to find GDP?

    A. A + B + C − D + E
    B. C + I + G + X − M
    C. D + S
    D. MC + MB

15. In terms of the business cycle, which of the following is most likely to increase faster during a contraction than during an expansion?

    A. The CPI
    B. The GNP
    C. Contractionary fiscal or monetary policy
    D. Unemployment

16. The horizontal and vertical axes on the aggregate demand/aggregate supply graph indicate which of the following, respectively?

    A. The price of a good and the quantity of a good
    B. The quantity of a good and the price of a good
    C. The price level and real output
    D. Real output and the price level

17. Decreasing taxes is a form of which of the following?

    A. Contractionary fiscal policy
    B. Expansionary fiscal policy
    C. Contractionary monetary policy
    D. Expansionary monetary policy

18. The national debt is less of a problem when

    A. the interest rate is high.
    B. less of the associated spending is on capital and technology.
    C. it permits projects that will benefit many generations.
    D. more of the debt is held by foreigners.

19. During a recession, the economy is most likely to benefit from

    A. an increase in the interest rate.
    B. contractionary fiscal policy.
    C. an increase in the discount rate.
    D. expansionary monetary policy.

20. Which of the following statements about the Federal Reserve System is NOT correct?

    A. It is a clearinghouse for checks.
    B. It prevents banks from having fractional reserves.
    C. It holds required reserves for banks.
    D. It serves as the central bank of the U.S.

21. Which of the following economic systems provides the most predictability regarding answers to the questions of what, how, and for whom to produce?

    A. Traditional
    B. Command
    C. Free Market
    D. Laissez-faire

22. Which type of unemployment is most likely to conclude with a more productive job-worker pairing than at the onset of the unemployment?

    A. Seasonal unemployment
    B. Structural unemployment
    C. Frictional unemployment
    D. Cyclical unemployment

23. Which of the following is not among the Fed's tools for adjusting the money supply?

    A. Antitrust legislation
    B. Open market operations
    C. Adjustments in the required reserve ratio
    D. Adjustments in the discount rate

24. If the Fed dumps dollars on the foreign exchange market, which of the following will result?

    A. The dollar will appreciate relative to other currencies.
    B. Foreign currencies will appreciate relative to the dollar.
    C. The demand curve for the dollar will shift to the left.
    D. The demand curve for the dollar will shift to the right.

25. Which of the following would increase the demand for U.S. dollars on the international market?

    A. A relative decrease in U.S. interest rates
    B. A relative increase in growth in the U.S. economy
    C. A relative decrease in the U.S. price level
    D. An increase in intranational trade

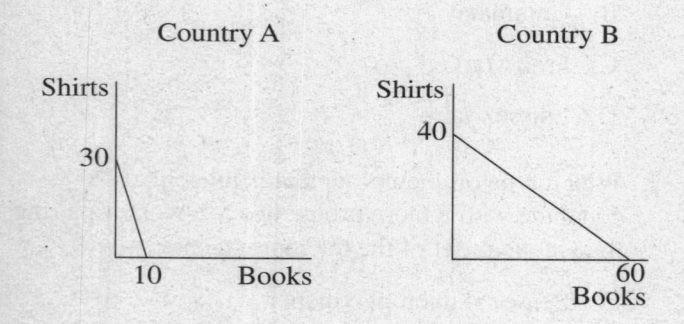

26. Countries A and B have the same resources and their simplified production possibilities curves are illustrated above. Which of the following statements is true?

    A. Country A has a comparative advantage in making shirts.
    B. Country B has a comparative advantage in making shirts.
    C. Neither country has a comparative advantage in making shirts.
    D. Country B has a comparative advantage in the production of both goods.

27. The balance of payments is a statement of

    A. payments by consumers to firms and payments to workers by firms.
    B. taxes collected and government expenditures.
    C. all international flows of money over a given period.
    D. payments by banks to creditors and payments by debtors to banks.

28. A tariff is

    A. the opposite of a tax.
    B. a regulation facilitating trade.
    C. a tax placed on imports.
    D. a fee placed on exports.

29. The law of diminishing marginal returns states that as

    A. the amounts of all inputs are increased proportionally, output will increase at a decreasing rate.
    B. time passes, a fixed level of resources will eventually produce less and less.
    C. more and more of a good is consumed, the utility derived from that good will eventually become negative.
    D. the amount of one input is increased and all other inputs are held fixed, the marginal product of the varied input will eventually decrease.

30. Which of the following do monopolies and monopolistically competitive firms have in common?

    A. High barriers to entry
    B. Downward sloping demand curves
    C. The potential for high long-run profits
    D. Very few firms selling similar goods

PART II: ESSAY QUESTIONS

The essay questions will allow you to demonstrate your graphing and analytical skills. You will have 45 minutes in which to write two essays. Your teacher will notify you when 20 minutes have passed.

Directions:

1. Read each of the essay topics carefully.

2. Organize your thoughts before you start writing. You may want to outline your essays or experiment with a few graphs first. You may write notes and practice diagrams on the test booklet. Only writing on the lined pages of the answer sheet will be scored.

3. Write your essays on the appropriate pages of the answer sheet.

4. The two essays receive equal credit, and you must write both essays to receive full credit. Allow yourself sufficient time to write each essay—an equal division of time would give you 22.5 minutes for each one.

5. Be sure to draw the relevant graphs, be specific, and use economic concepts, terms, and policies to reinforce your reasoning.

6. Don't waste time going off on tangents. Rather, address the given topic with well-supported responses.

1) Topic:

Sushi chefs stick together, agree to demand a minimum wage

Answer the questions below in an essay that employs economic concepts, reasoning, and supply and demand graphs. Assume that the minimum wage for chefs is higher than the wage sushi chefs were receiving previously.

A. Using a supply and demand graph, explain how the demand for a minimum wage for chefs will affect the sushi restaurant market?

B. How might other markets be affected by this wage increase?

C. Will all sushi chefs be better off as a result of this minimum wage? Explain why or why not.

2) Topic:

Consumer optimism grows with election of President Spendalot

Answer the questions below in an essay that employs economic concepts, reasoning, and an aggregate supply/aggregate demand graph.

A. Using a graph, explain the short-run and long-run effects of the new optimism.

B. What are the likely short-run and long-run effects on real GDP, employment, and the price level?

C. What government policy would have a similar effect on the economy? What government policy would have the opposite effect?

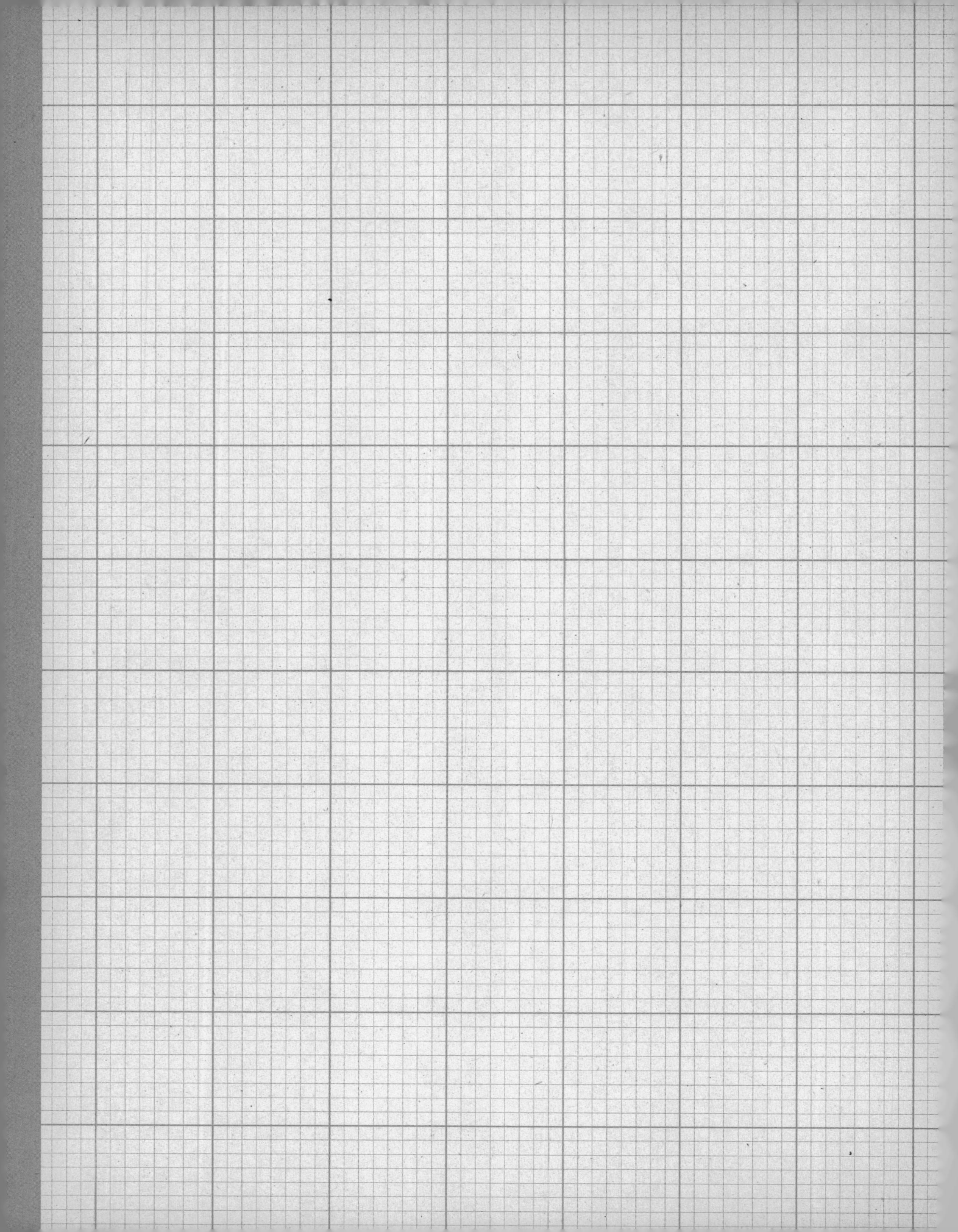

THE PRINCETON REVIEW

YOUR NAME: _____
(Print)   Last   First   M.I.

SIGNATURE: _____ DATE: ___/___/___

HOME ADDRESS: _____
(Print)   Number and Street

_____
         City   State   Zip Code

PHONE NO.: _____
(Print)

Completely darken bubbles with a No. 2 pencil. If you make a mistake, be sure to erase mark completely. Erase all stray marks.

Practice Test IV

1. Ⓐ Ⓑ Ⓒ Ⓓ
2. Ⓐ Ⓑ Ⓒ Ⓓ
3. Ⓐ Ⓑ Ⓒ Ⓓ
4. Ⓐ Ⓑ Ⓒ Ⓓ
5. Ⓐ Ⓑ Ⓒ Ⓓ
6. Ⓐ Ⓑ Ⓒ Ⓓ
7. Ⓐ Ⓑ Ⓒ Ⓓ
8. Ⓐ Ⓑ Ⓒ Ⓓ
9. Ⓐ Ⓑ Ⓒ Ⓓ
10. Ⓐ Ⓑ Ⓒ Ⓓ
11. Ⓐ Ⓑ Ⓒ Ⓓ
12. Ⓐ Ⓑ Ⓒ Ⓓ
13. Ⓐ Ⓑ Ⓒ Ⓓ
14. Ⓐ Ⓑ Ⓒ Ⓓ
15. Ⓐ Ⓑ Ⓒ Ⓓ

16. Ⓐ Ⓑ Ⓒ Ⓓ
17. Ⓐ Ⓑ Ⓒ Ⓓ
18. Ⓐ Ⓑ Ⓒ Ⓓ
19. Ⓐ Ⓑ Ⓒ Ⓓ
20. Ⓐ Ⓑ Ⓒ Ⓓ
21. Ⓐ Ⓑ Ⓒ Ⓓ
22. Ⓐ Ⓑ Ⓒ Ⓓ
23. Ⓐ Ⓑ Ⓒ Ⓓ
24. Ⓐ Ⓑ Ⓒ Ⓓ
25. Ⓐ Ⓑ Ⓒ Ⓓ
26. Ⓐ Ⓑ Ⓒ Ⓓ
27. Ⓐ Ⓑ Ⓒ Ⓓ
28. Ⓐ Ⓑ Ⓒ Ⓓ
29. Ⓐ Ⓑ Ⓒ Ⓓ
30. Ⓐ Ⓑ Ⓒ Ⓓ

THE PRINCETON REVIEW GSE ECONOMICS PRACTICE TEST IV

Multipl-Choice Answer Key

1	A	9	B	17	B	25	C
2	B	10	D	18	C	26	A
3	D	11	C	19	D	27	C
4	B	12	C	20	B	28	C
5	C	13	A	21	A	29	D
6	B	14	B	22	C	30	B
7	A	15	D	23	A		
8	C	16	D	24	B		

Part I: Multiple-Choice Explanations

1. **A** An effective price floor must be above the equilibrium price, causing the price to rise. At the higher price, the quantity supplied will increase, but the quantity demanded will decrease. Because each sale requires a buyer, the quantity sold will decrease with the quantity demanded.

2. **B** An increase in the cost of law school will shift the supply curve for lawyers to the left. At equilibrium, this will increase the wage and decrease the number of lawyers employed.

3. **D** The unemployment rate is the number unemployed divided by the number in the labor force. The population includes children, retirees, etc., who are not included in the unemployment rate calculation.

4. **B** Land is one of the factors of production (inputs), along with labor, capital—choice (A)—entrepreneurship, and human capital. Simplified models often shorten the list of inputs, and land is sometimes classified under natural resources. Land is an input into the production of outputs, choice (C), such as wheat. It is unlikely to be an inferior good, choice (D), which is something that people buy less of as their income increases.

5. **C** Public goods are nonrival in consumption, meaning that one person's enjoyment of them does not affect the enjoyment of others. They are also nonexcludable, meaning that if one person consumes them, others cannot be prevented from consuming them. Examples include streetlights and national defense. Public goods will be underprovided in the absence of intervention because "free riders" will try to enjoy

them without paying for them and not enough people will voluntarily pay for them. Thus, it is wise for the government to provide them using tax dollars.

6. **B** If they had their way, producers would sell at an infinite price and consumers would choose to pay zero, so answer (A) is imperfect. It would be correct if it said something like, "the lowest price at which producers are willing to supply the equilibrium quantity equals the highest price at which consumers are willing to buy the equilibrium quantity." The superior answer choice is that at equilibrium, the quantity that producers want to sell at the market price equals the quantity that consumers want to buy.

7. **A** Opportunity cost is the value of the next best alternative foregone when a decision is made. By deciding to go to the prom with Chris, the opportunity cost might be that you can't go with Pat. The other costs described in this question are limited to direct costs associated with the decision to go with Chris.

8. **C** An increase in supply increases quantity and decreases price. A decrease in demand decreases quantity and decreases price. Since there are opposing forces acting on quantity, it could increase or decrease depending on the relative strength of the two forces. Both the supply shift and the demand shift lower the price, so it is certain that price will decrease.

9. **B** Positive externalities are beneficial effects felt beyond or "external to" those creating the effects. For example, the immunization of one person prevents a lot of people from getting sick. At the same time individuals deciding whether or not to be immunized probably do not consider the benefits to others when weighing their costs and benefits from the immunization shot. Since the benefits are underrecognized, immunizations will thus be underconsumed. To reach the socially optimal number of shots, immunizations could be subsidized. They are not underpriced or in need of additional taxation, as an increase in prices or taxes would further reduce the purchase of this underconsumed service.

10. **D** The lower energy cost per pizza will allow Mamma Donna's to supply more pizzas at any given price, thus shifting the supply curve to the right.

11. **C** The demand for labor is derived from the demand for the output it produces. Thus, when the demand for output increases, the demand for labor increases. An increase in the workforce would increase the

labor supply curve, making choice (A) wrong. A decrease in the retirement age would decrease the labor supply curve, so you can get rid of choice (B). And a decrease in the marginal product of workers would decrease the marginal revenue product and thereby decrease the demand for labor; eliminate choice (D).

12. **C** Reductions in property, capital gains, or inheritance taxes, or in the highest marginal tax rates, will increase the incomes of the rich, thus increasing income inequality—so you know that all of these choices are wrong. In order to decrease income inequality, equalizing measures could be taken, such as making the rich pay more in taxes and redistributing it to the poor in the form of transfer payments.

13. **A** A perfectly competitive industry has a large number of firms selling identical products. Any economic profits that exist in the short run will be competed away in the long run as new firms enter to capture a share of the market.

14. **B** Gross domestic product (GDP) can be found by adding up consumption (C), investment (I), government spending (G), and exports (X), and then subtracting imports (M).

15. **D** A contraction means that real gross domestic product (GDP) is decreasing, which may dampen inflation as measured by the consumer price index (CPI)—eliminate choices (A) and (B). Contractionary fiscal or monetary policy is hastened during an *expansion* in order to slow the economy down, so choice (C) is wrong. Growth in unemployment is the most likely to increase during a contraction because there will be fewer workers needed to produce fewer goods.

16. **D** Aggregate demand and aggregate supply depict relationships between the real output of the whole economy (on the horizontal axis) and the general price level (on the vertical axis). They do not indicate the relationship between price and quantity for a particular good.

17. **B** When taxes are decreased, this leaves taxpayers with more money with which to make purchases. This increases or "expands" aggregate demand and real GDP. Contractionary fiscal policy, choice (A), would involve increases in taxes or decreases in transfers or government purchases. Monetary policy, choices (C) and (D), is the use of money and credit controls to influence the economy.

18. **C** When the interest rate is high, the debt costs us more. On top of that, borrowing by the government to fund the debt only makes things

worse because it competes with private borrowing and can make the interest rate higher still. Thus, (A) is out. It is better when *more* of the associated spending is on capital and technology, not less as in answer (B). This is because these types of expenditures create benefits for a long time to come, and as in the correct answer (C), some of those who must pay back the debt in the future will actually receive some of the benefits as well. It is also less of a problem when more of it is held by our *own* citizens, because this means that we effectively owe the money to ourselves, so choice (D) is wrong.

19. D An increase in the interest rate, contractionary fiscal policy, or an increase in the discount rate would all make a recession worse—get rid of choices (A), (B), and (C). On the other hand, expansionary monetary policy increases the money supply, decreases the interest rate, and encourages investment, which should help the economy out of a recession.

20. B Under a fractional reserve banking system banks hold a fraction of their deposits on reserve and lend out the rest. Rather than preventing banks from having fractional reserves, the Fed requires the banks to have fractional reserves and sets the reserve ratio, which is the fraction of deposits that must be held on reserve.

21. A Traditional economic systems guarantee a certain degree of predictability in the allocation of resources because answers to the questions of what, how, and for whom to produce are made based on tradition. The market mechanism in free markets, choice (C), and central planners in command economies, choice (B), may or may not continue allocating resources the way they have in the past.

22. C Frictional unemployment is that which occurs as workers and employers search for the optimal worker-job pairings. It often consists of workers who are between jobs because they are relocating or changing occupations so as to be more productive.

23. A Antitrust legislation consists of laws to prevent excessive market power and has no direct bearing on the money supply. Open market operations involve the purchase or sale of government securities by the Fed in order to increase or decrease the money supply respectively—get rid of choice (B). Increases in the reserve ratio, choice (C), or the discount rate, choice (D), will decrease the money supply and vice versa.

24. **B** With more dollars supplied by the Fed, the value of the dollar will decrease relative to other currencies. As the price of dollars in terms of other currencies falls, there will be movement *along* other nations' demand curves for dollars, not shifts in the demand curves.

25. **C** If U.S. interest rates fall, foreign investors will be less inclined to demand dollars for U.S. investments, so you can eliminate choice (A). If the U.S. is growing faster than other countries, it will purchase relatively more imports, thus increasing the demand for *other* currencies—get rid of choice (B). A relative decrease in the U.S. price level will attract more customers from other countries, and they will increase their demand for dollars with which to purchase the relatively cheap U.S. goods—this is choice (C) and the correct answer. Intranational trade is trade within a country, which has no necessary effect on the demand for dollars on the international market; choice (D) is wrong.

26. **A** A country is said to have a comparative advantage in the production of a good when it can produce that good at a lower opportunity cost (a smaller loss in terms of the production of another good) than another country. Country A gives up 1/3 of a book to make a shirt. This is clear because when it goes from making 0 shirts to making 30 shirts, it must give up 10 (1/3 as many) books. When country B goes from making 0 shirts to making 40 shirts, it must give up 60 (1.5 times as many) books. Thus A has a lower opportunity cost and a comparative advantage in making shirts.

27. **C** The balance of payments is a statement of all international flows of money over a given period. Included in the balance of payments are the merchandise trade account, the current account, and the capital account.

28. **C** A tariff is a form of trade restriction that constitutes a tax placed on imports.

29. **D** The law of diminishing marginal returns states that when one input is increased and all other inputs are fixed, the marginal (additional) product gained from additional units of the varied input will eventually decrease.

30. **B** Both types of firms face downward sloping demand curves. Only monopolies have high barriers to entry, the potential for long-run profits, and few (or no) firms selling similar goods.

Part II: Essay Explanations

Topic 1

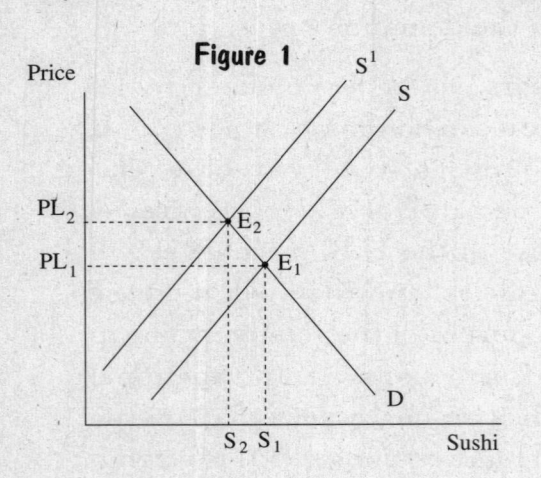

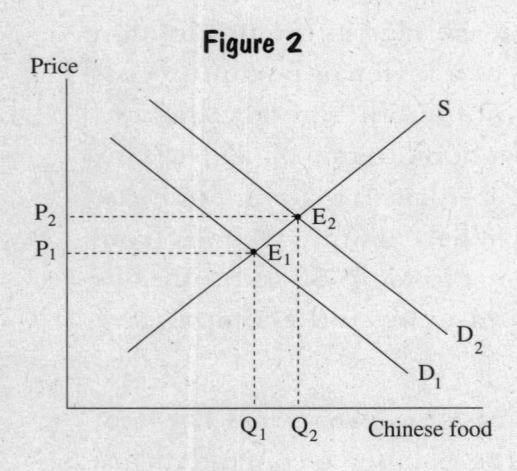

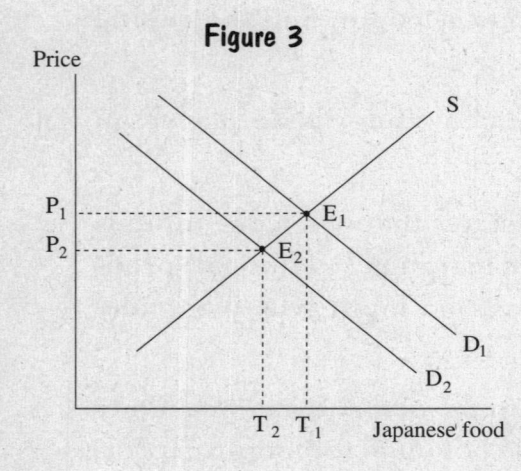

Figure 1 — Price vs. Sushi, showing supply curve shift from S to S¹ (labeled S₁ to S₂ on quantity axis), with equilibrium moving from E₁ (at PL₁) to E₂ (at PL₂), demand curve D.

Figure 2 — Price vs. Chinese food, showing demand shift from D₁ to D₂, equilibrium moves from E₁ (P₁, Q₁) to E₂ (P₂, Q₂), supply curve S.

Figure 3 — Price vs. Japanese food, showing demand shift from D₁ to D₂ (leftward), equilibrium moves from E₁ (P₁, T₁) to E₂ (P₂, T₂), supply curve S.

An excellent response:

A. As the wage paid to sushi chefs increases, the cost of supplying sushi also increases. Sushi restaurants will supply less sushi at any given price, thus shifting the supply curve for sushi to the left as illustrated in Figure 1. At the starting price of P_1 there will be a shortage of sushi as customers will want to buy more than the amount supplied at that price. Restaurants will respond to this by increasing prices until the quantity demanded decreases and the quantity supplied increases to reach a new equilibrium at E_2. At the new equilibrium, the price is higher and the quantity is lower than at the old equilibrium. Employment in sushi restaurants will also decrease with the quantity of sushi sold.

With higher prices and lower quantities in the sushi market, the demand for substitutes will increase and the demand for complements will decrease. For example, Chinese food may be a substitute for sushi. If so, as sushi prices rise, more Chinese food will be demanded at any given price, thus shifting the demand curve to the right as illustrated in Figure 2. The equilibrium price and quantity for Chinese food will increase, as will employment in Chinese restaurants.

B. Japanese tea is a complement to sushi. When people eat sushi, they often drink Japanese tea at the same time. With higher prices and lower quantities in the sushi market, less Japanese tea will be demanded at any given price to accompany sushi meals. This shifts the demand curve for Japanese tea to the left as in Figure 3, decreasing the equilibrium price and quantity.

Figure 4

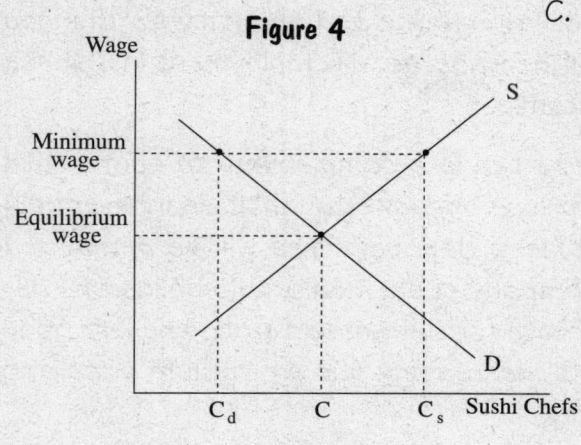

C. Figure 4 illustrates the labor market for sushi chefs. The minimum wage is above the equilibrium wage, resulting in an excess supply of chefs. At the minimum wage, Cs chefs would like to work, whereas restaurants want to hire only Cd chefs. The difference between Cs and Cd represents unemployment in the sushi chefs market. The Cd chefs who are still employed after the wage increase are better off. However, the C – Cd chefs who were working before the minimum wage will no longer be employed, so they are worse off. Unemployment grows by more than C – Cd because at the higher wage there are also Cs-C workers who would like to work but cannot. Since they joined the labor force at the higher wage but cannot find work, they are among the unemployed. The existence of unemployment in the market for sushi chefs will make it difficult to maintain the minimum wage demand. Unless there is a strong organization of sushi chefs that can effectively prevent unemployed chefs from offering their services at a lower wage, the wage demand might fail.

An average response:

A. As the wage paid to sushi chefs increases, the cost of supplying sushi also increases, shifting the supply curve for sushi to the left as illustrated in Figure 1. At the new equilibrium, the price is higher and the quantity is lower than at the old equilibrium. Employment in sushi restaurants will decrease with the quantity of sushi sold.

B. Chinese food may be a substitute for sushi. If so, as sushi prices rise, more Chinese food will be demanded, thus shifting the demand curve to the right as illustrated in Figure 2.

The equilibrium price and quantity for Chinese food will increase, as will employment in Chinese restaurants.

Japanese tea is a complement to sushi. With higher prices and lower quantities in the sushi market, less Japanese tea will be demanded to accompany sushi meals. This shifts the demand curve for Japanese tea to the left as in Figure 3, decreasing the equilibrium price and quantity.

C. Figure 4 illustrates the labor market for sushi chefs. The minimum wage is above the equilibrium wage, resulting in an excess supply of chefs. The chefs who are still employed after the wage increase are better off. However, those who were working before the minimum wage but are no longer employed are worse off. There are also new entrants into the labor force at the higher wage. They will be unemployed as well.

A poor response:

A. Figure 1 shows that there is a higher wage for chefs. Thus, demand will go down and supply will go up.

B. People will buy less Japanese tea and more Chinese food because the price of sushi went up.

C. Some will be better, some will be worse. It depends whether they are making more or not.

Topic 2

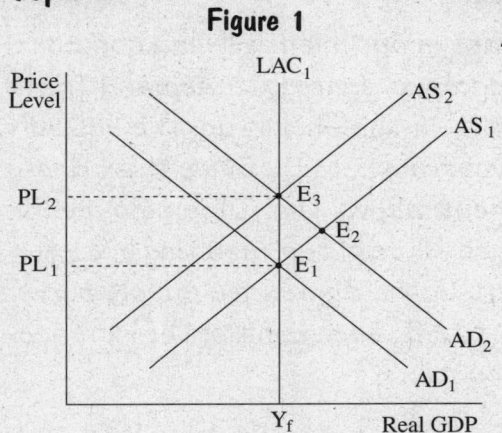

Figure 1

[Graph showing Price Level vs Real GDP with curves LAC₁ (vertical at Y_f), AS₁, AS₂, AD₁, AD₂, and equilibrium points E₁ (at PL₁, Y_f), E₂, and E₃ (at PL₂, Y_f)]

An excellent response:

A. The economy begins at equilibrium E_1 with output at the full-employment level Y_f. An increase in optimism will lead consumers to spend more at any given price level, increasing aggregate demand from AD_1 to AD_2. In the short run, the equilibrium moves from E_1 to E_2. Since this brings employment above the full-employment level, wages will be bid up, resulting in a leftward shift in the aggregate supply curve from AS_1 to AS_2 as a result of the increase in labor costs. The new long-run equilibrium is E_3, again at the full-employment level of output.

B. In the short run, both the price level and real output increase. After wages adjust to the increase in the price level and the aggregate supply shifts back to AS_2, real output returns to its original level of Y_f. However, the price level remains elevated because both the increase in AD and the decrease in AS result in an increase in the price level. Employment will exceed the full-employment level in the short run, meaning that unemployment will fall below its "natural" rate. Since real output is unchanged in the long run, there is no long-run effect on employment.

C. The government could bring about a similar increase in the aggregate demand curve with expansionary fiscal or monetary policy. For example, the government could increase its own purchases, decrease taxes to spur private consumption, or increase the money supply to lower the interest rate and spur investment demand.

The opposite effect—a decrease in aggregate demand—would result from contractionary fiscal or monetary policy. That is, the government could decrease its own purchases, increase taxes, or decrease the money supply.

An average response:

A. An increase in optimism will lead consumers to increase aggregate demand from AD_1 to AD_2. In the short run, the equilibrium moves from E_1 to E_2. Since this brings employment above the full-employment level, wages will be bid up, resulting in a leftward shift in the aggregate supply curve from AS_1 to AS_2 as a result of the increase in labor costs.

B. In the short run, both the price level and real output increase. After wages adjust to the increase in the price level, aggregate supply shifts back to AS_2. However, the price level remains elevated because both the increase in AD and the decrease in AS result in an increase in the price level. Employment will exceed the full-employment level in the short run, but there is no long-run effect on employment.

C. The government could bring about a similar increase in the aggregate demand curve with expansionary fiscal or monetary policy. The opposite effect—a decrease in aggregate demand—would result from contractionary fiscal or monetary policy.

A poor response:

A. The aggregate demand curve expands as in the graph.

B. Output and prices will increase. Employment will increase as well. In the long run everyone will be better off.

C. The government could spend more to have the same effect, or tax a lot to have the opposite effect.

ABOUT THE AUTHORS

John Gilleaudeau, PhD, is a fellow who was educated at Fordham University and has taught economics and related subjects at several institutions of higher learning in the New York City area.

David Anderson received his B.A. in economics at the University of Michigan and his M.A. and Ph.D. in economics at Duke University. He is currently an Associate Professor at Centre College and an Adjunct Associate Professor at Davidson College. He has been an AP Economics grader or exam leader for the past five years and has written and lectured on the teaching of AP economics. His numerous publications include articles and books on the economics of law, crime, education, social insurance, and dispute resolution. Dr. Anderson's recent awards include grants from the Mellon Foundation, the Associated Colleges of the South, and the 3M Foundation.

www.review.com

Expert Advice

Counselor-O-Matic

Pop Surveys

www.review.com

Paying for It

www.review.com

THE PRINCETON REVIEW

Getting In

Word du Jour

www.review.com

www.review.com

College Talk

Find-O-Rama College Search

www.review.com

Best Schools

SAT Survival

www.review.com

We have a smarter way to get better grades in school.

Find a tutor in 3 easy steps:

Find.
Log onto our website: **www.tutor.com**

Connect.
Sign up to find a tutor who fits all your needs

Learn.
Get **tutored** in any subject or skill

Visit www.tutor.com

More Expert Advice
on all your important exams

THE PRINCETON REVIEW

**CRACKING THE SAT & PSAT
2000 EDITION**
0-375-75403-2 • $18.00

**CRACKING THE SAT & PSAT WITH
SAMPLE TESTS ON CD-ROM
2000 EDITION**
0-375-75404-0 • $29.95

SAT MATH WORKOUT
0-679-75363-X • $15.00

SAT VERBAL WORKOUT
0-679-75362-1 • $16.00

**CRACKING THE ACT
2000-2001 EDITION**
0-375-75500-4 • $18.00

**CRACKING THE ACT WITH
SAMPLE TESTS ON CD-ROM
2000-2001 EDITION**
0-375-75501-2 • $29.95

CRASH COURSE FOR THE ACT
10 Easy Steps to Higher Score
0-375-75326-5 • $9.95

CRASH COURSE FOR THE SAT
10 Easy Steps to Higher Score
0-375-75324-9 • $9.95

CRACKING THE CLEP 4TH EDITION
0-375-76151-9 • $20.00

**CRACKING THE GOLDEN STATE EXAMS:
1ST YEAR ALGEBRA**
0-375-75352-4 • $16.00

**CRACKING THE GOLDEN STATE EXAMS:
BIOLOGY**
0-375-75356-7 • $16.00

**CRACKING THE GOLDEN STATE EXAMS:
CHEMISTRY**
0-375-75357-5 • $16.00

**CRACKING THE GOLDEN STATE EXAMS:
ECONOMICS**
0-375-75355-9 • $16.00

**CRACKING THE GOLDEN STATE EXAMS:
GEOMETRY**
0-375-75353-2 • $16.00

**CRACKING THE GOLDEN STATE EXAMS:
U.S. HISTORY**
0-375-75354-0 • $16.00

WE ALSO HAVE BOOKS TO HELP YOU SCORE HIGH ON

THE SAT II AND AP EXAMS:

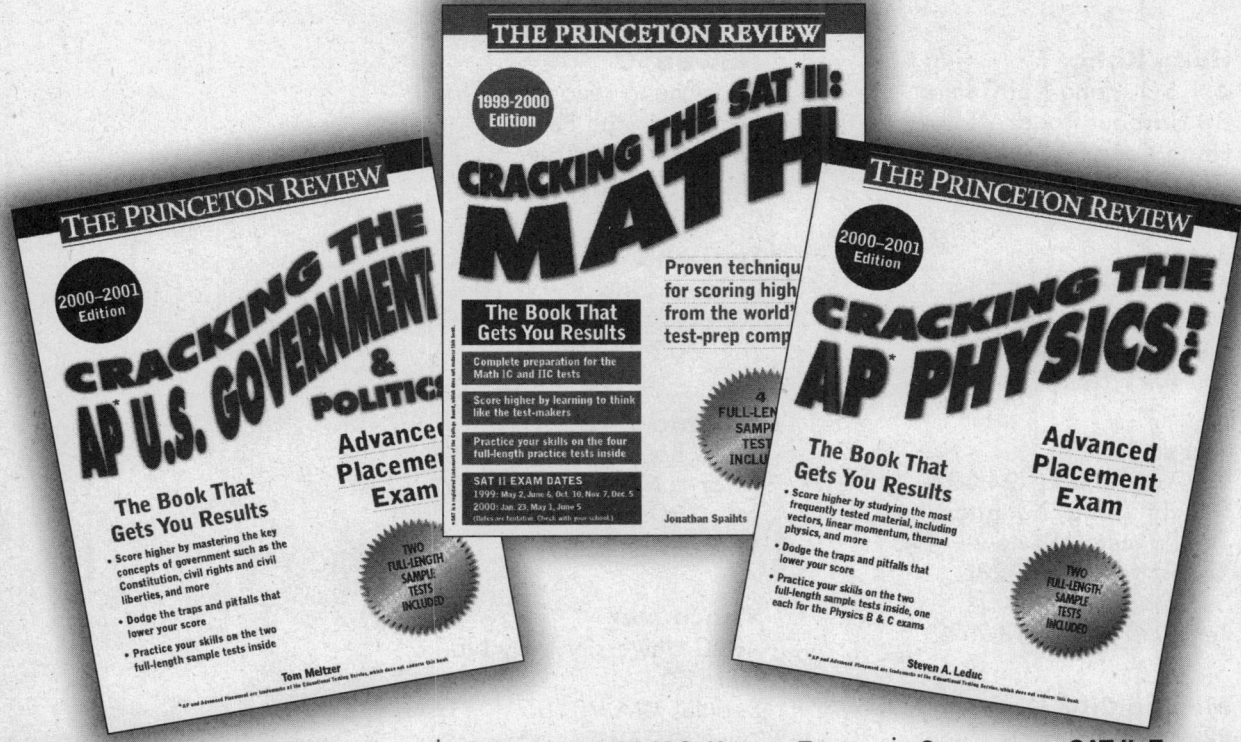

CRACKING THE AP BIOLOGY EXAM
2000-2001 EDITION
0-375-75495-4 • $17.00

CRACKING THE AP CALCULUS EXAM AB
& BC 2000-2001 EDITION
0-375-75499-7 • $18.00

CRACKING THE AP CHEMISTRY EXAM
2000-2001 EDITION
0-375-75497-0 • $17.00

CRACKING THE AP ECONOMICS EXAM
(MACRO & MICRO) 2000-2001 EDITION
0-375-75507-1 • $17.00

CRACKING THE AP ENGLISH LITERATURE
EXAM 2000-2001 EDITION
0-375-75493-8 • $17.00

CRACKING THE AP U.S. GOVERNMENT
AND POLITICS EXAM 2000-2001 EDITION
0-375-75496-2 • $17.00

CRACKING THE AP U.S. HISTORY EXAM
2000-2001 EDITION
0-375-75494-6 • $17.00

CRACKING THE AP PHYSICS
2000-2001 EDITION
0-375-75492-X • $19.00

CRACKING THE AP PSYCHOLOGY
2000-2001 EDITION
0-375-75480-6 • $17.00

CRACKING THE AP EUROPEAN HISTORY
2000-2001 EDITION
0-375-75498-9 • $17.00

CRACKING THE AP SPANISH
2000-2001 EDITION
0-75401-4 • $17.00

CRACKING THE SAT II: BIOLOGY
SUBJECT TEST 1999-2000 EDITION
0-375-75297-8 • $17.00

CRACKING THE SAT II: CHEMISTRY
SUBJECT TEST 1999-2000 EDITION
0-375-75298-6 • $17.00

CRACKING THE SAT II: ENGLISH
SUBJECT TEST 1999-2000 EDITION
0-375-75295-1 • $17.00

CRACKING THE SAT II: FRENCH SUBJECT
TEST 1999-2000 EDITION
0-375-75299-4 • $17.00

CRACKING THE SAT II: HISTORY
SUBJECT TEST 1999-2000 EDITION
0-375-75300-1 • $17.00

CRACKING THE SAT II: MATH SUBJECT
TEST 1999-2000 EDITION
0-375-75296-X • $17.00

CRACKING THE SAT II: PHYSICS
SUBJECT TEST 1999-2000 EDITION
0-375-75302-8 • $17.00

CRACKING THE SAT II: SPANISH SUBJECT
TEST 1999-2000 EDITION
0-375-75301-X • $17.00

Visit Your Local Bookstore or Order Direct by Calling 1-800-733-3000
www.randomhouse.com/princetonreview

FIND US...

International

Hong Kong
4/F Sun Hung Kai Centre
30 Harbour Road, Wan Chai,
Hong Kong
Tel: (011)85-2-517-3016

Japan
Fuji Building 40, 15-14
Sakuragaokacho, Shibuya Ku,
Tokyo 150, Japan
Tel: (011)81-3-3463-1343

Korea
Tae Young Bldg, 944-24,
Daechi- Dong, Kangnam-Ku
The Princeton Review—ANC
Seoul, Korea 135-280,
South Korea
Tel: (011)82-2-554-7763

Mexico City
PR Mex S De RL De Cv
Guanajuato 228 Col. Roma
06700 Mexico D.F., Mexico
Tel: 525-564-9468

Montreal
666 Sherbrooke St.
West, Suite 202
Montreal, QC H3A 1E7 Canada
Tel: 514-499-0870

Pakistan
1 Bawa Park - 90 Upper Mall
Lahore, Pakistan
Tel: (011)92-42-571-2315

Spain
Pza. Castilla, 3 - 5º A, 28046
Madrid, Spain
Tel: (011)341-323-4212

Taiwan
155 Chung Hsiao East Road
Section 4 - 4th Floor,
Taipei R.O.C., Taiwan
Tel: (011)886-2-751-1243

Thailand
Building One, 99 Wireless Road
Bangkok, Thailand 10330
Tel: 662-256-7080

Toronto
1240 Bay Street, Suite 300
Toronto M5R 2A7 Canada
Tel: 800-495-7737
Tel: 716-839-4391

Vancouver
4212 University Way NE,
Suite 204
Seattle, WA 98105
Tel: 206-548-1100

National (U.S.)

We have more than 60 offices around the U.S. and run courses at over 400 sites. For courses and locations within the U.S. call 1-800-2-Review and you will be routed to the nearest office.